The Guards 1915–17

An Elite Division at War

David Griffiths

Helion & Company

In Memory of Private Stephen Pickett
Dedicated to:
Augustina Prince-Griffiths
Ian & Richard Griffiths
Dania Prince-Griffiths

Helion & Company Limited
Unit 8 Amherst Business Centre
Budbrooke Road
Warwick
CV34 5WE
England
Tel. 01926 499619
Email: info@helion.co.uk
Website: www.helion.co.uk
X (formerly Twitter): @Helionbooks
Facebook: @HelionBooks
Visit our blog at https://helionbooks.wordpress.com/

Published by Helion & Company 2025
Designed and typeset by Mach 3 Solutions (www.mach3solutions.co.uk)
Cover designed by Paul Hewitt, Battlefield Design (www.battlefield-design.co.uk)

ISBN 978-1-804515-32-7

British Library Cataloguing-in-Publication Data.
A catalogue record for this book is available from the British Library.

For details of other military history titles published by Helion & Company Limited, contact the above address, or visit our website: http://www.helion.co.uk

We always welcome receiving book proposals from prospective authors.

Contents

Foreword

The formation of the Guards Division in August 1915 was a unique moment for the British Army. The Army had long operated Guards brigades, and both the 1st and 4th Guards Brigades had been part of the original British Expeditionary Force in 1914, but the creation of a full division was without precedent.

Much was expected of the new unit. The Regular Army was shaped by its strict understanding of class, which manifested in the separation between officers and men, and the ranking of individual regiments based on the nebulous concept of 'smartness.' The Guards stood at the very pinnacle of these scales. Its officers were drawn from the cream of the British aristocracy, while its regiments were ranked as the smartest in the entire Army. Maintaining this illustrious reputation was vital, which, in practice, meant strict discipline for the soldiers and uncompromising standards of behaviour for the officers.

These factors gave the new division several advantages. It benefited from a high standard of training and possessed considerable psychological cohesion. It was also fortunate to be commanded by the Earl of Cavan, a talented and experienced officer who had earned his stripes with the 4th Guards Brigade in 1914–1915. By all measures, the Guards Division looked to be an elite formation. Indeed, some contemporary commentators worried that concentrating the Guards battalions into a single division was a mistake, arguing that it would be better to distribute them throughout the army to bolster inexperienced New Army brigades.

This fascinating book explores the extent to which the Guards Division lived up to its impressive pedigree. As well as considering its formation, training, and trench-holding activities, it examines the division in three pivotal battles: Loos (1915), the Somme (1916), and Third Ypres (1917). Placing this unique division into the context of the British Army's wider development reveals both its strengths and limitations. The division's cohesion meant that it could always be relied on to attack with utmost determination. Yet, as the author shows, this alone was not enough to secure victory on the battlefields of the First World War. Coordination, planning, and combined arms were essential. Unfortunately, the British Army was still developing these concepts in 1915 and 1916, and as a result, the Guards Division endured heavy losses. It was not until its masterful set-piece attack at Pilckem Ridge in 1917 that the formation was able to fully capitalize on its considerable strengths. By placing the division within this context, the author materially enhances our understanding of the British Army in the First World War.

This is not merely a book about battles, however. The volume also explores the bonds that tied the Guards Division together. Its socially elite officer class was maintained despite a ghastly toll of casualties, and training for its soldiers remained uncompromisingly strict. It is no surprise that the Guards Division retained its 'regular' army status throughout the war. This powerful psychological strength meant that the Guards always believed they were an elite division, even when their battlefield successes were limited until 1917.

This book stands among the best of the literature on British Army divisions and expands our understanding of how the British Army functioned during the First World War. I learned much from it, and I look forward to the second volume, which promises to take the Guards Division to the end of the war.

Dr Spencer Jones
University of Wolverhampton, October 2024

Acknowledgements

My interest in the Guards Division owes much to Dr Spencer Jones who encouraged me to consider looking at them for my MA dissertation whilst studying at the University of Wolverhampton in 2016. As the reader will see, the original project has grown into something far more substantial, at times even all-consuming, but certainly always rewarding.

I would also like to thank Professor John Bourne for developing such a wonderful postgraduate programme at the University of Birmingham and Professor Gary Sheffield for taking the project to Wolverhampton and developing it still further with such expertise and enthusiasm. These are sentiments that I know my dear friend Geoff Inglis, a fellow student at Wolverhampton and battlefield companion who so sadly passed away before he was able to complete his PhD, would have shared.

I am especially indebted to Duncan Rogers at Helion & Company for giving me the opportunity to take this project through to publication and to Dr Michael LoCicero for his advice and support throughout.

Finally, but of course not least many, many thanks to my wife, Mary, for her love and support. Having to show an interest in a subject that was perhaps not too close to her heart and accompany me as a reluctant battlefield pilgrim has not always been easy!

David Griffiths
Cambridge, February 2024

Abbreviations

AA	Assistant Adjutant
BEF	British Expeditionary Force
CB	Order of the Bath
C-in-C	Commander-in-Chief
CO	Commanding Officer
CRE	Commander Royal Engineers
DCM	Distinguished Conduct Medal
FSR	Field Service Regulations.
GOC	General Officer Commanding.
GOCRA	General Officer Commanding Royal Artillery.
GSO1	General Staff Officer Grade 1
GSO2	General Staff Officer Grade 2
HQ	Headquarters
MC	Military Cross
OCB	Officer Cadet Battalion.
OTC	Officer Training Corps.
QMG	Quarter Master-General
RE	Royal Engineers
RFA	Royal Field Artillery
RFC	Royal Flying Corps
RQMS	Regimental quartermaster sergeant
SAA	Small Arms Ammunition
VC	Victoria Cross.

Introduction

The Guards Division was created at the instigation of Lord Kitchener, Secretary of State for War, in August 1915. Since the publication of Cuthbert Headlam's two volume *History of the Guards Division in the Great War 1915–1918* during 1924, there has been no further evaluation of what has always been regarded as an elite formation, if not the elite formation of the BEF in the First World War. This book looks at the period from August 1915 to July 1917 in which the Guards Division fought at the Battles of Loos, Flers-Courcelette and Morval on the Somme, and Pilckem Ridge near Ypres. It seeks to provide a readable narrative account of the Guards Division's development during this period within an academic framework.

The Guards 1915–17 is, therefore, not a traditional divisional history that typically covers the war in its entirety. I have taken time to provide an insight into the unique culture of this famous division, its characters and its 'way of doing things'. Each of the battles covered includes some discussion of the military context beforehand so that those readers unfamiliar with these turbulent years can fully appreciate what was being required of the BEF and the Guards Division in particular. There is also plenty of coverage of the division's activities between the short-lived intensity of battle which reveal so much of the more routine daily lives that Guardsmen faced. Wherever possible, I have endeavoured to illustrate events through the eye-witness testimony of those who were there.

Military historians have long struggled with developing a methodology to evaluate the military effectiveness of BEF divisions in the First World War. Back in the 1990s, the SHLM Project (named after its originators Peter Simkins, Bryn Hammond, John Lee and Chris McCarthy who gave their initials to its title) was intended to create a comprehensive database of these divisions, rating them individually and against each other according to a series of performance indicators including variables such as weather, terrain and the enemy but unfortunately it did not survive being overwhelmed by the weight of its own data.[1] Underpinning much research into divisional performance has

1 John Lee, 'The SHLM Project – Assessing the Battle Performance of British Divisions' in Paddy Griffith (ed.), *British Fighting Methods in the Great War* (London: Routledge,1998), pp.175–182.

been the concept of the BEF moving along a 'learning curve' of improvement.[2] However, this concept, as Jonathan Boff reminds us, was 'a metaphor rather than a formal process' and it has now evolved into the more nuanced concept of the 'learning process'.[3]

Peter Hodgkinson, writing in a recent history of the Sixth Division, noted that, 'Like the whole BEF, the division's career was not even. Progress was dependent on things that were both within its control and things which were not … The soundest competence could not guarantee success in the face of the friction of war and the independent will of a tenacious enemy.'[4] As will be seen, these factors applied equally well to the experience of the Guards Division. Two questions will be considered as part of this history. Can the Guards Division be regarded as an elite formation during the period of 1915 to 1917 and how effectively did it adapt to the learning process?

2 See for example, Simon Peaple, *Mud, Blood and Determination*, The History of the 46th (North Midland) Division in the Great War (Solihull: Helion, 2015)

3 Jonathan Boff, *Winning and Losing on the Western Front: The British Third Army and the Defeat of Germany in 1918* (Cambridge: Cambridge University Press, 2012), p.248.

4 Peter Hodgkinson, *A Complete Orchestra of War: A History of the 6th Division on the Western Front 1914–1919* (Warwick: Helion, 2019), pp.394–395.

1

Foundations: Establishing the Guards Division

Cavan: The Resurrection of a Military Career

In early July 1914 Rudolph Lambart, 10th Earl of Cavan, received a letter from a cousin inviting him to Germany for a fishing tour. Putting any concerns that he might have had about the deteriorating political situation in Europe to the back of his mind, Cavan bought a second-class ticket and travelled to Stuttgart via Ostend and Strasbourg. He had retired from the British Army in November 1913, at the age of 48, as a colonel after 28 years in the Grenadier Guards. His career had been a successful but not outstanding one. Now, he could dedicate himself to his estate at Wheathampstead near St Albans and spend his time fishing, golfing and being master of the Hertfordshire Hunt. Cavan certainly enjoyed himself in Germany. The weather was glorious and the fishing a delight.[1] He returned home after a fortnight having not read a newspaper at all and so he was blissfully unaware of how close things were to the outbreak of hostilities. As Cavan remarked in his unpublished memoir: 'A week later and I should have been interred for the duration of the war.'[2]

Within 10 days of his return, Cavan was recalled to the Army and given command of the 2nd Brigade of the 1st London Division of the Territorial Force. Whilst marching his troops from Bisley to Clandon Park in Surrey on 8 September, a dispatch rider pulled alongside to deliver a telegram; 'You are appointed to command 4th Guards Brigade. Vice [Brigadier] General Scott Kerr wounded. Report W.O. immediately'.[3] Cavan's military career was now on an upward trajectory from brigade to divisional to corps command in just 15 months and the history of the Guards Division was to be inextricably linked,

1 Churchill Archives Centre, University of Cambridge (CAC): GBR/0014/CAVN, The Papers of Field Marshal Lord Cavan. Cavan's Memoir, 'Recollections Hazy but Happy', Chapter 8, p.2. Unfortunately, the manuscript's pages and chapters are not arranged logically or necessarily in sequence.
2 CAC: GBR/0014/CAVN, 'Recollections Hazy but Happy', Chapter 8, p.4.
3 CAC: GBR/0014/CAVN, 'Recollections Hazy but Happy', Chapter 9, p.2.

either directly or indirectly, to Cavan's leadership throughout the period covered in this book.

The 4th Guards Brigade consisted of the 2/Grenadier Guards, the 2/Coldstream Guards, the 3/Coldstream Guards and the 1/Irish Guards and was part of the Second Division commanded by Major General Charles Monro. Cavan inherited a battle hardened and resourceful brigade when he arrived at Soupir on 17 September taking over from Geoffrey Feilding who had held temporary command as brigadier general. The Brigade had covered the retreat from Mons that had begun on 24 August. There had been a major four-hour engagement at Landrecies on 26 August in which the 3/Coldstream had borne the brunt of the German attack with the battalion losing five officers and 124 other ranks after the Germans had approached the Coldstream's piquets and answered the challenge in French. The retreat continued on 27 August under challenging conditions with excellent march discipline, although no further fighting had been needed. Soissons was reached on 30 August. The Brigade then covered the retirement of the 2nd Division at Villers Cotterets on 1 September which involved some tough, close quartered fighting in the wooded areas outside the town in which Brigadier General Scott-Kerr was severely wounded.

The Brigade next saw action as the Germans made a stand on the Aisne. They formed the infantry of the advanced guard of the 2nd Division helping to force the passage of the Petit Morin. On 14 September, the 2nd Division crossed the Aisne at Pont Arcy and the 4th Guards were the last of the brigades to cross the river, being directed on to the Soupir Spur.

Rudolph Lambart, 10th Earl of Cavan.

Brigadier General, later Major General, Geoffrey Feilding.

Heavy fighting ensued before the Guards had successfully entrenched on a line north and north-west of La Cour de Soupir Farm. The Brigade had suffered about 500 casualties on this day. The Guards remained here for three weeks suffering severely from the German artillery.[4] When Cavan reported to Monro, he appreciated his simple orders. 'Your Brigade is on that hill, see they stick to it.'[5] However, this was to be a demanding posting in the most challenging of circumstances.

By late September, it was clear further progress was impossible on the Aisne front and so the process of moving the BEF to Flanders began at the beginning of October. By 19 October, the First Battle of Ypres had begun and it was to last until 22 November. It was this battle that cemented Cavan's reputation as a highly competent battlefield commander although reading his response to orders received from Lieutenant General Douglas Haig, GOC 1st Corps, suggests that it was all relatively straightforward:

> On one warm October Day I was sound asleep under a well near Klein Zillebeke having been up all night. An officer of Sir Douglas Haig's staff galloped up looking very pale, and said to my Brigade Major: 'Lord Cavan is to take command of the next sector as well as his own, as General Bulfin has been wounded'. I dimly heard these words and had perhaps three more minutes of semi-conscious dozing, for I was very tired, while my Brigade Major noted the order in the diary.

Arriving at Brigadier General Edward Bulfin's 2nd Infantry Brigade HQ, Cavan continued:

> What was the situation? Obviously none too good as bullets had been zipping through the autumn leaves all the way and were reminding us of the near enemy as we were talking … I knew that I was called upon for a decision and wondered what I should do. It is a habit of mine to smoke under such circumstances; and without any thought, simply from habit, I felt my pockets, tapped my cigar case and lit a cigar. A highland Sergeant who was retreating saw me do this and I can only guess what went through his mind, but he stopped. Instantly my decision came. I sent Ruthven to the right, de Crespigny to the left and (I) stayed where I was… The cigar saved me and I am more than ever grateful to Lord Derby who sent me a dozen every month through the war.[6]

Of course, this rather self-deprecating account revealing a relaxed demeanour and calm approach belies the critical decisions Cavan was having to make under the greatest pressure. The First Battle of Ypres involved a complex series of fiercely fought battles which

4 Cuthbert Headlam, *History of the Guards Division in the Great War, 1915-1918* (London: Murray, 1924), vol.1, pp.3–7.
5 CAC: GBR/0014/CAVN, 'Recollections Hazy but Happy', Chapter 9, p.5.
6 CAC: GBR/0014/CAVN, 'Recollections Hazy but Happy', Chapter 9, p.5.

were part of an outflanking encounter on the eastern side of Ypres. A turning point, it marked the culmination of the mobile stage of the war and the effective destruction of the remainder of the professional pre-war British Army.

Cavan was referring in his memoir to a relatively short period of frantic and desperate fighting between 30 October and 1 November. On 30 October, the 3rd Cavalry Brigade and the 7th Division were pressed back towards Klein Zillebeke. Bulfin decided to form an impromptu force of six battalions to stem the German advance including three that Cavan had under his control: the 2/Grenadiers, the 1/Irish and the 2nd battalion, Oxfordshire and Buckinghamshire Light Infantry. This became known as 'Cavan's Force'. He was ordered to move down to the right of the 7th Division commanded by Major General Thompson Capper. In the evening the Irish Guards and the Ox and Bucks dug in on the edge of the wood known later as Shrewsbury Forest. The Grenadiers were on the right supporting the cavalry. Meanwhile Bulfin's group consisted of the 2/ Royal Sussex, the 1/Northamptonshire and the 2/Gordon Highlanders who were all on the eastern edge of Shrewsbury Forest.

On 31 October this line was heavily shelled by German artillery with the Irish Guards being the principal sufferers. On 1 November, Bulfin was seriously wounded in the head by a shell splinter in the fighting to hold on to the line held by his force. For a short time, it appeared that the 1/Irish had been broken. A message from Haig relayed through Cavan reached them in the early afternoon stated that the situation was critical, that they were to hold at all costs, and that he relied upon them 'to save the 1st Corps and possibly the Army'.[7] Haig then ordered Cavan to take over command of Bulfin's force.

A frantic day of heavy combat ensued. Remarkably, at dusk the line of Cavan's force was the same as in the morning except that it was shortened by blunting the salient at the corner of Shrewsbury Forest, which had proved a weak spot. At 7:00 p.m., Cavan drew the 2/Gordon Highlanders and the 2/Royal Sussex who had both been used to cover the readjustment out of the line which was then held by the 1/Irish, the 2/Grenadiers, the 2/Ox and Bucks and the 1/Northamptonshire battalions. The 7th Division's position was also intact. 'The fatigued troops of General Capper and Lord Cavan had held their ground against the whole *39th Division* and brigades of the *4th Bavarian* and *30th Divisions* on either flank of it'.[8]

At the end of First Ypres, Cavan said in a letter to Colonel Sir Henry Streatfeild: 'No words can ever describe what the devotion of the men and officers has been under the trials of dirt, squalor, cold, sleeplessness, and perpetual strain of the last three weeks … We came into this theatre 3,700 strong, and we shall go back about 2,000, but nothing finer to my mind has ever been done by human men.'[9] Cavan had made a big impression on those he commanded. For example, Major F.S. Garwood of the 7th Signal Company

7 Ian Beckett, *Johnnie Gough VC: A Biography of Brigadier-General Sir John Edmund Gough V.C., K.C.B., C.M.G.* (Staplehurst Kent: Spellmount,1989), p.189.
8 James Edmonds, *Military Operations, France and Belgium 1914, Volume 2* (Tennessee: Battery Press, 1995 [1925]), p.358.
9 Headlam, *History of the Guards Division,* p.12.

RE, 7th Division had not met him before but said in his diary: 'I was filled with admiration by the calm and quiet self-confidence of his manner. Here stood a man whose mere presence seemed equivalent to a brigade.'[10]

Cavan continued to impress in the following months. In February 1915, his brigade saw action at Cuinchy, a village along the La Bassée Canal. Cavan wrote that: 'I think that of all my war experiences the one that I look back to with the greatest pride was the very small affair at Cuinchy Brickstacks, only because it was a child of my own creation. I wrote the orders myself without instruction from above or assistance from below … based on Field Service Regulations. It was simply a matter of straightening a bit of line, but it was a complete success owing to the very careful arrangements made by Colonels Trefusis and Feilding commanding the 1/ Irish Guards and 3/ Coldstream Guards. Later victories on a larger scale were not due to me but to the troops and although one is responsible for the direction, that is dictated from above and put into shape from below.'[11] Cavan's 'small affair' had seen an intense German attack and successful British counter- attack. Rudyard Kipling wrote:

> Early in the morning of the 1st February a post held by the Coldstream in a hollow near the embankment, just west of the Railway Triangle—a spot unholy beyond most, even in this sector—was bombed and rushed by the enemy through an old communication-trench. No. 4 Company Irish Guards was ordered to help the Coldstream's attack. The men were led by Lieutenant Blacker-Douglass who had but rejoined on the 25th January. He was knocked over by a bomb within a few yards of the German barricade to the trench, picked himself up and went on, only to be shot through the head a moment later. Lieutenant Lee of the same Company was shot through the heart; the Company Commander, Captain Long-Innes, and 2nd Lieutenant Blom were wounded, and the command devolved on C.Q.M.S. Carton, who, in spite of a verbal order to retire 'which he did not believe,' held on till the morning in the trench under such cover of shell-holes and hasty barricades as could be found or put up. The Germans were too well posted to be moved by bomb or rifle, so, when daylight showed the situation, our big guns were called upon to shell for ten minutes, with shrapnel, the hollow where they lay. The spectacle was sickening, but the results were satisfactory. Then a second attack of some fifty Coldstream and thirty Irish Guards of No 1 Company under Lieutenants Graham and Innes went forward, hung for a moment on the fringe of their own shrapnel—for barrages were new things—and swept up the trench. [12]

10 Beckett, *Johnnie Gough V.C.*, p.194.
11 CAC: GBR/0014/CAVN, 'Recollections Hazy but Happy', Chapter 10/6.19. Some pages of this document have no page numbers.
12 Rudyard Kipling, *The Irish Guards in the Great War: The First Battalion* (Staplehurst: Spellmount, 2007 [1923]), pp.76–77.

At the Battle of Festubert, the 4th Guards Brigade went into action at 4:30 p.m. on 18 May, three days into the offensive. The 2/Grenadiers and the1/Irish immediately suffered heavy losses as they attacked across 600 yards of exposed ground. Cavan decided that digging in and consolidation was a better option than risking more lives in further attacks; a wise decision that revealed his priorities. The British had suffered over 16,000 casualties in just five days of fighting when the village of Festubert was eventually taken on 24 May and the front line had advanced just a couple of miles.[13]

Unsurprisingly, Cavan was promoted to GOC 50th Division on 29 June 1915 but he accepted the promotion with some personal regret:

> A Brigade is a glorious command and in my opinion it is the best of all the appointments for a regimental officer for he is in close touch with officers and men of four battalions. My heart was full and very sad when I said goodbye to the 2nd Grenadiers, 2nd and 3rd Coldstream and the 1st Irish Guards when I was promoted.[14]

A lot had changed for Cavan since his fishing holiday in Europe in the summer of 1914. He had risen to the challenges and opportunities created by the outbreak of the war and in doing so had resurrected his military career.

The Creation of the Guards Division

The Guards Division was formed in August 1915 although the details surrounding the circumstances of its foundation are rather lacking. Headlam states that: 'The idea of its creation appears to have been due solely to Lord Kitchener, who after first obtaining His Majesty's permission to carry out his project, proceeded to form the division without taking into confidence either the War Cabinet or the Commander-in-Chief in France.'[15] Sir John French first received notice of this development in a letter dated 13 July when he was told that: 'The King has approved of the formation of a Guards Division to be commanded by the Earl of Cavan.'[16] It has been argued that Kitchener 'was keen to curry favour by giving the Prince of Wales, who was attached to the Grenadiers, a bigger stage on which to perform' but is hard to imagine that such a major decision would have been made to accommodate the aspirations of the 21-year-old heir to the throne.[17]

Cavan himself was surprised to hear of its formation and that he would be its GOC. He had returned home to visit his wife who was suffering from diphtheria. His first

13 Simon Doughty, *The Guards Came Through* (London: Third Millennium, 2016), p.75.
14 CAC: GBR/0014/CAVN, 'Recollections Hazy but Happy', Chapter 9, p.6.
15 Headlam, *History of the Guards Division,* p.26.
16 Headlam, *History of the Guards Division,* p.26.
17 Simon Ball, *The Guardsmen, Harold Macmillan, Three Friends and the World They Made* (London: Harper Collins, 2004), p.40.

'intimation' that a Guards Division was to be formed was to his 'intense astonishment' when visiting the HQ of the Grenadier Guards in London. Colonel Sir Henry Streatfeild, who commanded the Grenadiers, produced a paper from the War Office ordering him to 'get the 3rd and 4th Battalion Grenadier Guards ready to go abroad at once as part of a Guards' Division'.[18]

On 19 July Cavan went to Windsor to receive the CB and the King was able to explain the proposed formation and 'told me to see Lord Kitchener'.[19] Cavan continued that: 'His Majesty informed me that I had been given the command of the "Guards Division" but it was not yet officially announced.'[20] On 20 July, he went to the War Office to see the Adjutant General. The proposed arrangements of the Guards brigades were discussed 'suggesting that the 1st Brigade should be the four Battalions of the Grenadiers. To this I demurred – arguing that if they went into action we might lose at one blow more officers and men of one Regiment than could be replaced.'[21] Further Cavan adds that: 'I deprecated breaking up the existing 4th Guards Brigade who had fought together for a year and whose experience and cohesion as a Fighting Unit made them of more than ordinary value to any Divisional Commander.'[22] Cavan clearly presented a very cogent argument because his thinking prevailed. Whilst there was little that could be done to stop the creation of the Guards Division, he was able to avoid the potential destruction of the Grenadier Guards when he insisted that all brigades should contain a mix of battalions from each of the Guards regiments.[23] At 6:30 p.m. he met Kitchener who said that: 'He intended the Divisional Formation to be permanent.'[24]

Indeed, Kitchener was 'a great admirer of the Brigade of Guards and had a profound belief in its discipline and training'.[25] There can be no doubt that, from its very inception, Kitchener viewed the Guards Division as an elite formation that was expected to play an important, if not pivotal role in what he believed would be a long-lasting war. There was an assumption that it was intended to use the division for special tactical roles, whether in attack or to restore stability where tactical disasters had occurred.[26]

Headlam pointed out that 'some military authorities considered that it was a mistake to concentrate so many fine battalions in a single division' and that 'their training and discipline would be more widely felt if the Guards battalions were distributed throughout the Army'.[27] Brigadier General Sir John Ponsonby, who was to be appointed as GOC, 2nd Guards Brigade, realised that there was a genuine fear within the various Guards

18 CAC: GBR/0014/CAVN, 'Recollections Hazy but Happy', Chapter 7.
19 CAC: GBR/0014/CAVN, 'Recollections Hazy but Happy', Chapter 7.
20 CAC: GBR/0014/CAVN, 'Recollections Hazy but Happy', Chapter 7.
21 CAC: GBR/0014/CAVN, 'Recollections Hazy but Happy', Chapter 7.
22 CAC: GBR/0014/CAVN, 'Recollections Hazy but Happy', Chapter 7.
23 Ball, *The Guardsmen*, p.40.
24 CAC: GBR/0014/CAVN, 'Recollections Hazy but Happy', Chapter 7.
25 Headlam, *History of the Guards Division*, p.27
26 Oliver Lyttelton (Lord Chandos), *From Peace to War: A Study in Contrast 1857–1918*. (London: The Bodley Head, 1968), p.137.
27 Lyttelton, *From Peace to War*, p.137.

regiments about the potential problems of assimilating a different quality of recruit but believed the Guards culture and traditions would prevail:

> The flooding of the army with new recruits might produce an entirely new stamp of man. Was the system alone good enough, to produce the fighting man who had hitherto, rightly or wrongly, been associated with the regiments of Guards? It might be necessary to take any men who were willing to join. Would there be a sufficient nucleus of old Guardsmen to ensure that the traditions carefully preserved through many generations were strictly maintained? The mill through which men of the Guards have to pass, however, is so severe, and the discipline so stern, that no one need have doubted that the new recruits would prove equal to their predecessors.[28]

Brigadier General Sir John Ponsonby.

Clearly, then, there was a Guards way of doing things and new recruits to the constituent parts of this elite formation would be expected to meet these standards.

Cavan was fortunate in being able to appoint some experienced staff to his Divisional HQ. His team, with the exception of Major N. Davidson R.A., who was appointed GSO2, were all Guardsmen. Of these, Lieutenant Colonel W. Hore-Ruthven, Scots Guards GSO1 and Lieutenant Colonel W. Darell, the Coldstream Guards AA and QMG were both Staff College graduates with considerable staff experience gained in the early months of the war.[29] The appointment of the Prince of Wales to the divisional staff, however, spoke more of the Guards social exclusivity rather than of his experience and competence.

On Cavan's insistence then, the Guards Division from the outset consisted of three brigades. 1st Guards Brigade (GOC, Feilding) already had considerable battlefield experience as the 4th (Guards) Brigade, including a period under Cavan's command of course, consisted of the 2/Grenadier Guards, the 2/Coldstream Guards, the 3/Coldstream

28 Frederick Ponsonby, *The Grenadier Guards in the Great War* (London: Macmillan, 1920), vol.1, p.283.
29 Headlam, *History of the Guards Division*, p. 28.

Guards and the 1/Irish Guards. The 2nd Guards Brigade: (GOC, Ponsonby) consisted of the 3/Grenadier Guards which was the only regular Guards battalion to have been kept at home, the 1/Coldstream Guards, the 1/Scots Guards and the newly formed 2/Irish Guards. Although the latter had only been formed officially on 18 August, there was a good supply of men in reserve at Warley to fill it. [30] Finally, the 3rd Guards Brigade (GOC, Heyworth) which was the least experienced of the three brigades. It included the 1/Grenadier Guards, the 4/Grenadier Guards which was formed on 15 July, the 2/Scots Guards and the 1/Welsh Guards which had been created by Royal Warrant on 26 February. Two of the GOCs were already brigadier generals with Ponsonby being promoted from lieutenant colonel of the 1/Coldstream Guards.[31]

The creation of the Welsh Guards illustrates how every effort was made to build this new regiment firmly on the traditions of the Guards. Major W. Murray Threipland was recruited from the Grenadiers to be its lieutenant colonel. He was a career soldier who had been commissioned in 1887 and had seen action in the Sudan and the Boer War. The second name on the regimental roll was the Regimental Sergeant Major, W. Stevenson from the Coldstream Guards. Additionally, I. M. Smith came from the Grenadiers as RQMS and W. Bland from the Grenadiers as drill sergeant. [32] The more important warrant and other non-commissioned ranks were filled with volunteers from the Grenadier, Coldstream and Scots Guards.[33] Permission was obtained to appeal to Welshmen who had joined these regiments and were already at the recruiting depot at Caterham and this led to 503 Welshmen including 40 NCOs transferring.[34] By early June, the battalion's strength was 47 officers and 1,610 other ranks.[35] Training was done at the White City and then from early May at Esher where a number of new officers joined. The Welsh Guards then left for France on 17 August.[36]

'The Guards Way of Doing Things'

Those young men who joined this newly created division were soon exposed to the unique culture of the Guards regiments. To serve in the Guards was to have a very specific experience of the war. They were socially elitist, officered by aristocrats or those who aspired to be like aristocrats. They had an unshakeable *esprit de corps*. They were 'introverted', especially when an entire Guards division was created in 1915. A junior officer would rarely ever encounter a senior officer who was not a Guardsman. 'Although they were part of the process by which the army transformed itself from a small professional army

30 Headlam, *History of the Guards Division*, p.31.
31 Headlam, *History of the Guards Division*, p.28.
32 C.H. Dudley Ward, *History of the Welsh Guards* (London: Murray, 1920), p.10.
33 Ward, *History of the Welsh Guards*, p.9.
34 Ward, *History of the Welsh Guards*, pp. 9–10.
35 Ward, *History of the Welsh Guards*, p.14.
36 Ward, *History of the Welsh Guards*, pp.13–15.

into a 'people's army', those in the Guards were inoculated against this experience ... Many 'hostilities only' officers entered the Guards regiments, but 'dilution' was strictly limited: the Grenadier Guards had doubled in size from two to four battalions by 1915, but the process went no further for the rest of the war'.[37]

They were, of course, regarded as a combat elite. Robert Graves wrote that the British Army in France was divided into three equal parts: units that were always reliable, units that were usually reliable and unreliable units. The Guards were on his 'always reliable' list. He commented that: 'It was a matter of pride to belong to one of the top-notch divisions – the Second, Seventh, Twenty-ninth, Guards', First Canadian, for instance.'[38]

Simon Ball's *The Guardsmen* is the story of Harold Macmillan, Oliver Lyttelton, Bobbety Cranborne and Harry Crookshank who all arrived at Eton in 1906, then served in the Great War in the same battalion of the Grenadier Guards, and finally entered the Cabinet under Winston Churchill during the Second World War. Macmillan, the most successful member of the group, rose to be Prime Minister between 1957 and 1963.

> In the carefully cadenced world of Edwardian society, the four had started out not as a quartet but as two distinct pairs. Cranborne and Lyttelton were patricians, Macmillan and Crookshank 'new men'. Eton was the clasp, a link sought quite consciously by the Macmillan and Crookshank families, that bound patrician and plebeian together. In the event this link was annealed by the Grenadier Guards.[39]

It was natural for those young men from the appropriate social background to aspire to a commission in the Guards regiments and they were able to depend upon the social exclusivity of their family backgrounds to find the placement that they felt they were entitled to. Lord Salisbury, who had a proprietary interest in the 4/Bedfordshire Regiment promised his son, Viscount Cranborne and his friend Oliver Lyttelton (whose late father had been a close friend), that he would fix commissions for them. Initially they joined the 4/Bedfordshires. When it became obvious that this battalion was likely to be broken up, they feared for their positions: 'We are angry because it seems possible that we may be gazetted to K(itchener)'s army'. Salisbury intervened and 'raised hell' with the War Office which led to their commissioning in the Guards during December 1914.[40]

Harold Macmillan was initially commissioned to the King's Royal Rifle Corps but fearful that his battalion might be used as a training establishment, decided to use his mother's influence to gain a transfer. Macmillan's family background was not aristocratic, but his father was Maurice Crawford Macmillan, a publisher and his mother Helen was an artist and socialite born in the United States. They might be fairly

37 Ball, *The Guardsmen*, pp.27–28.
38 Robert Graves, *Goodbye to All That* (London: Penguin,1998 [1929]), p.152.
39 Ball, *The Guardsmen*, p.1.
40 Ball, *The Guardsmen*, p.29.

described as being very well connected and socially aspirant. Macmillan was satisfied with the outcome:

> It seemed to me that we were so low down in the list of battalions in this vast Kitchener's Army that we must be forgotten. Our hope of getting overseas seemed more and more remote. I felt I must do something about it, and effect an exchange into some other regiment where there would be a better chance. Naturally I turned to my mother, and by her help and the recommendation of one or two of my Oxford friends I was sent for by the Lieutenant-Colonel of the Grenadier Guards, Sir Henry Streatfeild. I could not help feeling the contrast when I went to see him at the Regimental Headquarters in Buckingham Gate. The smart saluting of the sentry and of the sergeant put me to shame. I was conscious that when I went in to see the Lieutenant-Colonel my bearing would be ignominiously unsoldierly. However, he asked only a few questions and put me at my ease. After a few weeks, I heard that my application had been successful. I was gazetted to the Reserve Battalion of the Grenadier Guards in March 1915. Of course readers today will exclaim that this was all wrong. It was all done by influence. It was privilege of the worst kind – and so it was. It was truly shocking. But, after all, was it so very reprehensible? The only privilege I, and many others like me, sought was that of getting ourselves killed or wounded as soon as possible.[41]

The new recruits would soon come across the regimental 'characters' whose reputations went before them; regular officers who had joined the Guards in the late 1890s. Their years of peacetime soldiering had inculcated them with the proper Grenadier 'attitude'. Promotion for them had been very slow so that when the new arrivals encountered them, they were still captains or majors. 'They were attractive monsters, the ideals to which a new boy must aspire.'[42]

Lyttelton joined the 2/Grenadier Guards in February 1915 as a second lieutenant in No.4 Company. By August 1915, he had been promoted to lieutenant before transferring the following October to the 3/Grenadiers. He identified several such colourful 'characters' in his *Memoirs* published in the early 1960s. Lieutenant Colonel George Darell Jeffreys of the 2/Grenadiers, known to all as 'Ma', was absolutely dedicated to doing things in the 'Grenadier Way' and was somewhat of a reactionary. 'The three pillars of 'Ma' Jeffrey's beliefs and loyalty were Eton, the Brigade of Guards and the Conservative Party … 'Ma' wanted the Brigade of Guards to be composed only of the three oldest regiments'.[43] Another character was Lieutenant Colonel B.N. Sergison-Brooke or 'Boy Brooke' who was brigade-major of the 4th Guards Brigade and later CO of the 3/Grenadiers. He never spoke before luncheon. Treating his subordinates to 'intimidating silences, when the most that could be expected was a curt order delivered between

41 Harold Macmillan, *Winds of Change: 1914–1939* (London: Macmillan, 1966), pp.64–65.
42 Ball, *The Guardsmen*, pp.30–31.
43 Oliver Lyttelton, *The Memoirs of Lord Chandos* (London: The Bodley Head, 1962), p.50.

clenched teeth, derived from a slow acting digestion, which clothed the world in a bilious haze until the first glass of port brought a ray of sunshine'. After luncheon he was 'charming, helpful and humorous'.[44]

However, Lyttelton's particular favourite was Lieutenant Colonel Claude de Crespigny or 'Crawley' de Crespigny:

Lieutenant Colonel Claude de Crespigny.

> He was 'soon my company commander, and I fell completely under his charm. He had been one of the best-known gentlemen jockeys of his day. Once, when he had taken a bad fall on a favoured animal, and was walking past the silver ring towards the enclosure, someone shouted out that he must have backed the other. Crawley jumped the railings and chastised the offender with his cutting whip. He was, however, the kindest and most understanding of men, brave as a lion, most considerate and friendly to his subalterns. He was sometimes known to temper discipline with leniency, and when a young officer ran in one of his men for gambling in billets, he gave the man no more than a caution, and in private damned the eyes of the complainant.
>
> He was wracked by pain of a stomach disorder … would not report sick, and sometimes used to lie groaning in the trench for the best part of the night. He usually recovered the next day, and took his glass of port or two as a sharp but unwise reminder to his stomach that he was having no nonsense with his digestion. He did not entertain a great respect for generals and the high command, and was reputed to begin most battles by cutting his own telephone wire.[45]

The royal connection that the Guards enjoyed could be a beneficial one. Writing fondly about the Prince of Wales, Lyttelton recalled that:

> He used to lend his large grey Daimler to any brother officer who could find the courage to ask for it … I later got some leave and asked to borrow the car to get to Boulogne, because by this means you could get an extra day in England. He sent

44 Lyttelton, *The Memoirs of Lord Chandos*, p.52.
45 Lyttelton, *The Memoirs of Lord Chandos*, pp.40–41.

> me a slip of paper agreeing at once, but asking me whether I would take a letter to 'my people' at home … As I reached the quay the leave boat had just cast off, but I was not the Prince's messenger for nothing and, waving his letter to the King, I persuaded the embarkation officer to order the ship to put back. I swept up the gangway in triumph and delivered the letter at Buckingham Palace in a few hours.[46]

Looking back on his varied career Lyttelton remarked that he had known many institutions in his life but 'the best human organisation, the most efficient and the most closely knit … is the Brigade of Guards'. A battalion 'well turned out, the men with their heads up … in step and in some awe of their officers and NCOs, will stand the strain of battle better than bodies which follow looser rules'.[47] Quite simply then, the Guards had an entirely different outlook and culture to the rest of the army.

However, it should not be forgotten that, like the rest of the BEF's component parts, the Guards Division would be expected to follow the set requirements of the *Field Service Regulations 1909* and that, as an elite force, be particularly mindful of them. The regulations stipulated, for example, that 'generals should be supported by collegiate staffs, collating military intelligence' who should 'consider all relevant factors before issuing "brief" orders of intent'. They were to be 'transmitted down the command hierarchy for tactical implementation with time allowed for planning and organisation at battalion level.' In successfully mounting an attack the aim was 'not overwhelming numbers, but fire-power superiority from concealed artillery' which would not be in the front line but would be providing close supporting for the infantry. Initiative during battle at a local level was to be encouraged.[48] In essence then the *Field Service Regulations* were a 'set of principles for application by trained and experienced officers, which specifically avoided going into too much detail, since those applying them should, through experience and training, know what detailed actions to perform within their framework.'[49]

Training: Assimilating Guards Traditions and Preparations for Loos

Basic training, of course, began in Britain. We are fortunate to have two memoirs written by Guardsmen who write evocatively and vividly of their experiences of training which are even more valuable because of their different perspectives. However, both Stephen Graham's *A Private in the Guards* and Norman D. Cliff's *To Hell and Back with the Guards* leave us in no doubt about the often brutal approach used to inculcate the unique culture of the Guards.

46 Lyttelton, *The Memoirs of Lord Chandos*, p.47.
47 Lyttelton, *The Memoirs of Lord Chandos*, pp.35–36.
48 50. David Hutchinson, *FSR: An Analysis*, <https://fieldserviceregulations.co.uk/>, accessed 20/12/23.
49 Andy Simpson, *Directing Operations: British Corps Command on the Western Front 1914–18* (Solihull: Helion, 2019), p.20.

Whilst Graham's book was published in 1919, Cliff's was not published until 1988. They both write about 'the draconian treatment' handed out by 'harsh and sometimes sadistic NCOs' at the Guards Training Depot at Caterham known as 'Little Sparta' although they come from different perspectives.[50] Graham was an older man, widely travelled and an experienced journalist whereas Cliff was younger, less tolerant of the prevailing class system and, ultimately, a pacifist. Further Cliff's memoir is based on his experiences from the very outset of the war whereas Graham's experiences are based on 1917 and 1918. However, it is reasonable to assume that the basic, initial 'breaking in' of raw recruits did not change much over these years.

For Graham:

> To be struck, to be threatened, to be called indecent names, to be drilled by yourself in front of a squad in order to make a fool of you, to be commanded to do a tiring exercise and continue doing it whilst the rest of the squad does something else; to have your ear spat into, to be marched across parade-ground under escort, to be falsely accused before an officer and silenced when you try to speak in defence – all these things take down your pride, make you feel small, and in some ways fit you to accept the role of canon-fodder on the battle ground.[51]

Recruits were from all social backgrounds and included 'crocks' and 'duds'. Graham provides clear evidence of the social mix that went into the 'melting pot' of Guards recruitment: 'we had men with weak chests, with weak ankles, with weak brains, and lung trouble and rheumatism and neurasthenia. But they all seemed to make good in time and they filled up the gaps in the heroic line – which illustrates the point that in this war, out of almost any material, first-class soldiers could be made.'[52] Graham is also accepting of the gulf between the officers and their men:

> Our officers are brave men; from a rankers point of view they are not themselves particularly disciplined. Their discipline is of a different type from that of the men and refers to higher things. For leadership personality is required, and that the system leaves to the officer. He is a 'sportsman', a 'good sort', he's 'the finest man ever was in this regiment' – these are common ever repeated remarks about officers. Not that the officers are really near the men: a great gulf divides them socially, and must do so, but the men would not follow so well an officer who was too free with them.[53]

50 Brian Bond. *Survivors of a Kind, Memoirs of the Western Front* (London: Continuum, 2008), p.63.
51 Stephen Graham, *A Private in the Guards* (London: Macmillan, 1919), pp.50–51.
52 Graham, *A Private in the Guards*, p.63.
53 Graham, *A Private in the Guards*, p.17.

By comparison, Cliff is highly critical of the dehumanising nature of the training and the obsession with perfect turn out together with immaculate drill even in the immediate aftermath of battle.[54] He realised that the more a soldier reverts to a savage, the better a killer he will become. 'Mercy, kindliness and chivalry have to be replaced by brutality, hatred and ruthlessness.' He believed that 'by giving priority to smartness and almost mechanical precision on parade the Guards tended to dull the mind and kill initiative and responsibility'.[55] As Cliff put it: 'The effect of the whole system of drill was not to inculcate self-respect and to fire enthusiasm, but to humiliate and rob a man of his dignity, thus instilling hatred of and contempt for those in authority.'[56] He retained a particular contempt for his former company commander Captain (Viscount) Lascelles. Whilst disliking his pompous, 'rakish' appearance and awkward lisp, his particular 'crime' was the belief that he was responsible for the unnecessary death of a sentry who he ordered to look over the top of the trench. Nonetheless, he did accept that Lascelles and certain other officers certainly displayed bravery in action.[57]

A review of Graham's book by Captain John Reeve of the Grenadier Guards, who was at Caterham during the war, was published in the 'Victory' edition of the *Guards Brigade Magazine* in 1920. It largely endorsed his account of Little Sparta finding it to be generally 'excellent' with some 'exaggeration' on occasion. 'It is not for me', Reeve contends, 'to make excuses for Officers, but if abuses occurred through want of supervision, when we had about three officers per thousand men, and when Captains in charge of regiments there had anything from 500 up to 4,000 men with their accompanying bedding, rifles, and other stores; we probably averaged not less than a thousand men under our charge'. He believed training was generally close to peace time standards and completed in 10 to 12 weeks as against 16 beforehand. Recruits may have been very occasionally humiliated by 'blows' but he was 'giving a very wrong impression' to suggest this was a normal procedure. Reeve addressed Graham's contention that 'although the process of being disciplined is hard, it is difficult to understand why the discipline and training of our Spartan division were not applied to the whole Army … Indeed if all had been trained like the Guards, it seems probable the German Army would have been defeated in the field earlier'. For Reeve, the answer was simple: 'The Army did not have the wherewithal to apply it'. He recalled that an Australian Officer who spent three weeks at Caterham had wasted his time 'for it was an ideal they would never attempt or hope to attain'.[58]

Once the Guards Division was brought together in France, how effective was the training of what would be, as Graham and Cliff both confirm, highly disciplined troops encouraged to view themselves as an elite force? There was just four or so weeks to prepare them for the Battle of Loos. By looking at the war diaries of the Guards Divisional

54 Bond, *Survivors*, p.66.
55 Bond, *Survivors*, p.64.
56 Norman Cliff, *To Hell and Back with the Guards* (Braunton: Merlin, 1988), pp.25–26.
57 Bond, *Survivors*, p.65.
58 John S. Reeve, 'Little Sparta in the War', *Household Guards Magazine*, 'Victory' Edition (1920), pp.89–91.

HQ and three different battalions some judgements can be made. The battalions chosen are the 1/Welsh and the 4/Grenadiers which were both newly formed together with the 1/Irish who were already 'battle-hardened' by their experiences in the fighting of 1914 and 1915. In truth, the battalion war diaries convey a vague picture with frequent references to daily 'company training'. However, there was a 'Conference of Officers Commanding Battalions' held on 24 August and the notes kept in the war diary of the 1/Welsh are instructive in indicating what would have probably happened during these training activities. There would be a particular focus on bombers who were to be trained by the Brigade Grenade Company as well as by battalions. All officers were to be trained and as many men as possible. The 4/Grenadiers and the 1/Welsh were to receive 'double lot training'. Bombers would be expected to work with companies in training. Two machine gun officers per battalion were to be trained and employed with the Machine Gun Section. Double teams were to be trained with each battalion training gunners. As with bombing, the machine gunners were to work with companies in training. Other priorities that were identified included: the selection and training of battalion snipers, the training of company wiring sections, night digging, a focus on the importance of 'digging in at every opportunity', and the use of rifle ranges. With regard to smoke helmets or anti-gas hoods, attention was focussed on methods of carrying them and a drill to utilise them within 17 seconds.[59]

Tactical exercises took place on the instruction of the divisional HQ. On 1 September, all three Guards Brigades plus the attached RFC Squadron, cyclists, pioneer and signals companies practiced march discipline, inter-communication and concealment from aircraft. Three separate brigade tactical exercises were witnessed by Cavan: the 3rd Guards Brigade at Le Biberou near Heuringhen on 6 September, the 2nd Guards on 8 September, the 1st Guards on 15 September. On 18 September, he watched a tactical exercise near Setques involving a combination of the 2nd Guards Brigade, 74th RFA, 55th Field Corps, detachments from the Divisional Squadron and Divisional Mounted Troops. Finally, on 21 September he attended a tactical exercise near Helfault by 3rd Guards Brigade, 76th Brigade RFA and Divisional Mounted Troops.[60] Meanwhile artillery training included temporary detachments. On 2 September, 61st (Howitzer) Brigade RFA and 74th Brigade had been temporarily attached to the Indian Corps for training with the 61st returning on 17 September after the 74th's return on 14 September. The 75th Brigade RFA had temporarily joined III Corps for instruction on 6 September.[61]

The war diary of the 1/Welsh gives a good picture of what was achieved on the tactical exercise held on 6 September. They marched out of billets at 8:30 a.m. and returned at 4:00 p.m.

59 The National Archives (TNA): WO95/1224, 1/Welsh Guards War Diary, 24 August 1915.
60 TNA: WO95/1190 Guards Brigade HQ, 1 –21 September 1915.
61 TNA: WO95/1190 Guards Brigade HQ, 2 –17 September 1915.

> Not a heavy day's marching, much time spent lying down. An attack practice carried out with skeleton enemy'. 1st bn. Welsh bn. 4 bn Grenadier Guards in firing line, 2 bn. Scots, 1 bn. Grenadiers in reserve. Firing line held up and reserves passed through line and carried on. Bn work and attack in my opinion well done which included a change of direction in the middle of the attack and reallocation in firing line. Machine guns did well and Bn signallers were specially good during 3 changes of direction … continued communication by telephone with Brigade HQ – messages went through quickly and efficiently.[62]

The 3rd Brigade's tactical exercise on 21 September was less useful to the 1/Welsh, however: 'Bn. marched 7.30 am returned billets by 2 pm. Being a Brigade Reserve, did nothing only marching 4 or 5 miles and returning same distances'.[63] Other snippets of interest from their war diary include references to the problems of logistical preparations and the ongoing training of bombers. So, on 12 September, 'Practice of transport move to Haut Schoubrouck went badly' with 'far too much stuff on GS wagon'. Also, on the following day, 'Morning attack practice with Brigade near Clairmarais Foret attended by GOC Division and Brigadier. GOC congratulated on morning's work but still problems with loading transport. 26 bombers returned from Brigade Bombing School.'[64]

The war diary of the 1/Irish has some clear evidence of training targets and, ultimately, a tragic event. On 7 September we find: 'The companies were exercised in extended order drill and fire control, also in advanced guards under their company commanders.'[65] Then, 'the CO prepared a scheme for an attack by the battalion against village of Drionville for 9 September.'[66] On 16 September: '20 Motor buses were sent to their billets at Thiembronne- battalion practiced occupying them as quickly as possible, half a battalion at a time.'[67] Meanwhile, on 20 September, 'Capt. Hargreaves gave a lecture on Lewis machine guns to all officers, and to selected NCOs and men.'[68] On 22 September: 'Bn exercised in musketry by co. commanders – each man had to fire 10 rounds rapid with his helmet on … Lewis gun teams from each co. which had been under instruction for some days were … instructed in the actual firing of the gun with ball ammunition'. The 'company and bn bombers were instructed under 2nd Lt. Tisdall in throwing live bombs'. To remind us of just how dangerous this kind of training could be, one bomber was killed and Tisdall himself, together with two others, were wounded.[69]

The war diary of the newly formed 4/Grenadier Guards has an entry on 23 August to what was most likely to have been some kind of team building exercise when they

62 TNA: WO95/1224, 1/Welsh Guards War Diary, 6 September 1915.
63 TNA: WO95/1224, 1/Welsh Guards War Diary, 21 September 1915.
64 TNA: WO95/1224, 1/Welsh Guards War Diary, 12–13 September 1915.
65 TNA: WO95/1216, 1/Irish Guards War Diary, 7 September.
66 TNA: WO95/1216, 1/Irish Guards War Diary, 9 September 1915.
67 TNA: WO95/1216, 1/Irish Guards War Diary, 16 September 1915.
68 TNA: WO95/1216, 1/Irish Guards War Diary, 20 September 1915.
69 TNA: WO95/1216, 1/Irish Guards War Diary, 22 September 1915.

'experimented in embarking on barges at Arques on the canal'.[70] Other entries have a more relevant focus, however. On 31 August, the 'Company Training CO and Machine Gun Officers attended a machine gun demonstration at the Machine Gun School at Wisques'.[71] On 1 September: 'Divisional Field day … The Brigadier complimented the Battalion on its march discipline and on the way it kept out of sight of aeroplanes. Total march of 17 miles, not a man fell out.'[72] On 7 September: 'Nos 1 and 4 Coys marched to Avroult to dig new defences returning on 9/9' and on 13 September: 'The Battalion had an object lesson in putting up wire entanglements from the RE.'[73] Meanwhile, on 15 September: 'Ellison and Thompson went to Wizernes for a course of instruction in the Lewis Gun' and on 17 September, Cavan received the Brigade and 'greatly complimented me on the appearance of the battalion, he stated that the men's packs were the best he had ever seen'.

Undoubtedly then, the Guards Division HQ did its utmost to prepare the troops for battle in what would be just a 'window' of a few weeks. The various tactical exercises where battalions worked together proved useful in the attacks around Hill 70 at Loos and beyond, the stress on training more bombers was especially valuable in the intense fighting around the Hohenzollern Redoubt in October and march discipline was important in bringing the Guards Division up to the front lines on 25 to 27 September. However, the reality of what was ultimately to be faced at Loos was beyond what could be achieved in such artificial and time-limited circumstances. Further, we cannot be sure of the consistency in the quality of training across the Guards Division as a whole. The discipline that was the foundation of all Guards training back in Britain would, however, be vital in the Guards Division's 'baptism of fire' at Loos.

70 TNA: WO95/1223, 4/Grenadier Guards War Diary, 23 August 1915.
71 TNA: WO95/1223, 4/Grenadier Guards War Diary, 31 August 1915.
72 TNA: WO95/1223, 4/Grenadier Guards War Diary, 1 September 1915.
73 TNA: WO95/1223, 4/Grenadier Guards War Diary, 7–13 September 1915.

2

The Battle of Loos: 25–28 September 1915

Military Context

During 1915 the BEF fought with little success at Neuve Chapelle in March, at nearby Aubers Ridge and Festubert in May, and at Givenchy in June. At Neuve Chapelle, there had been an initial breakthrough but a failure to consolidate these gains allowed for a highly effective German counter-attack. Losses were heavy with 7,000 British and as many as 4,200 Indian casualties. The attack had revealed significant deficiencies in communication and especially with the artillery bombardment which led Sir John French to blame the BEF's ineffectiveness on a shell shortage. The ensuing 'Shell Crisis' brought about the collapse of Asquith's Liberal administration together with the appointment of David Loyd George as Minister of Munitions. The subsequent Battles of Aubers Ridge and Festubert were characterised by inadequate barrages, yet more high casualty levels, and no significant ground was gained. At Givenchy, the BEF fought alongside Canadian troops. Two attacks were made on successive days despite a lack of ammunition but were repulsed on both occasions.

The inexperienced volunteers from the New Armies lacked adequate preparation and suffered variable standards of leadership whilst the Old Army had been battered by its experiences in 1914 and its established battalions were 'filled with new drafts – half trained, only partially disciplined and new to battle'. Whilst they did not lack courage, these new men 'had neither the skill with the rifle nor the resource in battle of old soldiers.'[1] The BEF was also still in a transitionary stage of procurement; antiquated 4.7-inch guns were still used by some batteries and 'Long' Lee-Enfield rifles that dated from the Boer War were still issued to most Territorial infantrymen.[2]

1 Spencer Jones, '"To make war as we must, and not as we should like": The British Army and the Problem of the Western Front, 1915' in Spencer Jones (ed.), *Courage without Glory: The British Army on the Western Front 1915* (Solihull: Helion, 2015), p.40.
2 Jones, 'To Make War', pp.44–46.

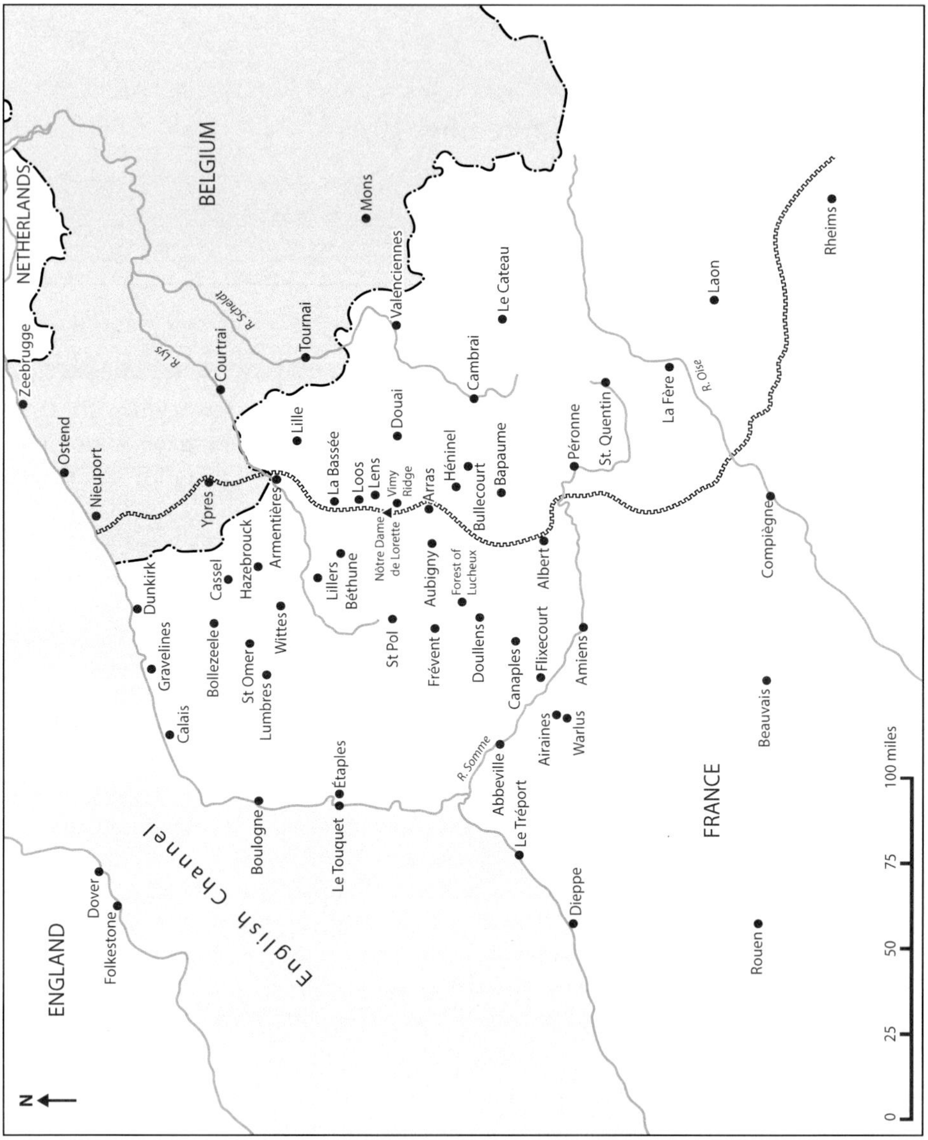

The Western Front, September 1915.

The Battle of Loos was fought in September and October 1915 and was the biggest British offensive action on the Western Front up to that point of the conflict. Whilst Joseph Joffre, C-in-C of the French forces, believed that an assault by the French First and Tenth armies in the Lens-Arras region together with a British attack in the La Bassee-Loos area could bring about a decisive breakthrough. The BEF's view was somewhat different and General Sir Douglas Haig (now promoted to GOC First Army) both believed that the ground in the area proposed for the attack was totally inappropriate for such an enterprise. It was dominated by German-held slag heaps and colliery towers integrated into a very substantial defensive network. This view was only strengthened in July when it became obvious that the Germans were building a second defensive position behind the front lines. However, on 21 August, Lord Kitchener, the British Secretary of State for War, committed the BEF because of his belief that the Entente's very survival depended on the BEF fighting alongside their French allies so avoiding the possibility that 'otherwise France or Russia might sue for peace'.[3] Kitchener, facing the terrible reality of this situation, commented that 'unfortunately we had to make war as we must, and not as we should like'.[4]

With inadequate supplies of ammunition and heavy artillery, Haig decided on the use of chlorine gas in the opening attack on 25 September. Although the BEF suffered heavy casualties, they enjoyed a good deal of success on the first day in penetrating the German positions near Loos and Hulluch. Events then turned on the ineffective utilisation of the reserves (the Cavalry Corps and three infantry divisions from XI Corps; the Guards, 21st and 24th) which Sir John French had opted to hold too far back from the battle front to be able to exploit these initial successes. Overnight, the Germans reinforced and reorganised their forces overwhelming the massed ranks of the inexperienced 21st and 24th Divisions after they were released from the reserves. The debate about the use of the reserves and the role of Haig and French is well documented elsewhere; suffice to say that the delay in releasing all three divisions made it very difficult, if not impossible, to maintain the initial momentum of the attack.[5] The Battle of Loos soon became bogged down in attritional warfare for relatively minor gains. The *Official History* identified several key problems with the attack. Chief amongst these was the lack of proper road control which was an indication of poor staff work. Thus, the delays and unnecessary hardships inflicted on the 21st, 24th and Guards Divisions on their way up to the battlefield might have been averted by a good system of road control, and the marking and policing of 'Up' and 'Down' routes. The time allowed for orders to reach the front companies and be acted upon was insufficient. Even the normal pre- war number

3 David Stevenson, *1914–1918: The History of the First World War* (London: Allen Lane, 2004), p.159.

4 Jones, 'To Make War', p.55.

5 See Tim Travers, *The Killing Ground: The British Army, the Western Front & The Emergence of Modern Warfare 1900-1908* (London: Leo Cooper, 2003) pp. 16–20, Robin Prior and Trevor Wilson, *Command on the Western Front: The Military Career of Sir Henry Rawlinson 1914-1918* (London: Blackwell, 1992), pp.130–134.

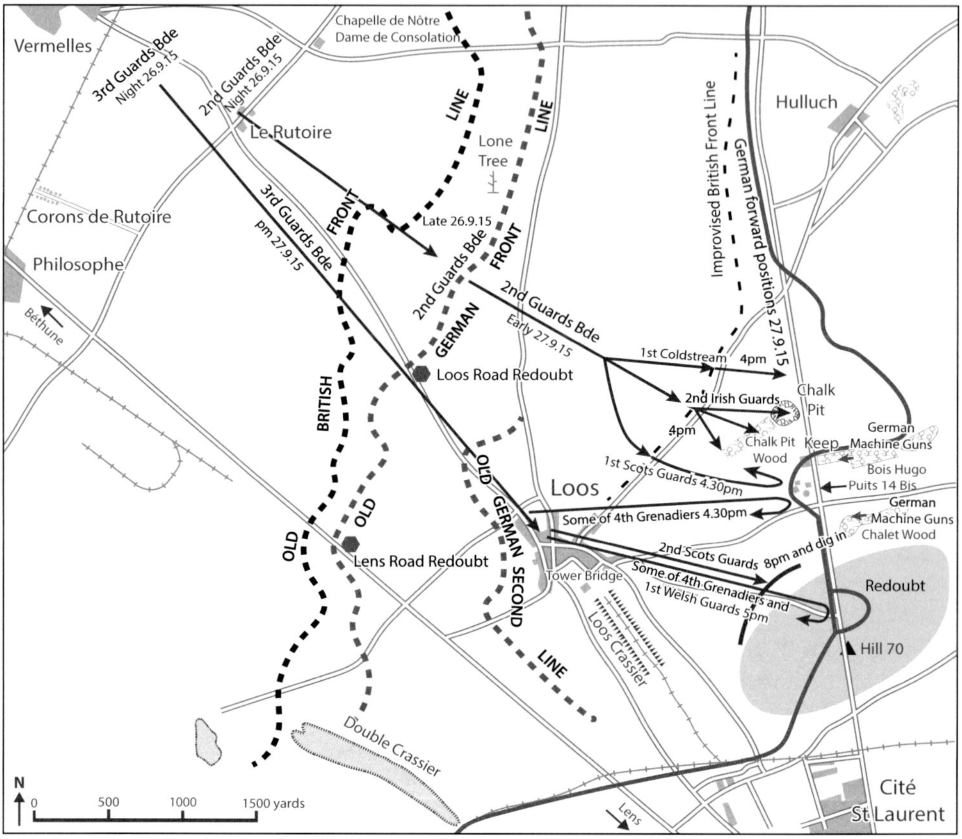

The Battle of Loos, the attack on Puits 14 Bis and Hill 70, 27 September 1915.

of heavy guns per division was lacking, the artillerymen were even less well trained than infantry, equipment for close fighting such as trench-mortars and hand grenades were mainly improvised and inferior to that of the enemy.[6] Yet some regard Loos as a missed opportunity. As Major General Richard Hilton, at the time a Forward Observation Officer, said: 'The real tragedy of that battle was its nearness to complete success'; a point that both Nick Lloyd and Gordon Corrigan have made.[7]

6 James Edmonds, *Military Operations, France and Belgium 1915* (Tennessee: Battery Press, 1995 [1928] vol.2, p. 395.

7 Philip Warner *The Battle of Loos* (William Kimber, 1976), p.1, Michael Woods, 'Gas, Grenades and Grievances: The Attack on the Hohenzollern' in Spencer Jones (ed.) *Courage without Glory: The British Army on the Western Front 1915*, p.432.

The Entry of the Guards Division to the Battlefield, 26 September

With the BEF's attack stalling on September 26, the urgent priority now was to close the gap in the British lines left by the rout of the 21st and 24th Divisions before launching a fresh assault on the dominant German position of Hill 70 just to the east of Loos itself. This responsibility would be borne by the Guards Division which, having been brought out of the reserves, was finally placed under Lieutenant General Sir Richard Haking's control as XI Corps GOC at 2:30 p.m. on 26 September.[8] Cavan felt a great opportunity had been lost:

> I shall always regret that at Loos, our first battle as a Division, we were not allowed to come under Sir Douglas Haig's immediate orders until too late. It is my firm conviction that had we been allowed to follow up the first successful attack, as originally intended, and been supported by the 21st and 24th Divisions, the results of the battle would have been far more decisive than they were. There is nothing more difficult for inexperienced troops than to meet the onslaught of a counter-stroke – on unknown ground freshly won with the trenches battered in, and all defences the wrong way round. Such things had been the almost daily routine of the Guards Battalion [sic] engaged at Ypres in the previous autumn and I believe their greater experience would have won the day.[9]

From this point, Haking's role as XI Corps GOC took on a tactical dimension; arguably one in which he was not successful in at Loos.[10] At Loos, the role of Haking was pivotal, yet the exact role of a corps commander was still undergoing refinement in 1915. Originally conceived of as a channel of communication between the GHQ, army and divisions, Andy Simpson observes that the job was morphing into something of much greater importance. For example, after the Battles of Festubert and Aubers Ridge, responsibility for artillery control would come to rest within the corps. Significantly by the time of Loos, the corps had been given responsibility for traffic control up to the front.[11] At Aubers Ridge on 9 May, Lieutenant General James Willcocks, GOC Indian Corps, had vividly described the impossibility of movement through blown away trenches, noting that 'the nearer one got to the front, the more of a shambles it became'.[12] Yet as Simon Robbins states, the 'poor management of operations continued at Loos when no proper arrangements were made to

8 TNA: WO95/880, XI Corps War Diary, 26 September 1915.
9 CAC: GBR/0014/CAVN, 'Recollections Hazy but Happy', Chapter 7.
10 Michael Senior, *Lt. Gen Sir Richard Haking: A Dutiful Soldier, XI Corps Commander 1915-18: A Study in Corps Command* (Barnsley: Pen & Sword, 2012), p.65.
11 Andy Simpson, 'British Corps Command on the Western Front, 1914-1918.' in Gary Sheffield, and Dan Todman (eds), *Command and Control on the Western Front: The British Army's Experience 1914-1918*. (Staplehurst: Spellmount, 2004), pp.101–102.
12 Cited in Jones, 'To make war as we must', p.50.

clear the roads for the advance of XI Corps to exploit the initial success of the assaulting divisions'.[13]

Prior to the battle itself, there had already been some worrying signs. At a briefing of 2nd Guards Brigade officers on 15 September at Lumbres, Haking had spoken optimistically about prospects for the forthcoming attack in which he estimated the German defences consisted of only 40,000 men in comparison to the BEF's 200,000.[14] Remarkably, when he stressed how important the role of platoon leaders would prove, 'he instructed them always to push on boldly whenever an opportunity offered, even at the expense of exposing and leaving unguarded their flanks'.[15] Surely, this was a potential recipe for disaster and the fact that there are three exclamation marks at the end of the entry indicated 'at least a degree of incredulity on the part of the writer'.[16] Lieutenant Colonel Murray Threipland does not seem to have been impressed noting in the Welsh Guards' war diary that: 'He spoke for about ¾ of an hour' in explaining the operation but he 'spoke indistinctly and too fast to allow for note taking'.[17] Haking's optimism when speaking at Lumbres was certainly not borne out by events.

Indeed, the movement of the Guards up to the front-line on 25 and 26 September was badly managed, as Simon Robbins has stated, and meant that when they entered it, many soldiers were already exhausted. It exposed poor staff work and preparation on the part of Haking's team. The Guards had already spent 25 September moving forward in anticipation of a breakthrough with a 6:00 a.m. start. By 10:30 a.m. they were at Ferfray and at 11:30 a.m. they were ordered to move towards Noeux-les-Mines at 2:00 p.m. which proved a frustrating experience: 'The move of the Division was greatly delayed by troops of the 21st Division and transport of 21st and 47th Divisions. The tail of the column was cut off by the Cavalry Corps, orders having been received that it was to be allowed to pass. The rear troops did not reach their destinations until after mid-night.' At 10:00 p.m. it 'was placed under GHQ in General Reserve – to be ready at 5.00 a.m. to move at 2 hours' notice'.[18]

This is confirmed by Harold Macmillan who described the delays suffered by his battalion, the 4/Grenadiers, on 25 September. In a letter to his mother, he says that at Marles-les-Mines, they waited from 3:30 p.m. to 9:30 p.m. They were kept standing most of the time in heavy rain. The rest of the brigade had gone on ahead and they could not communicate with them. 'This of course means shocking staff work … we had no idea where we supposed to get to or what to do.' They eventually got to their billets at 1:30 a.m. before being woken again just three hours later.[19]

13 Simon Robbins, *British Generalship on the Western Front, 1914–1918: Defeat into Victory* (London: Routledge 2006), pp.21–22.
14 Cited in Senior, *Haking*, p.65.
15 Senior, *Haking*, p.65.
16 Senior, *Haking*, p.65.
17 TNA: WO95/1224, Welsh Guards War Diary, 15 September 1915.
18 TNA: WO95/1190, Guards Brigade HQ War Diary, 25/26 September.
19 Macmillan, *Winds of Change*, pp.72–73.

On 26 September at 12:40 p.m. orders were issued by XI Corps HQ 'to occupy a portion of original British front line' but this was amended at 2:10 p.m. 'to occupy German instead of British trenches'. The Guards Division:

> …marched in accordance with orders and during the night to take over a portion of the German line from 21st on the right (2nd Guards Brigade) and 24th Division on left (1st Guards) with 3rd Guards in Reserve. Touch was obtained with 3rd Cavalry Division on the right and 1st Division on the left. Advanced Guards Division HQ opened at SAILLY LABOURSE with Brigade HQs at Le Rutoure Farm for the 1st and 2nd Brigades with 3rd Brigade just south of Vermelles.[20]

Kipling's account of the 2/Irish Guards experience is based closely on their war diaries and makes salutary reading. He outlines the gruelling nature of the task in merely getting to the front. When they eventually arrived at Haquin 'very wet and tired' at about 1:00 a.m. on the 26 September, their billets were inadequate. They 'had been on their feet standing, marching, or variously shifted about, for twenty odd hours. The men's breakfasts were issued at half-past four that same dawn as there was a possibility of an early move.'[21] In fact, they waited until mid-day on 27 September when the brigade moved to trenches in front of La Rutoire. They eventually reached their allocated position after great difficulty moving over congested roads and the battle-scarred terrain, just before midnight. They were experiencing difficulties in establishing exactly where they had been expected to position to: 'There was no one to tell them exactly which trenches were to be taken over.'[22] Kipling, whose own son, Second Lieutenant John Kipling of the 2/Irish Guards died at Loos on 27 September, comments that they had now been on foot and awake for 48 hours in which time they had been largely unfed. At 2:30 a.m. they received 'verbal instructions to push forward to another line of captured German trenches, some five hundred yards, relieving any troops that might happen to be there'.[23] Kipling's account confirms the ongoing inadequacy of XI Corps staff work and the highly fatigued state of troops who were just hours away from combat.

Back at XI Corps HQ, at 11:30 p.m. on 26 September, Haking received orders to submit plans for the capture of Hill 70, the Chalk Pit and Puits No 14 to be enacted during the following afternoon. Hill 70 was the dominant feature of the battlefield, and any further progress made its capture vital. Puits No.14 was a fortified mining complex on its north-westerly slope with the Chalk Pit immediately beneath it. Whilst little could be accomplished during the night, the morning hours were a period of intense activity. The lack of adequate time for preparation is clear in the following telephone

20 TNA: WO95/1190, Guards Brigade HQ War Diary, 26 September 1915.
21 Rudyard Kipling, *The Irish Guards in the Great War: The Second Battalion* (Staplehurst: Spellmount, 1997 [1923]), p.22
22 Kipling, *The Irish Guards*, p.22
23 Kipling, *The Irish Guards*, p.22

message (unfortunately without an exact time) sent to the First Army HQ which clearly indicates the sense of improvisation that was taking place:

> Genl. Haking is not in a position to decide the details of the attack against Hill 70 this afternoon until he has seen Lord Cavan, who is out now looking at the ground ... Meanwhile if the attack is not to be delayed, he suggests that all available heavy artillery should be turned on to Hill 70, PUITS 14 bis and the CHALK PIT to the North of it as early as possible this morning, and the wire should be out on Hill 70. If the bombardment begins in good time, he hopes to be able to commence the attack early in the afternoon ... General Carey will be over later when the definitive plan is decided to discuss details of artillery preparation and support with General Mercer.[24]

By 8:40 a.m., IV Corps HQ was able to report that 'it was pretty clear that both Puits No. 14 and the CHALK PIT were in enemy hands'.[25] However, beyond that Haking had no precise detail of the enemy's strength. The *Official History* states that the German forces that faced the Guards were units of the *7th, 8th* and *117th Infantry Divisions*. Specifically, *IR 165* and *IR 26* were from *7th Infantry Division*, *IR 153* was from *8th Infantry Division* and *IR 157* was from the *117th Infantry Division*.[26] The *7th* and *8th Infantry Divisions* had both been recruited in Prussian Saxony and by the Battle of Loos were already battle hardened. The *117th* was newly created in April 1915 but had been unfortunate to experience a real baptism of fire during May and June north of Souchez and at Notre Dame de Lorette where the division lost 107 officers and 5,255 other ranks.[27]

The basic facts of what then happened are well established. Haking settled on a plan to attack Hill 70 from the north and west simultaneously. Initially, the 2nd Guards Brigade would move eastwards from North Loos Avenue across the Loos valley and the Loos–Hulluch road towards Puits 14 bis and Chalk Pit Wood. Moving through Bois Hugo and Chalet Wood, they would then assault the Hill 70 redoubt from the southern edge of Chalet Wood. Meanwhile, a frontal attack from the west would be made by the 3rd Guards Brigade approaching from Vermelles during the afternoon.[28] Strangely, the most experienced of the Guards brigades, the 1st, was destined to remain on the periphery of these events and one wonders why, in the original disposition of the forces towards the front lines and knowing the likely objectives of the forthcoming assault, it was not placed further south in the line at the very outset by Haking.

24 TNA: WO95/880, Appendix 8 XI Corps HQ War Diary, 27 September 1915.

25 TNA: WO95/158, First Army HQ Diary, 27 September.

26 Edmonds, *Military Operations, France and Belgium 1915, Volume 2* [1928]). The map on p.355 states that IR 106 was involved, whereas Anon., *Histories of Two Hundred and Fifty-One Divisions of the German Army Which Participated in the War (1914–1918).* (Naval and Military Press Reprint, 1989 [1920]) has this as *IR 165*.

27 Anon., *Histories of Two Hundred and Fifty-One Divisions* pp.145–146, pp.157–158, pp.608–610.

28 Edmonds, *Military Operations, 1915 Volume 2*, p.355.

According to the *Official History*, the supporting bombardment by No. 1 Group HAR and IV Corps Artillery was from 12:30 p.m. to 3;00 p.m. and there was a shorter one between 3:30 p.m. and 4:00 p.m. by the Guards Division artillery.[29] The only record of the instructions which Cavan gave to his artillery for both brigades are timed at 12:45 p.m. on 27 September: 'Following is artillery timetable – Artillery lifts off Chalk Pit at 4 pm, Puits No 14 bis at 4.20 pm and Hill 70 4.50 pm.'[30]

Verbal instructions were issued by Haking to Cavan at 1:50 p.m. with a confirming written order issued by XI Corps at 2:00 p.m.[31] Meanwhile, at this precise time, the news of the loss of Fosse 8, reached First Army HQ. Fosse 8 with its dominating slagheap had been taken by the 9th (Scottish) Division on 25 September. After meeting both Lieutenant Generals Hubert Gough and Henry Rawlinson commanding I and IV Corps respectively, Haig telephoned Haking at 3:10 p.m. asking about the possibility of either postponing or stopping the attack of the Guards Division. Whilst Haking doubted it would be possible to inform the advance battalions of the 2nd Brigade, he thought that the 3rd Brigade, which was now advancing from Vermelles, could be stopped. Consequently, Haig gave directions for the attack to be limited 'and not to be pressed beyond the line Hill 70–Puits 14 bis–Chalk Pit Wood, that is practically the line of the Lens Road'.[32] Cavan amended the orders to the three brigadiers, and the attack went ahead although the assault from Chalet Wood southwards against Hill 70 Redoubt was now called off. However, Brigadier General Feilding, GOC 1st Guards Brigade, was ordered to provide a smoke barrage to protect the 2nd Brigade's advance which would be undertaken across completely open ground.[33]

It is reasonable to ask whether Haking could have been expected to formalise a plan so quickly. As we have seen, instructions to do so were only issued at 11:30 p.m. on 26 September.[34] This left Haking with little time to review his options. As will be seen below, the artillery plan that was devised to support the Guards was flawed as was the decision to make the success of the 3rd Brigade's attack depend on that of the 2nd Brigade. Moving on to the actual merits of launching the attack in the first place, it is clear that Haig still believed that the momentum of the battle had to be maintained and that the seizure of Hill 70 was both possible and strategically essential if a breakthrough was to be effected. Any delay would probably allow the Germans to strengthen their forces and positions around Hill 70 at this critical point as well as elsewhere along their lines offering a springboard for counter-attacks. For both Haig and Haking, the elite Guards Division would have seemed the ideal vehicle to press on. However, we have seen plenty of evidence to show that these forces were not fresh enough to go into battle on 27 September. With the situation at Fosse 8 being so critical in the early afternoon, it

29 Edmonds, *Military Operations, 1915 Volume 2*, p.355.
30 TNA: WO95/1190, GR270 Guards Division HQ, 27 September 1915.
31 TNA: WO95/1190, Appendix A Guards Division HQ, 27 September 1915.
32 Edmonds *Official History 1915 Volume 2*, p.356.
33 Edmonds *Official History 1915 Volume 2*, p.356.
34 TNA: WO95/1190, Guards Division HQ, 27 September 1915.

may have been more prudent to postpone the entire attack. The fact that there was time to modify the attack itself suggests that the 50-minute period available might have been enough for Haking to stop the advance battalions of the 2nd Brigade and so facilitate a complete postponement. However, the condition of the ground and the availability or otherwise of working field telephones was likely to have made quick communication with these battalions difficult so Haking may well have been right in his judgement.

We will now look at the 2nd Brigade's attack before going on to that of the 3rd Brigade. The attack began at 4:00 p.m. as planned. The smokescreen provided by 1st Guards Brigade was a great success. The report of Brigadier General Feilding states that he subjected the German trenches in Hulluch and to the south to heavy machine gun and rifle fire. Sargeant Danks and brigade bombers were ordered to go forward with 144 smoke balls to commence just before 4:00 p.m. for not less than 30 minutes. Feilding continued that:

> After about six had been thrown the whole country was absolutely lost to sight. The enemy's trenches, Wingles and Pont a Vendin could no more be seen. Gun fire balls were at once fired in the air from the German trenches south of Hulluch and the enemy turned the whole of their artillery on to the smoke and fired with rifles as well … the 2nd Battn. Irish Guards advanced … about 1500 yards across the open and across the enemy's front without being subjected to any artillery fire … The 144 smoke balls were able to keep up a thick cloud of smoke from 3.57 to about 4.40 pm. With a favourable wind I feel certain that there are great possibilities in these smoke balls and I feel certain that they should be used in this manner away on the flank of an attack.[35]

The 2/Irish Guards were able to form an effective firing line along the eastern edge of Chalk Pit Wood securing the 2nd Brigade's flank. The 1/Scots Guards crossed the valley at speed with few casualties and the two companies of the 4/Grenadiers from Loos extended to their right. Regrettably, at this point, the attack lost cohesion. A number of the Irish Guards were swept along with the Scots and were drawn to the Puits where they came under heavy fire from machine guns above the Puits itself, Bois Hugo, and especially from the German trenches on Hill 70.[36] Clearly the artillery suppression of these positions had failed. Only a small party managed to reach the Puits led by Captain J.H. Cuthbert of the Scots Guards along with Second Lieutenant Crabbe and half a dozen Grenadiers. They fought on for a while reinforced by a platoon of the 3/Grenadier Guards under Lieutenant Ayres-Ritchie, but without further help these forces fell back. Some sought cover in Chalk Pit Wood thereby causing confusion amongst the Irish Guards

35 TNA: WO95/1190, Guards Division HQ, Report by Brigadier General Feilding GOC, 1st Guards Brigade, September 29, 1915.

36 Kipling *Irish Guards, 2nd Battalion* pp.24–24, Edmonds, *Official History 1915 Volume 2*, pp.357–358.

who had been digging in on the further side of the wood.[37] Captain Barne of the Scots Guards confirms the disorder and indiscipline: 'I met a stream of battle stragglers. Many were wounded, but with them there was also a liberal accompaniment of unwounded "friends" and others who obviously should not have been there'. He tried to turn them but left the job to Lieutenant Browne, the adjutant, who set about them 'with a heavy hunting crop which he carried'.[38] Whilst the situation was thereby stabilised, these episodes reflect two features. On the one hand, we have the remarkable bravery and resilience shown by those who were able to enter the Puits, but on the other hand, the lack of order and discipline shown by the subsequent retreat, albeit under intense pressure. As darkness fell, the Irish Guards retraced their steps, spending the night consolidating Chalk Pit Wood.

Meanwhile, what of the attack by the 3rd Guards Brigade? As we have already noted, the movements of the 3rd Guards Brigade depended on the success of the 2nd Brigade. The advance, which began at 3:00 p.m. along the Vermelles-Douai road, was in full view of the Germans once the reverse slope of the Grenay Ridge was reached with the 4/Grenadiers and the 1/Welsh deploying very effectively in artillery formation. Their truly remarkable advance is confirmed in the following two extracts which certainly reflected genuine discipline under heavy fire but one might question why there had not been more effective artillery suppression of the German guns.

> Attention was first drawn to them by a sharp increase in the number of German shells passing overhead … Quite quickly the opposite slope took on the appearance of a gigantic moving chessboard as the platoons approached with intervals between them. The steadiness of the march was impressive, and those who thought that Guardsmen were only ornamental soldiers revised their opinions speedily. So inspiring was the sight that scores of the 23rd men of their own accord clambered out of their trenches and, under machine gun fire, pulled aside wire entanglements and threw duckboard bridges over the ditches to facilitate the way for the Guards when it was seen that they had to pass through their lines.[39]

The *Times* Special Correspondent noted evocatively that the brigade:

> …advanced with the steadiness of men on parade, and men of other battalions who could see the manoeuvre from their own trenches have spoken again and again of that wonderful advance as being one of the most glorious and impressive sights of the war, and how they were thrilled to see those large silhouettes pressing silently and inexorably forward against the skyline.[40]

37 Edmonds, *Official History 1915 Volume 2*, pp.357–358.
38 Randall Nicol, *Till the Trumpet Sounds Again: The Scots Guards 1914–1919 in Their Own Words, Volume 1* (Solihull: Helion 2016), p.417.
39 Captain G.A. Brett, 1/23rd Londons, cited in Andrew Rawson, *Loos–Hill 70* (Barnsley: Pen & Sword, 2002), pp.144–145.
40 Doughty, *The Guards Came Through*, p.83.

However, things soon began to deteriorate for the 3rd Brigade and much of the blame for the course of events must be with Brigadier General F.J. Heyworth who wilted under the intense pressures of battlefield command. Harold Macmillan provides an interesting indication of the chaotic nature of the command and control situation and Heyworth's part in it although he certainly does not apportion blame to Heyworth for what happened. The 4/Grenadiers were leading the 3rd Brigade's attack.

> When we got to Loos our battalion was met by my Captain, Aubrey Fletcher, and was ordered to double down the slope and get into a trench which ran through some ruined houses. Loos was being heavily shelled, and a lot of gas shells were falling … When we had got some way down the trench, the Brigadier (Heyworth) was seen gallantly and somewhat unexpectedly galloping down the road. He ordered No. 3 Company and No. 4 Company not to go into the trench any further, but to follow him. From then on our battalion was separated into two parts. At the time, of course, we had no idea that this was happening, but much trouble followed from it. In the general confusion of the rest of the day, I recall only my own experience and those of my own company. What happened to the other half of our battalion I was unaware of until much later.[41]

Heyworth's mystifying decision to split the battalion had fateful consequences. In fact, the party that followed Heyworth's orders were Nos. 6, 7 and 8 platoons from No. 2 company, No. 10 platoon from No. 3 company and a few men from No. 4 Company. Once in Loos itself, they found themselves under very heavy bombardment and a 'hand to mouth' command and control situation. Heyworth initially directed these men to go on through Loos and put themselves under the command of Lieutenant Colonel Hamilton, 4/Grenadier Guards, but he had, unfortunately been gassed. Heyworth then put Major Ponsonby in command who made a failed attempt to bring up the rest of the battalion. Regrettably, the orderly carrying the message was killed. The Welsh Guards now arrived under Lieutenant Colonel Murray Threipland who told Ponsonby that Heyworth wanted the attack to begin at once. Despite, Ponsonby's concerns that the paucity of forces available made any attack potentially a futile and costly endeavour, Threipland pressed ahead. The attack was made, therefore, by a combined force of Welsh and Grenadier Guards.[42] Threipland wrote that at this point:

> I informed the Brigadier of the launching and time of the attack, and heard shortly after from my liaison officer with the Brigade that before my order to attack had arrived, the Brigadier had found that the attack of the 2nd Brigade had failed, and had sent me orders to cancel my attack. As those orders had not however left the Brigade office, and the attack had commenced, the cancellation order was destroyed.[43]

41 Macmillan, *Winds of Change*, pp.74–75.
42 Ponsonby, *The Grenadier Guards in the Great War, Volume 1,* pp.310–312.
43 TNA: WO95/1190, Guards Division HQ War Diary Letter from Lieutenant Colonel W. Murray Threipland to Colonel G.R.C. Lord Harlech. 28 September 1915.

Chaos then ensued. The attack began at 5:30 p.m. and lacked any element of surprise. Threipland remarked that: 'I was then for some time without any information: darkness came on in less than half an hour of my attack, and I received no artillery support.'[44] Heyworth had given explicit orders that there should be no advance over the crest of the hill and that consolidation should take place on the reverse slope when it had been occupied. However, the Grenadiers were totally unaware of this order with Hamilton incapacitated, and so they pushed on whilst the Welsh Guards remained just below the hill's crest.[45] There appears to have been a vacuum in over-all command with Heyworth unable to ensure that his orders were being followed.

In his after battle report, Heyworth wrote that when the 4/Grenadiers 'debauched' from the communication trenches, they faced a German gas shell attack. It caused 'delay and confusion'. With Hamilton gassed, Ponsonby took over with 'about one third of the battalion getting detached under Captain Morrison who worked round the North-Eastern end of the town.'[46] However, Heyworth took no personal responsibility for what happened. There was no acknowledgement that the delay and confusion was due to his own action in splitting the battalion. With reference to his decision to proceed with the attack on Hill 70, he said:

> I should have noted that my instructions were that I was not to attack if the 2nd Guards Brigade attack failed, but having myself seen the attacking force of the 2nd Guards Brigade enter Puits no 14, I concluded the attack was successful and went to organise my own attack. I was not aware that the attacking troops had subsequently to retire.[47]

He failed to explain what evidence he saw that persuaded him that it was satisfactory to continue with the attack. An entry into the Puits did not equate to control of it. However, in a footnote to his report added in pencil, it states that:

> Communication was very difficult owing to wires cut. But as soon as GOC Guards Division knew the CHALK Pit was gained but Puits No 14 was not gained, he ordered the 3rd Guards Brigade to press their attack on Hill 70. This order dated 5.20 pm tho sent in duplicate by wire did not reach General Heyworth until much later.[48]

44 TNA: WO95/1190, Guards Division HQ War Diary Letter from Lieutenant Colonel W. Murray Threipland to Colonel G.R.C. Lord Harlech. 28 September 1915.
45 Ponsonby, *Grenadier Guards Volume 1*, pp.312–313.
46 TNA: WO95/1190, Guards Division HQ War Diary, App7D. Account of the Capture of Hill 70 by 3rd Guards Brigade by Brig. Gen. Heyworth October 2, 1915.
47 TNA: WO95/1190, Guards Division HQ War Diary, App7D. Account of the Capture of Hill 70 by 3rd Guards Brigade by Brig. Gen. Heyworth October 2, 1915.
48 TNA: WO95/1190, Guards Division HQ War Diary, App7D. Account of the Capture of Hill 70 by 3rd Guards Brigade by Brig. Gen. Heyworth October 2, 1915.

In other words, it confirmed that Heyworth did the 'right thing'.[49] Heyworth then continued to gloss over the chaotic situation However, his referencing to the inaccurate map is interesting and was confirmed in Threipland's report:

> After seeing the two Commanding Officers of my attacking force and explaining what I wanted them to do I returned to the spot from where I had seen the attack of the 2nd Guards Brigade. I then learned of the failure of the 2nd Guards Brigade attack but it was too late to stop my advance … Both battalions had been instructed on no account to carry the attack beyond the ridge, but they carried on owing to the fact that the map shows the trenches and redoubt on the North slope of the Hill, whereas in reality they are some yards down on the reverse slope.[50]

Threipland's detailed report described a night of great uncertainty as he struggled to gain an accurate overview of events although he was in no doubt about the bravery of his men. Eventually his own inspection of the most forward positions persuaded him that it would be impossible to dig-in at this point because of their exposure to German machine-gun fire. A decision was taken therefore to withdraw and consolidate to a point approximately 100 yards behind the crest of Hill 70.[51]

A final attempt to take the Puits complex was made on 28 September with two companies of the 1/Coldstream Guards starting from the cover of Chalk Pit Wood. This attack was made in the hope that a rapid advance with the element of surprise would succeed. Enfiladed by machine gun fire on three sides, a small party reached the objective but could not hold it. This marked the end of the Guards Division's first major engagement.[52]

Brigadier General Ponsonby's after battle report is especially interesting in what it tells us about the inadequacy of artillery suppression in support of the 2nd Brigade's assault.[53] For example, on 27 September: 'The Scots Guards were now sent forward to assault the PUITS. They advanced in extended order and doubled down the Hill. A heavy shrapnel fire was opened up on them as they moved forward' or that 'an assault was organised on the KEEP and PUITS. At this moment, the Companies emerging from the Wood and up the slopes of the Hill came under a terrific fire from the enemy's maxim guns which are in concealed positions in BOIS HUGO and in the KEEP and PUITS.'[54]

49 TNA: WO95/1190, Guards Division HQ War Diary, Letter from Lieutenant Colonel W. Murray Threipland to Colonel G.R.C. Lord Harlech. 28 September 1915.
50 TNA: WO95/1190, Guards Division HQ War Diary, Letter from Lieutenant Colonel W. Murray Threipland to Colonel G.R.C. Lord Harlech. 28 September 1915.
51 TNA: WO95/1190, Guards Division HQ War Diary, Letter from Lieutenant Colonel W. Murray Threipland to Colonel G.R.C. Lord Harlech. 28 September 1915.
52 Headlam, *History of the Guards Division*, pp.66–67.
53 TNA: WO95/1190, Guards Division HQ War Diary, Operation of 2nd Guards Division. Report by Brigadier General Ponsonby, 27/28/29 September.
54 TNA: WO95/1190, Guards Division HQ War Diary, Operation of 2nd Guards Division. Report by Brigadier General Ponsonby, 27/28/29 September.

In Bidwell and Graham's seminal work *Fire-Power*, their analysis of the artillery's weaknesses is especially useful in light of the events at Loos.[55] Artillery doctrine had been, theoretically, laid down in *Field Artillery Training, 1914* but left much unresolved. For example, there was vagueness about the exact stage in a battle when divisions should reinforce each other's fire and the relative role of the reserve artillery, little was said about concealment of gun emplacements and 'arrangements for making fire plans remained ad hoc, for infantry plans were made before the gunner was asked what he could do to help'.[56] At Loos, they point out that much of the British artillery was obsolete, for the Territorial and New Army divisions were not equipped with the weapons that the BEF had used in 1914, there was a severe shortage of heavy calibres, with which the French were already well supplied and the artillery ammunition 'was unreliable and the standard of shooting of the new divisions was unsatisfactory'.[57] In addition, Paddy Griffith argued that in the 1915 battles, 'artillery plans rose to major prominence among the infantry man's concerns, especially the question of their precise timing and density, for which effective formulae were glimpsed but not yet grasped'.[58]

Indeed, an article written in 1930 by Captain T.B. Trappes-Lomax of the Scots Guards stated that the artillery plan was totally ineffective in the attack of 27 September.[59] Whilst this article has been ignored by subsequent generations of historians, his observations are as valid now as they were at the time of its publication.[60] For example, the Irish began their advance at 4:00 p.m. at the exact time the artillery lifted off the Chalk Pit. The Scots then started at 4:30 p.m. which was 10 minutes after the artillery lifted off the Puits and the Keep. The result, according to Trappes-Lomax, was what might have been anticipated: 'Throughout the whole of the attack by the 2nd Brigade not a round was fired to keep down the heads of the German machine gunners who swept the long open slopes in front of the Puits.'[61]

Significantly, Trappes-Lomax argued that:

> … to make the 3rd Brigade's attack contingent on the success of the 2nd Brigade was to prejudice the former's chances of artillery support. It was clearly necessary to fix a time after which the artillery should not fire on Hill 70, otherwise it might shell our own troops. This time was fixed at 1650 by which time

55 Shelford Bidwell and Dominick Graham, *Fire-Power: The British Army Weapons and Theories of War 1904-1945* (London: George Allen & Unwin, 1982).
56 Bidwell and Graham, *Fire-Power*, pp.20–21.
57 Bidwell and Graham, *Fire-Power*, p.77.
58 Paddy Griffith, *Battle Tactics of the Western Front: The British Army's Art of Attack, 1916-1918* (New Haven: Yale University Press, 1994), p.53.
59 Thomas Byrnand Trappes-Lomax was commissioned on 10 April 1915 in the Royal Lancashire Regiment, transferred to the Scots Guards on 19 March 1917 and eventually became a Brigadier General in 1942.
60 Capt. T.B. Trappes-Lomax, 'Artillery Support at Loos', *Household Brigade Magazine*, Spring Number 1930.
61 Trappes-Lomax, 'Artillery Support at Loos', p.88.

> it was presumably anticipated that the 2nd Brigade would have got the Puits. It followed that if the attack by 3rd Brigade was launched after 16.50 hours, it would be totally unsupported by artillery fire, unless communication was established between the infantry brigadier and his supporting artillery. This was never done. Consequently, the defenders of Hill 70 had been untouched by shelling for one hour before the assault.[62]

In fact, we know from other sources that at Loos this kind of communication was problematic to say the least. Major J.D. Anderson (CO, XCVII Brigade RFA, 24th Division) went into Loos to consult with Heyworth to ascertain how the artillery would best assist his attack. He found that the village was under a heavy barrage which had cut all telephone wires making it impossible for him to make contact with his batteries.[63] Niall Barr, in his analysis of the Battle of Neuve Chapelle, noted that the use of an extensive telephone system was important in giving 'unrivalled flexibility and rapid artillery response to infantry requests for fire support' but this broke down after the initial phase of the attack.[64] Certainly, had the telephone system been intact at Loos, artillery support might have been improved. Thus, command and control became increasingly difficult. It is perhaps worth noting that Major R.G.A. Hamilton (CO, CVIII Brigade RFA, 24th Division) had a similarly wasted journey in the 1st Brigade's sector. Tasked with co-ordinating with Brigadier General Feilding:

> I had to walk about a mile up our own communication trench and came to our old fire trenches, the ones we had been in till two days ago. After that it was necessary to get into the open and pass through the wire into the neutral zone. Crossing the space of some 400 yards before reaching the German trenches was simply Hell incarnate. It was being swept continuously by the German heavy guns and also with shrapnel, to say nothing of rifle bullets which were coming over the crest.[65]

He eventually made contact with Feilding, but the meeting proved pointless because he was unable to report back directly.[66]

Returning to Trappes-Lomax's analysis, he observed that the artillery was in effect 'distributed' along the whole 3,500 yards of front but there was no flexibility in its use. No attempt appears to have been made to switch all or some of the artillery from one sector of the front to another as, for example, in supporting first the attack of the 2nd

62 Trappes-Lomax, 'Artillery Support at Loos', pp.88–89.
63 Lloyd, *Loos*, p.192.
64 Niall Barr, 'Command in the Transition From Mobile to Static Warfare, August 1914 to March 1915' in Gary Sheffield and Dan Todman, *Command and Control on the Western Front: The British Army's Experience 1914-1918* (Staplehurst: Spellmount, 2004), p.33.
65 R.G.A. Hamilton, *The War Diary of the Master of Belhaven* (London: John Murray, 1924), pp.77–79.
66 Hamilton, *The War Diary of the Master of Belhaven*, pp.77–79.

Brigade before moving on to support the 3rd Brigade assault. Quite fairly, he concluded that: 'It is prodigal of life to allow artillery to stand by idle during the minutes your infantry is advancing against machine guns.'[67] Perhaps the fact that there was no definite zero-hour for the 3rd Brigade's final assault precluded this possibility but there should have been some thought given to this, but, as we have seen the artillery plan was a rushed affair.

We can conclude then that the Guards Division were placed in an almost 'no-win' situation in their attack on Hill 70. Brought up from the reserves at a time that was too late, facing a time-consuming and gruelling move to the front positions as result of poor staff work, they entered the line fatigued only a few hours before the assault began. Haking had too short a period to plan the detail of the attack, but the artillery plan was deeply flawed and it was a mistake to make the attack by the 3rd Guards Brigade contingent on that of the 2nd. However, whether the entire 2nd Brigade's attack could have been postponed rather than just modified once news of the events at Fosse 8 had arrived is uncertain. The 2nd Brigade's attack was undoubtedly helped by the effectiveness of the smokescreen laid down by the 1st Guards Brigade and was pursued with good discipline and genuine courage at first before order broke down amidst a retreat. Meanwhile the assault by 3rd Brigade, although showing quite remarkable discipline and courage under fire in crossing the Grenay Ridge, was undermined by ineffective command and control and Brigadier General Heyworth must bear the blame for much of what ensued. Whilst the forces led by Lieutenant Colonel Murray Threipland fought with great commitment and bravery, the objective of gaining control of Hill 70 was always going to be an illusion in the circumstances.

67 Trappes-Lomax, 'Artillery Support at Loos', p.89.

3

The Battle of Loos: The Hohenzollern Redoubt, 8–22 October 1915

The Hohenzollern Redoubt was positioned on a slight slope in the form of a salient thereby providing excellent observation and fields of fire for the Germans. It was the most heavily defended position in the Loos sector and as such was a truly formidable fortification. It was linked to the German front line by two trenches, known as Big Willie and Little Willie, which were deep and very well fortified. The former was partially occupied by British forces. There were also three communication trenches known as North Face, South Face, and Quarry trench which led to Fosse and Dump trenches situated close to a slagheap known as the Dump. Fosse 8 was situated close to the Dump. The German position known as the Quarries lay to the east of Quarry trench. The Guards Division saw a good deal of bloody, close combat action between 8 and 22 October in this relatively confined area where the role of the bomber was critical. The evidence suggests that the Guards genuinely rose to the occasion and, in doing so, Cavan began to develop the basis of an effective battlefield methodology for bombing, learning directly from experience and quickly adapting and refining techniques.

According to the *Official History*, the German attack to regain Loos and Lone Tree had been scheduled for 27 September but, because more troops were required along their lines at Vimy, not enough could be spared to enable the new action to begin before 8 October. The bombardment duly began at 12:00 midday with an increasing intensity for the last hour before the assault began at 4:00 p.m. Subsidiary enemy bombing attacks were also made from the direction of the Quarries and Fosse 8 against the former German lines at Quarry Trench and Big Willie.[1]

The line of the 3/Grenadier Guards along Big Willie was very exposed. As Colonel N.A.L. Corry, commanding, said in his after battle report: 'It being a finger sticking out into HOHENZOLLERN with saps round both flanks and liable to attack from three

1 Edmonds, *Official History, 1915 Volume 2*, pp.372–373.

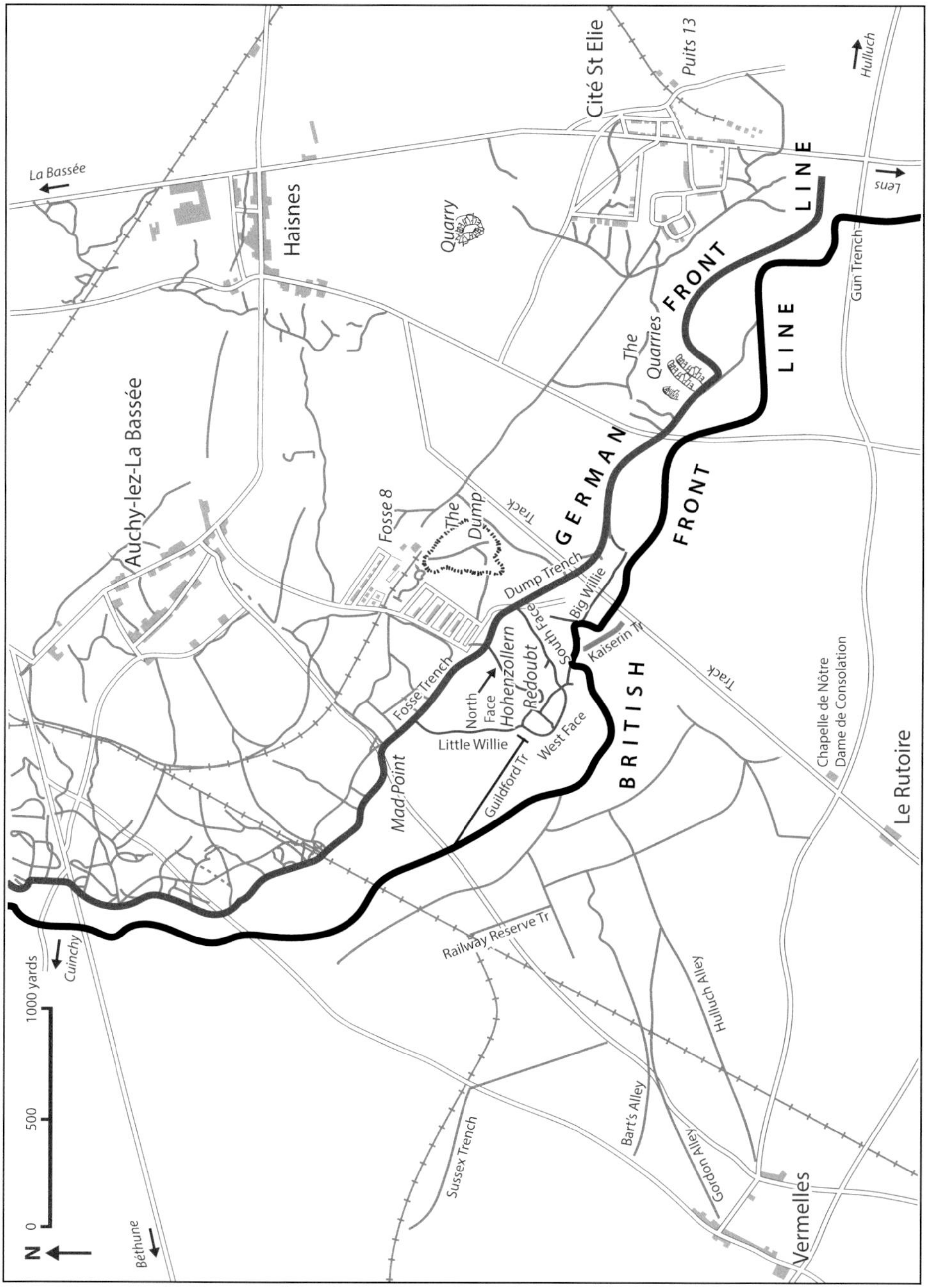

The Battle of Loos, the Hohenzollern Redoubt, October 1915.

sides.'[2] Bombers of the German *57th* and *104th Regiments* rushed this end of the trench from three sides, and broke through the British front line with nos. 2 and 3 companies deciding to withdraw in order to be able to launch a counter-attack which Corry thought was a wise decision on the part of his captains.[3]

Corry described what happened next:

> As all bombers had been killed, I thought it best to let them through and reorganise. I ordered No.1 company to hold my second line … and to block the communication trenches. The 3rd Battn Coldstream realizing the situation then organized a bombing party and started bombing down the lost trenches. I ordered O.C. No.1 to co-operate with them and went back to organize fresh bombers and get supplies of Mills grenades. The 1st Scots Guards, Irish Guards and the 2nd Irish supplied bombers and the grenades came up in the nick of time and were forwarded up the two communication trenches. In the meantime I heard that No.1 had joined the Coldstreams and were working up the old trench and supplying Bombs, that the Germans were retiring and suffering heavy casualties.[4]

This extract shows that Corry reacted quickly to events displaying outstanding qualities of leadership. The various Guards battalions appear instinctively to have worked well together and initiative was not in short supply. The forward supply of bombs was especially well executed. In particular, Corry is full of praise for:' the action of the bombing Officer of the 3rd Battn Coldstream (who) was magnificent and it is entirely due to him that the situation was restored.'[5] The bombing officer was Lance Sergeant Oliver Brooks who subsequently received the VC for his actions. His citation is well worth noting in full:

> A strong party of the enemy having captured 200 yards of our trenches, Lance Sergeant Brooks, on his own initiative, led a party of bombers in the most determined manner, and succeeded in regaining possession of the lost ground. The single bravery by this non-commissioned officer, in the midst of a hail of bombs from the Germans, was of the first order, and the complete success attained in a very dangerous undertaking was entirely due to his absolute fearlessness, presence of mind and promptitude. [6]

2 TNA: WO95/1190, Guards Division HQ War Diary Appendix 4.4 Guards HQ, 9 October 1915.
3 TNA: WO95/1190, Guards Division HQ War Diary Appendix 4.4 Guards HQ, 9 October 1915.
4 TNA: WO95/1190, Guards Division HQ War Diary Appendix 4.4 Guards HQ, 9 October 1915.
5 TNA: WO95/1190, Guards Division HQ War Diary Appendix 4.4 Guards HQ, 9 October 1915.
6 Cited in Doughty, *The Guards Came Through*, p.92.

Lance Sergeant Oliver Brooks VC.

It would also appear that artillery support provided by 3rd Brigade RFA was highly effective as it bore down accurately on the German communication trenches.[7] Losses were however, heavy in this action reflecting the intensity of the close combat: 'Officers 7 killed, 10 wounded plus 2 missing, believed killed. Other ranks totalled 136 killed and 390 wounded'.[8] There is a good deal of truth in Headlam's judgement about the events of October 8 when he concluded that: 'The action proved that in modern warfare – and particularly in intricate trench to trench warfare – everything may ultimately depend upon the bravery and resource of the individual soldier.'[9]

Captain Viscount Gort, who was the brigade major for 1st Guard's Brigade, reported on 10 October that German bombing attacks were a continuing menace and, even on a 'quiet' day, there were ongoing threats and challenges. He commented that the 2/Grenadier bombers made sure that the enemy were 'cleared out of the trench leading from point 89 left handed round to our former bombing post and a block was established at point 89'.[10] A serious problem arose when it was found that a 'large number of undetonated bombs which had been sent up, had got mixed up with the detonated ones' so 'it was decided not to press the attack further'.[11] During the night: 'The enemy made two bombing counter-attacks … which were repulsed after a very hard fight of over an hour'.[12] To add to the Guards' discomfort: 'The enemy shelled the line from 2.30am to 3am doing considerable damage.'[13] There was an ongoing pressure to repair trenches and 'the trenches captured last night will also require to be made into good

7 TNA: WO95/1190, Guards Division HQ War Diary, Cavan's introductory remarks to Appendix 4.4 Guards HQ, 9 October 1915.
8 TNA: WO95/1190, Guards Division HQ War Diary, RHS 156 10 October.
9 Headlam, *History of the Guards Division*, p.77.
10 TNA: WO95/1190, Guards Division HQ War Diary, App. 55 Capt. Gort's Daily Progress Report 11 October 1915.
11 TNA: WO95/1190, Guards Division HQ War Diary, App. 55 Capt. Gort's Daily Progress Report 11 October 1915. 'Undetonated bombs' were those that had not had their detonators inserted.
12 TNA: WO95/1190, Guards Division HQ War Diary, App. 55 Capt. Gort's Daily Progress Report 11 October 1915.
13 I TNA: WO95/1190, Guards Division HQ War Diary, App. 55 Capt. Gort's Daily Progress Report 11 October 1915.

fire trenches'. He concluded by saying that this work had to be undertaken under the ongoing threat caused of sniping and bombing and 'aerial torpedoes' were a real concern.' All in all, there were approximately 56 casualties on 10 October.[14]

For Cavan, the events of 8 October to 10 October, provided some clear lessons. He was anxious that any weaknesses in the Guards approach to bombing should be identified and potential improvements be identified and implemented. On 11 October, he sent a remarkable report to Haking that is worthy of analysis. Firstly, Cavan believed successful bombing necessitated good forward planning. This can be seen in his judgement that stores of bombs and some bombers needed to be kept at the tail as well as the head of each sap or point that jutted towards the enemy. He stated that parties for bringing up the bomb reserves to the firing line must be organised as a permanent fatigue which should be formed from those troops kept in reserve. An orderly should be based at the brigade bomb store with the ability to liaise with the divisional store to ensure continuity of supply and the division should issue specific instructions to the unit allocated to bring them forward.[15]

At the front line, Cavan had a clear view of how the defences should be best organised. For example, he believed that blocks must be made double, and that the trench between blocks must be straight, with a machine gun placed behind the rear block, firing through a low loophole. He argued that: 'In every trench by which it is possible for the enemy to get round behind our advanced points … must be outposted and blocked. Such places can only be discovered by night reconnaissance'. Cavan realised that repelling violent bombing attacks often depended on acts of individual bravery (he would have been very mindful here of Lance Sergeant Brooks) and that it was important that 'their names will be at once sent forward for immediate reward'.[16] Cavan clearly had a strong sense of combat motivation and what made his men 'tick'.

He stressed the value of the Mills bomb which he believed was well-shaped and there was no fear of their exploding in the hand. The bomber was therefore less likely to rush. This, he felt gave the Guards bomber a five-yard advantage over his German counterpart. The greatest threat lay in the preliminary bombardment before a German bomb attack. 'This is well directed and blows in our communication trenches in many places, and therefore cuts off the regular system of supply.'[17]

Cavan's final remarks reveal that he has an enlightened attitude to command and a sharp sense of the realities facing inexperienced soldiers and the pressures upon their commanding officers. New battalions, he observed, 'who have not had hard experience of this war, cannot be expected to do as well as the older hands, and if a new Battalion is holding such intricate and difficult points as BIG WILLIE, POINT 89, and ST ELIE AVENUE, they should at least have the moral support

14 TNA: WO95/1190, Guards Division HQ War Diary, App. 55 Capt. Gort's Daily Progress Report 11 October 1915.
15 TNA: WO95/1190, Guards Division HQ War Diary, App. 47 and 48, 11 October 1915.
16 TNA: WO95/1190, Guards Division HQ War Diary, App. 47 and 48, 11 October 1915.
17 TNA: WO95/1190, Guards Division HQ War Diary, App. 47 and 48, 11 October 1915.

of seasoned bombers behind them. This of course means a tremendous demand on the older warriors, but each fight will improve the young ones.' He felt that had 'one of the old Guards Battalions been holding BIG WILLIE on 8th inst. It would not have been temporarily lost, chiefly because the CO would have realized the danger of the projecting left flank, and would have made his blocks further East, denying the intervening ground to the enemy.' Anticipating criticisms that are likely to come the way of these inexperienced commanders, he said that: 'In this connection I am sure that new comers feel that even a slight tactical re-arrangement of their line will be construed adversely into a withdrawal, and they are consequently afraid to take the steps that would ensure absolute protection.' To relieve such anxieties, he concluded that: 'I feel very strongly that a carefully worded memo on this point would give many new COs a little more confidence.'[18]

Haking reacted positively to these ideas forwarding them to the other divisions in XI Corps on the very next day, 12 October.[19]

There was another 'bombing fight' on 12 October confirming the unrelenting pressure on the Guardsmen. Gort described how at:

> About 3.30 pm the enemy commenced to bomb sapheads … held by the 2nd Battn. Grenadier Guards. The Germans threw a great quantity of hand bombs and at the same time opened a heavy fire of aerial torpedoes and trench mortars on the whole of our trenches in the vicinity … simultaneously he heavily bombarded other parts of the line with Artillery, damaging the trenches in many places and wrecking SPURN HEAD communication trench … The hand bomb contest continued at the saphead till 4.30 pm … But continued at the barricade for another hour.[20]

Once again, the casualties of 81 were not insignificant with Gort judging that as many as three-quarters came from 'aerial torpedoes'.[21]

The Guards anticipated a well-earned relief which was made overnight by the 7/ Suffolks and the 1/5th South Staffs on 12 October into the early hours of 13 October but they were quickly recalled when the attack by the 46th (North Midland) Division failed. Haking, feared that the Germans might regain their old positions and so ordered the Guards to rejoin the line on the nights of 14/15 and 15/16 October. They were now tasked with capturing and holding Dump and Fosse trenches and forming a defensive flank facing north to cover a further advance on Fosse 8. There were real concerns about the feasibilities of such an attack. Heyworth, after his own personal reconnaissance of the line, believed that the condition of ground was so bad that no offensive

18 TNA: WO95/1190, Guards Division HQ War Diary, App. 47 and 48, 11 October 1915.
19 TNA: WO95/886, XI Corps HQ War Diary, RHS 178 XI 12 October 1915.
20 TNA: WO95/1190, Guards Division HQ War Diary, App. 59 Capt. Gort's Report on a Bombing attack 12 October, dated 14 October.
21 TNA: WO95/1190, Guards Division HQ War Diary, App. 59 Capt. Gort's Report on a Bombing attack 12 October, dated 14 October.

could be carried out before 17 October. Cavan was in agreement.[22] A conference was held on 14 October which Haking attended. It was decided that it would be unwise to attempt to carry out the complete operation allocated to the Guards Division in a single attack. The objectives agreed would be secured by a series of bombing attacks supported by both artillery and trench-mortar fire. The 3rd Brigade would operate on the right at the junction of Slag Alley trench and the Dump trench plus the triangle formed by the south face of the Hohenzollern Redoubt and the southern section of Dump trench. Meanwhile, 2nd Brigade would be on the left at the chord of the Hohenzollern Redoubt and the northern part of Little Willie. Artillery and trench-mortar support would be provided.[23]

Despite very heavy and accurate German shelling overnight, the attack began on time at 5:00 a.m. It involved the 1/Grenadiers and the 2/Scots supported by the 4/Grenadier Guards on the 3rd Guards Brigade front while the 2nd Guards Brigade front saw the 1/Coldstream supported by the 3/Grenadiers. It soon became obvious to both brigadiers that the enfilade machine-gun fire and terrible condition of the ground meant 'it was not humanly possible for their troops to reach their objectives'.[24] As soon as Cavan was aware of this, he ordered the attack to cease, and any ground gained to be consolidated. In his after battle report, Cavan noted that: 'The enemy fired an enormous quantity of shells at our trenches, far more than on 8th October, of every sort of size and kind. In fact from dawn to mid-day my Brigadiers agree that there has been no more severe shell fire this War. This was of course because it was concentrated on us.'[25] He confirmed the intensity of the fighting and some satisfaction in the supply of bombs to the front positions: 'We used 15,000 bombs and the chain of supply was well organized.' He reported that 'a block with second block behind it' had been established by the Germans 'with the foremost block 2 yards east … of the cross trench running up the South Face. A very gallant effort was made to pass this trench, but Captain Orr leading it with 10 volunteers was killed, and most of the party of the 2nd Scots Guards.' Optimistically, Cavan observes that: 'There is no doubt the enemy were much alarmed. They lost to us 200 yards of trench that is very precious to them.' However, in reality very little progress had been made by either Guards brigade and losses were severe: four officers had been killed and seven wounded plus 400 other ranks were killed or wounded. Yet, Cavan, typically, tried to take something positive in terms of a learning experience from these events:

> The defence against a bomb attack is so to cut your trench that it forms an arrow with the head away from the attacker. As the attacker advances from Z to X he is met by 3 to 1, and no bombers can meet this – they are all blown to pieces. All the 2nd Scots Guards bombers were killed in this way. Our own sap-heads are now

22 Headlam, *History of the Guards Division*, p.83.
23 TNA: WO95/1190, Guards Division HQ War Diary, App 62, 17 October.
24 Headlam, *History of the Guards Division*, p.85.
25 TNA: WO95/1190, Guards Division HQ War Diary, App 75. 17 October.

> being constructed as far as possible on this principle, but the great difficulty is to get a line anywhere, owing to shell holes and buried corpses.[26]

The very limited results of 17 October persuaded Haig that it was useless to attempt the recapture of Fosse No. 8 and the network of trenches around the Dump until the Germans had been systematically driven out of their outlying trenches.[27] Back on 14 October, Haking had advocated a change in tactics towards 'biting off' the enemy's trenches trench by trench by means of constant bombing attacks and persistent sapping in a report written for Haig.[28] His thinking seems to have been behind the attack on the night of 20/21 October which saw the final Guards action at Loos when the 2/ Irish Guards made an attempt to storm the trenches held by the Germans behind the west front of the Hohenzollern Redoubt. Two parties of bombers, converging from the north and south, were employed in this attack which was covered by the guns of the Guards divisional artillery directed on Little Willie, North Face and South Face, and by the rifle fire of the 2/Coldstream Guards on the right flank. It achieved only modest results.[29] The 'Preliminary Report' prepared at Guards HQ by Lieutenant Colonel W.P. Hore-Ruthven makes for gloomy reading: 'The Left party was met immediately by a very strong German bombing party who were either waiting for them or were just intending to attack themselves. This hostile party drove our head back to behind our barricade, but was then checked.' A second attack was only successful in getting a few yards, when it was also driven back. However: 'The Right party made progress … driving the enemy's advance post back by bombing, but could get no further on account of bombs from three sides. It succeeded in making a barricade just South of the little loop – an advance of 40 yards.' The report concludes that: 'Every effort will now be made to join the heads of the Left and Right parties but the difficulties are really enormous, as digging is made almost impossible by the number of half buried corpses, the broken nature of the ground, and the fact that the enemy's Snipers … command all visible ground South West of the Chord'.[30] Thus Haking's change of tactics had failed miserably despite the best efforts of the guardsmen involved.

On the very next day, 22 October, Cavan produced yet another set of recommendations outlining further his thoughts on good bombing practice. He was clearly determined that lessons would be learned from the Guards period at the Hohenzollern and that their experiences would serve to formulate more successful bombing techniques for the future. Cavan initially stressed that he 'does not wish to lay down hard and fast rules' suggesting that he believed there must always be scope for initiative and flexibility. Prior to an attack, he argued the need, if possible, to carry out a careful reconnaissance of the

26 TNA: WO95/1190, Guards Division HQ War Diary, App 75. 17 October.
27 Headlam, *History of the Guards Division*, pp.85–86.
28 TNA: WO95/1190, Guards Division HQ War Diary, App 75. 17 October.
29 TNA: WO95/1190, Guards Division HQ War Diary, App 75. 17 October.
30 TNA: WO95/1190, Guards Division HQ War Diary, Preliminary Report on the Action on the Northern End of the West Face', 21 October 1915.

trench to be attacked to ascertain such things as what obstacles lie ahead, whether any wire exists on top of the trench, how many saps run into the trench to be attacked and 'what arrow head trenches or cross trenches the enemy have prepared'. Always aware of the potential advantage to be gained from R.F.C. support, he remarked on the great value of air photographs. Indeed , he gave an example of a recent bombing attack which ended in failure because a previous reconnaissance had not discovered that the Germans had formed an 'arrow-head' enabling them to bomb the advancing Guards from in front and both sides resulting in 'the whole of the forward bombing party being killed and the attack held up'.[31]

Cavan then moved on to the actual implementation of the attack. During the night prior to an attack, he argued, our own barricades should be prepared for easy removal once it begins. 'The Company to attack the trench should be formed up and so organised into parties that every man in each party knows exactly what he and his party are expected to do.' Cavan then illustrated how this should be done by providing a recent example of good practice in which the assault forces were organised in three groupings:

i) Escort of 3 men with fixed bayonets. 3 Bombers for forward drive. Rifle Grenade Party (5 men)
ii) Blocking parties for blocking all saps and side trenches running into the main trench to be attacked
iii) The main body of the Company to hold and consolidate all new ground gained. They were headed out by the dug-out clearers..[32]

Additionally, he added specific detail about what numbers of bombs, shovels and sandbags should be carried by the men in a 'rough diagram of a Company organized for a bombing attack with two hostile communication trenches to block'. It is in a remarkably sophisticated format showing the specific responsibilities of an advanced party for 'forward drive up a hostile trench' to include an order of attack with specific numbers of men required for optimal exploitation including attention to such responsibilities as blocking side trenches and a final 'bombing party of 4 men in case any hostile party is overlooked'.[33]

However, Cavan's thinking did not stop at this point. Each attack, he contended, would require at least 5,000 bombs and good numbers of rifle grenades. As in the document of 11 October, he reminded fellow commanders of the need for a continuity of forward supply and how this should be achieved and then maintained once the objective was reached. He stresses that: 'It is absolutely essential that every Mills bomb is

31 TNA: WO95/1190, Guards Division HQ War Diary, App 95, Notes on the Experience gained during recent bombing by the Guards Division, 22 October 1915.
32 TNA: WO95/1190, Guards Division HQ War Diary, App 95, Notes on the Experience gained during recent bombing by the Guards Division, 22 October 1915.
33 TNA: WO95/1190, Guards Division HQ War Diary, App 95, Notes on the Experience gained during recent bombing by the Guards Division, 22 October 1915.

inspected' and has a detonator inserted 'before being sent up to the firing line', and that 'the trench must be kept clear of other men otherwise it will get blocked and the attack will break down'.[34]

Finally, Cavan returned to the subject of the most effective use of bombs. As on 11 October, he stressed that the Mills is the best bomb to use as, 'it is the only bomb that can be retained in the bombers hand until he has an opportunity to throw with advantage'. However, Cavan was not blind to the heavy physical toll that bombers experience and recommended that bombers should be 'be supplied with a left handed glove or finger stall. We discovered that the men's fingers got absolutely raw from pinching in the split pin and drawing out the ring from the Mills bomb.' He suggested design improvements such 'a larger ring and better devices than the present split pin'. 'The casualties amongst the bombers are necessarily very heavy. It is absolutely essential that every officer, NCO and man in the ranks should be instructed in how to throw a Mills bomb'. Further, fire discipline is vital to stop indiscriminate throwing. 'The carriers start throwing and even some of the chain passing up bombs to the carriers. This tendency must be sternly repressed. Hundreds of bombs were thrown without the pins being pulled out.' Bombers should be well trained, he urged, in both accuracy and rapidity to work, ideally, as a body of three with the work shared in rotation.[35]

Once again, Haking seemed impressed by Cavan's suggestions and his 'instructive notes' were forwarded to Advanced First Army for further consideration.[36] Interestingly, Haking just focused on one single area to highlight:

> There is no doubt that the MILLS hand grenade is by far the best, and the advantages of using only one kind of hand grenade, with which all grenadiers are familiar, is so great that I strongly recommend that no others should be issued. I consider that that men should not be trained in the use of any other hand grenade other than the Mills … the great point of the Mills Grenade is the confidence it gives because there is no danger of it going off until the holder chooses to throw it.[37]

The Guards Division had done very well indeed in these actions around the Hohenzollern. Their tenacious fighting spirit and battlefield discipline seems to have been especially well suited to these conditions of intense close quartered combat. Indeed, the gallant initiative shown by Lance Sergeant Oliver Brooks VC on 8 October is the very epitome of the qualities displayed by the Guards during this period. The leadership displayed by Cavan is also very worthy of note. He had a very clear sense of what his men were experiencing in these circumstances and was determined to develop a methodology of

34 TNA: WO95/1190, Guards Division HQ War Diary, App 95, Notes on the Experience gained during recent bombing by the Guards Division, 22 October 1915.
35 TNA: WO95/1190, Guards Division HQ War Diary, App 95, Notes on the Experience gained during recent bombing by the Guards Division, 22 October 1915.
36 TNA: WO95/886 XI Corps HQ War Diary, G954, 24 October 1915.
37 TNA: WO95/886 XI Corps HQ War Diary, G954, 24 October 1915.

best bombing practice based on their experiences. The reports that Cavan submitted to Haking on 11 and 23 October are a testimony to his ability to learn from events and to think of ways to apply this newly gained knowledge.

Loos, Conclusions

Looking back after the end of the war in 1920, Lieutenant Colonel Frederick Ponsonby commented that: 'As the first appearance of the Guards Division, Loos was somewhat disappointing. Although there were splendid bits of fighting the three Guards Brigades hardly had a fair chance, for the original attack had failed and all element of surprise had been eliminated when they were thrown in.'[38]

This was a fair judgement. As we have seen, when the Guards were released to XI Corps, they were moved hastily in a chaotic way in order to stop a collapse in the front lines and then launch an attack which was unlikely to succeed. Simon Robbins' view that the staff work was very poor indeed as XI Corps grappled inadequately with their critical responsibilities of traffic control and forward movement to the front line is confirmed by the evidence. Andy Simpson's analysis of the pressures created by the changing role of the corps commander is exemplified by the inept performance of Haking as GOC XI Corps. It is true that he had just a few hours to plan the attack on Hill 70 but to make the 3rd Brigade's attack depend on that of the 2nd Brigade was courting disaster in the fog of war, and the artillery fire plan, as suggested by Nick Lloyd, was deeply flawed. As Bidwell and Graham together with Paddy Griffith have stated, the nature of artillery fire planning was in an early stage of development at this point and the Guards were offered scant protection as they attacked well-fortified positions that had been barely, if at all, suppressed. [39] In terms of command and control, Brigadier General Heyworth's part in the 3rd Brigade's attack on Loos of 27 October was especially damaging. However, Lieutenant Colonel Murray Threipland's willingness to take the initiative and attempt the assault on Hill 70 as darkness fell is commendable as is the bravery of all of the Guardsmen involved. Whilst discipline did break down further north as elements of the Guards withdrew, they were soon rallied. Ponsonby also, quite rightly, eulogised about the 3rd Brigade's famous advance on Loos as it moved over the Grenay Ridge on 27 October: 'The spectacular advance under heavy fire was a fine performance and created a great impression at the time: officers and men of other Brigades expressed their admiration at the precision and parade-like regularity with which this advance was made.'[40]

38 Sir Frederick Ponsonby, 'The Finest Achievements of the House–Hold Brigade in the War', *Household Brigade Magazine*, Victory Number 1920, p.45.

39 Simon Robbins, *British Generalship*. Andy Simpson, *British Corps Command on the Western Front*, Nick Lloyd, *Loos*, Bidwell and Graham, *Firepower*, Paddy Griffith, *Battle Tactics*, page numbers as originally cited.

40 Sir Frederick Ponsonby, Lieutenant Colonel, 'The Finest Achievements of the House-Hold Brigade in the War.', p.45.

The Guards' action around the Hohenzollern Redoubt between 8 and 22 October which received only very limited coverage in the *Official History*, reveals the remarkable foresight that Cavan's leadership offered as the Guards became embroiled in resisting intense bombing raids by the German forces. It shows that Cavan had a true grasp of the dangers and realities faced by his men and that he was determined to establish a methodology of best bombing techniques to build on their success.

What of the famous culture that the various Guards regiments believed marked themselves out as a truly elite force? Headlam concluded that at Loos: 'If no large measure crowned their efforts, they yet gave a striking example of the physical and moral endurance which can only be achieved by good discipline, long training and *esprit de corps*.[41] Whilst this statement might be taken to contain a good deal of hyperbole, it holds a considerable degree of truth. During the attack on Loos and especially around the Hohenzollern, in the most demanding of situations, the Guardsmen worked well collectively across battalions when needed and fought with great bravery. Those long, 'de-humanising' weeks training in Britain meant that these men were hardened for battle and, to an extent, inculcated in the culture of their regiments. The evidence of the effectiveness of their training in France is sketchy but the stress on good march discipline would, without doubt, have been important as the Guards Division moved out of reserve towards the front, helping it to cope with inadequate XI Corps staff work and we know that a good deal of time had been spent in France on bombing practice and technique in the weeks prior to Loos.

Having been kept back in reserve, to exploit any breakthrough, the Guards Division at Loos stepped in to secure the line after the unfortunate rout of the 21st and 24th Divisions and this was achieved commendably. The failure of the attack on Hill 70 will have seemed to be almost a stain on the Guards reputation for some but in reality, it only ever had a minimal chance of success and its failure cannot be fairly attributed to the Guards Division. At the Hohenzollern in October, once again the Guards' role in thwarting a series of intense German attacks was critical. Losses had been heavy; a total of 2,041 including 244 killed and 607 missing.[42] Corrigan points out that they lost an average of 32 men per battalion killed between 26 and 29 September, whereas 21st Division lost an average of 53 men per battalion. The intensity of action and danger were the same. 'The difference is that the Guards, even with their casualties to date, were led by officers and NCOs who, by and large, knew what they were about.'[43]

The Guards Division may not have enjoyed an historic success at Loos but their battlefield performance was very sound indeed and Cavan's leadership was impressive. For both the Guards Division and for Cavan himself, the events at Loos augured well for the BEF in the coming years of the Great War. That was no small achievement.

41 Headlam, *History of the Guards Division*, p.109.
42 Edmonds, *Official History 1915, Volume 2*, p.392.
43 Gordon Corrigan, *Loos 1915: The Unwanted Battle* (Staplehurst: Spellmount, 2006), p.108.

4

November 1915 to July 1916: Dominating the Enemy, Christmas Fraternisation and Trench Raiding

Adapting to Winter Warfare and Maintaining the Offensive Spirit

After Loos, the Guards Division was stood down and billeted to the west and south-west of Bethune. On 24 October, XI Corps received notification that King George V was to spend the day touring the First Army area culminating in an inspection of the Guards Division during the afternoon.[1] The diary of the Guards Division HQ reveals the meticulous planning that was made, and a highlight would be the award of the VC to Oliver Brooks on a specially created stand.[2]

However, these detailed plans were all in vain. On the morning of 28 October 1915, the King visited the Royal Flying Corps Aerodrome at Hesdigneul, close to Bethune where he suffered a very serious riding accident. General Sir Douglas Haig wrote that:

> We were within 50 yards of the place at which he was to dismount and look round the aeroplanes … The mare was so quiet all through the day, but the waving caps and the sudden cheering would have upset any horse at such a close distance … the King seemed to clutch the reins very firmly and pulled the mare backwards. The grass was very wet and slippery, so that the mare's hind legs slipped from under her, and she fell with the King partly underneath her. The King seemed to have his wind taken and his leg hurt. Several of us undid his collar, and we lifted him to his car which was close at hand.[3]

The King had sustained a fractured pelvis which caused great discomfort to him for the rest of his life. Nonetheless, on 1 November, Brooks received his VC from the King on

1 TNA: WO95/880, XI Corps HQ, First Army C/405.
2 TNA: WO95/1190, Guards HQ WD, App.111.
3 Robert Blake, (ed.) *The Private Papers of Douglas Haig* (London: Eyre & Spottiswoode,1952), p.110.

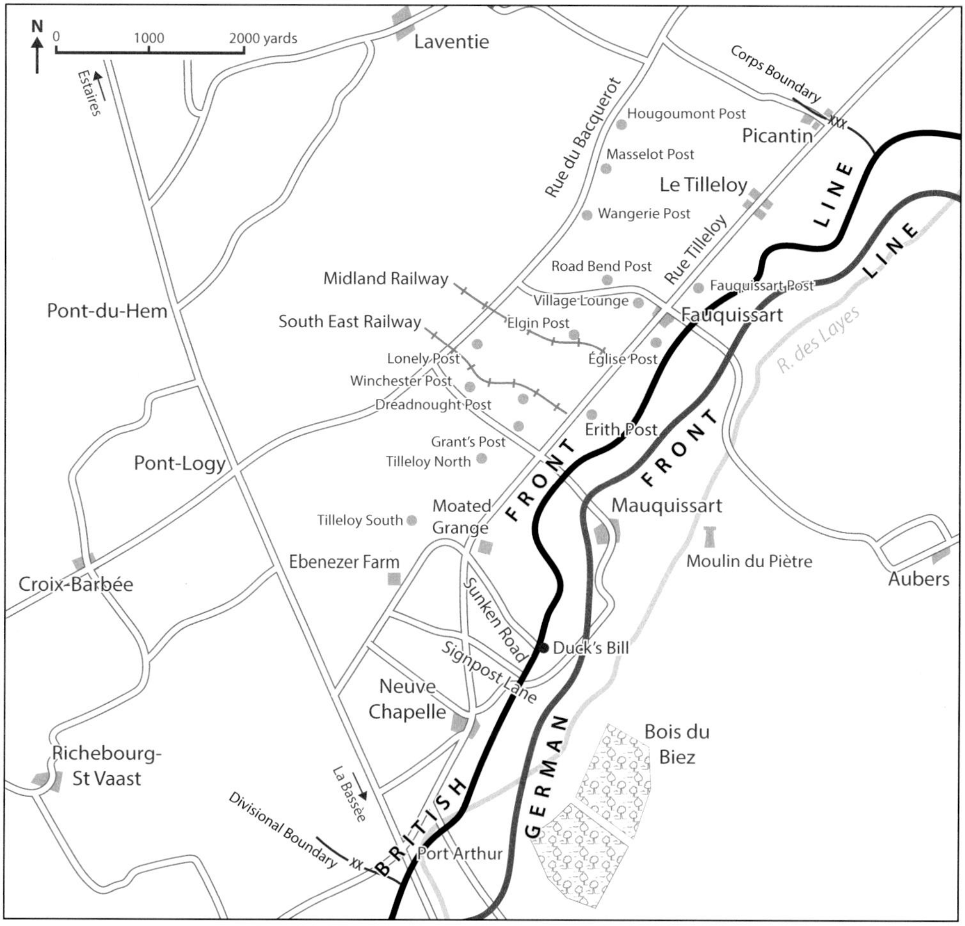

The Neuve Chapelle area, winter 1915-1916.

a hospital train at Aire-sur-la-Lys station. *The War Illustrated* printed an artistic impression of the occasion. The magazine remarked that: 'Though the King was suffering considerably from his fall ... His Majesty endeavoured to pin the VC to the heroic Coldstreamer's tunic, but was not strong enough to do so without assistance'.[4] Clearly the King took his responsibilities to the Guards Division very seriously indeed.

Shortly afterwards, XI Corps was reconstituted. Concerned about the wisdom of letting Indian forces spend a second winter in France, it was decided that XI Corps would take over the sector north of the La Bassee Canal which had been occupied by the Indian Corps. However, there were still active operations around Fosse No. 8 and

4 *The War Illustrated*, 27 November 1915.

it was decided that 12th Division would remain in that sector and that they would be replaced by the 19th Division so that XI Corps now consisted of the Guards together with the 19th and 46th Divisions. The new XI Corps front extended from La Quinque Rue to Picantin which was a village about two miles east of Laventie. The Guards were allocated the northern part of XI Corps' sector. Effectively this meant from a position around 1,000 yards south east of Neuve Chapelle to a ruined hamlet north of Fauquissart on the Rue Tilleloy and then north east to Picantin which was about 2,500 yards north east of Fauquissart. The transfer of this sector to the Guards was achieved in stages between 9 November and 25 November and the division remained in these positions until the start of February 1916.[5]

For Cavan, the winter would provide an opportunity for the Guards Division to recover from its first battlefield experience at Loos but he was well aware that these months would be taxing and gruelling in a different way. He was determined that the Guards would continue to display the same qualities expected of their elite status. The sector would be well maintained, discipline would remain tight, and the men would still be expected to show an offensive spirit in trench raiding. No doubt, the potential for promotion to corps command would, at the very least, have been at the back of his mind. It is with these objectives in mind that we can proceed to evaluate the winter of 1915–1916.

The Guards faced immediate problems as they took control of this new sector. The marshy ground meant that the front-line defences were breastworks rather than trenches which had been neglected and in need of serious repair. In an area where the Germans enjoyed excellent observation over the British lines, the water-logged trenches meant understanding the hydrology that underpinned local conditions was imperative. An artificial channel that ran behind German lines caught and distributed the flow of water that descended from Aubers Ridge and a network of open drains and channels then controlled the water flow into the River Lys. The CRE and his staff were able to discover which of these waterways in the network could be used to channel water away from the front line. Because of the huge amount of heavy manual labour involved a Land Drainage Company was allotted to the Guards Division as new channels were constructed, often under fire, and a new pumping station was constructed on the River Lys opposite Estaires.[6]

A vital task, therefore, was the repair and then the relentless maintenance of the front-line breastworks and the communication trenches. It was decided at a conference at Guards Division HQ on 18 November that battalions, who would spend a period of 48 hours in the front line, should be responsible for the upkeep of these trenches when on duty. The reality of life in these front-line trenches in often freezing conditions was challenging but could provide, surprisingly, some relief. As the historian of the Welsh Guards wrote:

5 Headlam, *History of the Guards Division*, pp. 92–93. TNA: WO95/1190, Guards Division HQ.
6 Headlam, *History of the Guards Division*, pp.94–97.

> On the night of the 16th the battalion relieved the 2nd Battalion Scots Guards in the line. It was held in a series of posts, some of them being a considerable distance apart. At night each post found double sentries while the rest could sleep in the shelters, which were small dog-kennel arrangements built of mud-filled sandbags and roofed over with bits of tin on which earth was piled. As shelters against anything but the mildest sort of weather these concoctions of tin and sandbags were absolutely useless, but the distance from the enemy, combined with his unenterprising disposition, permitted the use of fires to an extent never again encountered by the battalion. Not only did each shelter have its brazier but the company cooks prepared and served hot dinners and teas in the line, frequently raising by their efforts clouds of smoke in the daytime and a blaze of light at night. The work in this line was one long struggle against water, and the Welsh Guards spent weeks making water run uphill by 'swishing' it along from one to another with spades. The first few days in the line were very wet and cold and the nights frosty. The enemy knew at once that a relief and change of troops had taken place.[7]

This account goes on to mention the kind of 'banter' that ensued as soldiers called across the lines. Cavan, as we shall see, had no intention of the Guards Division falling into anything that remotely resembled what became known as the 'Live and Let Live' system.[8]

Faced with a long winter, important decisions were now made about the best way that the line could be held, how the Guards Division would organise its defences and finally, how the division could maintain its offensive spirit and seek to 'dominate' no man's land and the Germans forces opposite. The health and well-being of his troops and effective training were also very much in his mind. Just as he had done in the Battle of Loos, Cavan showed clear, logical thinking and effective leadership as he made his plans.

It was assumed that no large-scale German attack would be made in the winter period but because of the proximity of the front lines, a sound defensive system had to be decided upon as a precautionary measure. The ideal solution was to utilise the smallest number of men in this forward zone. A decision was made at Army level to locate two divisions in the front line with one in Army reserve to allow appropriate training. Haking's initial proposal for XI Corps was to place the Guards and the 46th Division on the front line, with the 19th Division in reserve.[9]

Cavan was quick, however, to envisage a better option. After consulting the GOCs of the other two divisions, he sent his preferred solution to Haking on 14 November. Showing great confidence in his division, he suggested that the Guards remain permanently in the front line with the other two divisions being rotated:

7 Dudley Ward, *History of the Welsh Guards*, pp.52–53.
8 Tony Ashworth, *Trench Warfare 1914–1918: The Live and Let Live System* (London: Pan, 2000).
9 Headlam, *History of the Guards Division*, pp.97–98.

> I make this suggestion with a full sense of responsibility but as I always have a Brigade in Reserve in roomy and comfortable billets, for 6 days out of every 18 days, as, also, I can arrange that no Battalion is actually in the line for more than 48 hours. I am convinced that all ranks will get their proper share of rest. Secondly – as regards training–I would point out that the Guards Division went through a full month's training between August 18th to September 22nd – including Battalion, Brigade and Divisional Exercises over ground – also a course of musketry for every man – at and about LUMBRES – the Division would not therefore be losing in efficiency … This system has the obvious advantage that each Division of the Corps knows its own ground thoroughly and well – and it also ensures continuity of policy and more efficient work. From the point of view of offensive action it has everything to recommend it. Thorough knowledge of ground, strength of opposing forces, weak spots, position of enemy Machine Gun emplacements – good sniping posts and lastly but by no means least such intimate and close connection with the Artillery that any portion can be instantly engaged – owing to familiarity with names and places. Meanwhile all our regular training courses would be working under a regular and settled system.[10]

Haking was happy to accept Cavan's proposal for an initial two-month period but he cautioned that proper consideration must be given to pressures on the brigadiers and their staff.[11] In reality, this method of holding the line 'proved so entirely satisfactory that it remained in force throughout the winter'.[12] Having gained his favoured position in the line, Cavan was now free to establish his modus operandi for the Guards Division in the coming months. The division's defences were divided into three zones with the front line being defended whatever the cost by its garrison of two battalions in each brigade area. The second line's garrisons were manned at the discretion of the brigadiers by a battalion billeted as close by as possible and the third line was not permanently manned but had 'caretakers' located in them.[13]

On 19 November 1915, Cavan was now in a position to outline his plans in some detail. He was in no mood for the Guards to wrest on their laurels; the 'offensive spirit' would be maintained. He considered that, once again, the winter months would preclude any significant forward movement just as they had in the previous month. However, he noted that the circumstances had changed. The previous winter had seen British forces 'just hanging on with a thin line and no depth in it'. There had not been enough artillery ammunition and guns whilst the trenches were badly constructed and water-logged with communication trenches together with supporting trenches in short number. However, Cavan believed that the Guards Division could now look forward

10 TNA: WO95/1190 Guards Division HQ 14 November 1915, appendix 144.
11 TNA: WO95/1190 Guards Division HQ 14 November 1915, Haking's handwritten notes on Appendix 144.
12 Headlam, *History of the Guards Division*, p.99.
13 Headlam, *History of the Guards Division*, pp.102–103

more optimistically to a winter where 'many of these disadvantages have been removed'. There was now a significant increase in manpower to insure strongly defended lines in good depth. Additionally, the supply of artillery ammunition had improved. He pointed out that 800,000 Mills bombs were now being made available to British forces. Further, with improved communications, British trenches benefitted from effective second lines and strong points which meant that a 'break through on the part of the enemy may be considered an impossibility'.[14]

Clearly Cavan believed that the Guards Division was well placed to take advantage of this position 'to dictate to the enemy the form the winter campaign should take' and so 'allow him no respite'. Trench raids would be at the very heart of this offensive strategy. The division would select places where four or five lanes of about 50 to 100 yards in the enemy's wire could be cut by the artillery. These lanes would be kept open permanently by shrapnel and machine gun fire. If the Germans attempted any repairs, they would need to be stopped immediately. The division was then expected to carry out raids at these points during the night. A force of about two companies would rush into the German front lines. Specifically, Cavan ordered that:

> All Germans in the front line trenches to be killed or captured, machine guns, minewerfers etc to be destroyed or brought back, traverses and trenches blown up and generally as much damage to be done as possible and all our troops to be back in their trenches within a short time. These raids may be assisted according to local conditions by a short intensive bombardment, the employment of gas, or a combination of both.[15]

Cavan realised that it might only take a week before the Germans realised that these activities were not attempts to gain and hold their ground but were raids. He anticipated that their response would be to 'hold the trenches opposite the lanes very lightly and … create strong positions on each flank'.[16] The Guards Division's response would be to wait for advantageous weather, then simulate an attack opposite one of the 'lanes' before discharging gas on each flank without committing any forward movement by the infantry. Enfilading guns would be brought forward to fire shrapnel into the German trenches that were well manned.

This approach brought many distinct advantages according to Cavan. Firstly, the enemy could be kept in a state of heightened anxiety because of the combined effect of having different 'lanes' always open to utilise in an unpredictable way by a combination of stimulated and real raids. Secondly, in small attacks the German front line could be reached with minimal losses without the likelihood of heavier losses if these lines had to be subsequently held. 'By these raids we ought therefore to be able to inflict the maximum

14 TNA: WO95/1190, Guards Division HQ 19 November 1915, appendix 148.
15 TNA: WO95/1190, Guards Division HQ 19 November 1915, appendix 148.
16 TNA: WO95/1190, Guards Division HQ 19 November 1915, appendix 148.

losses on the enemy without incurring heavy losses ourselves'. Thirdly, it would help the men's spirit avoiding 'the boredom and possible slackness occasioned by the monotony of ordinary trench life'. Finally, there was the obvious impact on the enemy which would confirm Cavan's desire to dominate the Germans on the Division's front:

> The enemy's method is to hold his front line very lightly. Our policy is almost certain to have the effect of making him use more troops in the front line. He will have to keep some of his best fighting troops in front, instead of using untrained Landstrum for the purpose which he does at present in many places, and the strain of expecting an attack at any one of about a hundred places on any night is bound to effect the morale of the rank and file.[17]

Filmer's Raid

On the night of 11/12 December a bombing raid was carried out by the 4/Grenadier Guards that is worthy of a detailed analysis as an exemplar of expectation and practice. Described by Haking as 'a well-planned and well-executed operation reflecting the highest credit on all concerned from Col. Seymour, Comdg. 4 th Bn. Grenadier Guards, downwards'.[18] We are fortunate to have detailed accounts from the key participants that show just how closely the raids planning and implementation was based on Cavan's thinking, although its execution left plenty of scope for further refinements.[19]

Captain Sir Robert Filmer.

The raid was planned and led by Captain Sir Robert Filmer, who commanded No. 3 Company. The son of Sir Edmund Filmer, 9th Baronet, a Grenadier Guards officer and MP for

17 TNA: WO95/1190, Guards Division HQ 19 November 1915, appendix 148.
18 TNA: WO95/1190/, Guards Division HQ: First Army No.52 (G).
19 TNA: WO95/1190, Guards Division HQ; 'Summary of Report on Bombing Raid Carried Out by the 4th Battalion Grenadier Guards 3rd Guards Brigade on the11th–12th December Against the Enemy's Trenches to the N.E. of Neuve Chapelle', (M.35.d. And M.36.C) 20 December 1915.

West Kent. Born in 1878, Robert had inherited the baronetcy at the age of just eight years old. After Eton and Sandhurst, he too gained a commission in the Grenadier Guards. He was at Omdurman in 1898 and had served in the Boer War. He eventually resigned his commission in 1904 and transferred to the reserves, where he held the rank of major in the Royal East Kent Yeomanry. He then stood, unsuccessfully, as the Conservative candidate for Lincoln in the two general elections of 1910. He had re-joined his old regiment on 1 February 1915.

Filmer had originally sent out a patrol under Sergeant Higgins at 6:00 a.m. on 7 December from the head of Sign Post Lane about 500 yards northeast of Neuve Chapelle to find out if the enemy wire on this road in front had been cut by the artillery bombardment. Higgins reported a gap of 15 yards in width which he penetrated and crawled close to the parapet; he believed a platoon or party of bombers could have rushed the trench. This was confirmed by a patrol sent out by the 1/Grenadiers. On 10 December Filmer 'sent out Lieutenants Ponsonby and Nairn with Higgins to thoroughly reconnoitre the ground from Sign Post Lane through the gap in the wire as near to the enemy's parapet as was possible. They reported the gap in the wire was still open, but they had not been able to get further.'[20] Filmer and Ponsonby then met at Battalion HQ on the morning of 11 December to receive their orders. Filmer requested artillery support to form a barrage and for Lieutenant Stevenson (1/Grenadier Guards) to continue in command of the machine gun at Sign Post Lane. Filmer had previously discussed with him how that gun might co-operate in the attack. Both requests were granted. Lord Henry Seymour, who commanded the 4/Grenadiers, was clear about the objectives of the raid: to kill Germans, gain information of their trenches and how they were held, damage their morale, capture and destroy machine guns.[21]

The following narrative comes from Filmer's report. The composition of the attacking party was 33 volunteers together with three officers. The left and right parties consisted of six bombers, three carriers and two bayonet men. The central party consisted of three bombers, two carriers and six bayonet men. Lieutenant Ponsonby was in command of the bombers, Lieutenant Nairn the assault and Captain Filmer the attack as a whole. Filmer then issued orders to Ponsonby and Nairn and explained arrangements in detail to the NCOs and men of his company who had already volunteered, and to the NCOs and men of the battalion bombers. These meticulous orders covered the allocation of men to the various parties, their duties, his plan of attack in which responsibilities were clearly delineated. The centre party were charged with clearing the enemy trench 20 yards approximately on either side of central file. The right and left parties would not go beyond the second German communication trench. The flanking parties were to bomb

20 TNA: WO 95/1190, Guards Division HQ; 'Copy of Report on Bombing Attack carried out by Battalion Bombers and Volunteers from my Company the night of 11/12 December, 1915'. R. Filmer.

21 TNA: WO95/1190, Guards Division HQ; 'Report on Surprise Attack, by O.C. 4th Bn. Grenadier Guards, by party of 4th Bn. Grenadier Guards on December 11th 1915'.

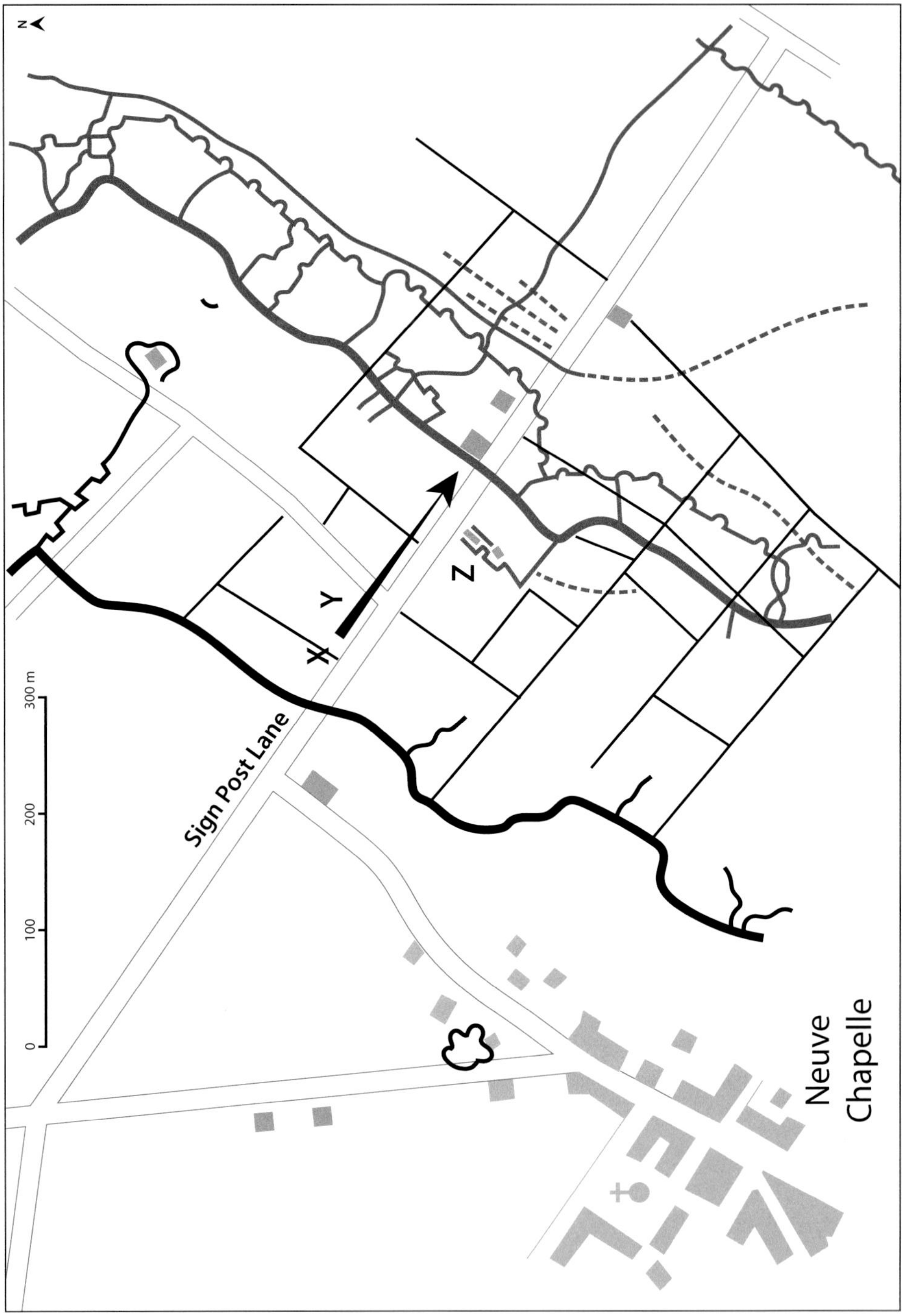

The Filmer Raid, 11/12 December 1915.

outwards, the centre party was to secure and hold the central position. The plan was to be subject to modifications after Filmer's personal reconnaissance when it became dark. The limit of time to be spent in the German trench was set at 20 minutes and there would be three blasts on the whistle for the retreat. The method of retirement was settled with the left party to fall back first, followed by the right and when all clear, the centre party. Arrangements were made for a connecting or covering party to be placed half-way between the enemy's and the Guards' lines to cover the retreat and pass on any prisoners taken. The men were required to wear clean fatigue dress, leather waistcoats and stocking caps and to carry bombs, bayonets, and revolvers but no rifles. Bombs were to be carried in sandbags. All identification marks, letters, maps etc were to be left behind. Machine gun fire would be arranged to cover any sounds made by the three parties and make the situation appear normal.

Filmer then met the commanding officer of Battery 75 at the head of Sign Post Lane who lent him a large scale map of the German trenches. He proposed to start the attack from the trench at X with a line of advance towards the German trench at Z but he needed to carry out a personal reconnaissance to confirm it was still occupied. If it was. Filmer proposed to get the CO's permission to attack at that point 'as I did not consider it safe to have it on my right rear'. Filmer set out to reconnoitre the situation at 8:15 p.m. together with Sergeant Higgins and four others. Corporal Lord was charged 'to cut a good wide passage through our own wire', whilst he also 'dropped one man as connecting file between our wire and the German, and two more at the gap in their wire'. From the gap he crawled 'all around the houses at Z' to find that the German trenches there 'had been abandoned by the Germans, are waterlogged and smashed up by our shell fire, and could be disregarded as far as my attack was concerned. I also settled the exact line he was to lead the attacking party along' before returning whilst 'leaving out the three connecting files.'

Having gained the CO's approval on his return, Filmer issued the final verbal orders that Higgins was to guide and command the right party, followed by the left party under Ponsonby, the centre party under Nairn, and the connecting party under Filmer himself together with CQMS Hayward. Filmer posted the connecting party at Y 'a good position to cover the retirement of the attacking parties, which I had selected while out on patrol.' He then took forward the two reserve bomb carriers to post them at the gap in the enemy wire 'in case the Bombers ran short of bombs after the attack'. He then discovered that the attacking party had halted so he 'pushed to the front and ascertained from Sergt. Higgins who had slightly lost direction to the left, that there was a German trench full of men to his immediate front'. Filmer crawled forward after him, and 'asked him after a further reconnaissance whether he could get through the short strip of low barbed wire which the enemy had erected immediately at the bottom of their parapet'.

Higgins replied that 'he would make an attempt' but as he was moving forward and 'stepping over the wire, our Artillery (Battery B.75) opened fire and placed a barrage on both flanks and in front'. Seymour said that this fire was 'most excellent in its accuracy of aim and moral effect. This barrage continued until the entire party returned and could not have been more satisfactory'.[22] Filmer confirmed the positive impact of this artillery support:

> Nothing was observed or heard till 11.30 pm when bombs were seen exploding in German trench near SIGN POST LANE. From this time onward, bombing, shelling and Very lights were incessant. Very little rifle fire or enemy shell fire commenced till the signal for retirement was given … This may have partly accounted for the fact that no fire was opened on us, although we were only a few feet from the parapet, but the enemy's sentries, if posted, must have been off their fire positions. From the sounds of pumping, singing and talking, there must have been a considerable number of men in the trench.

Afterwards Filmer ascertained from Nairn and Higgins that 'the gap in the old German wire through which we crawled at this spot led directly on to a covered Machine Gun Emplacement. The fire of this gun must have weakened the wire in front of it, which accounted for the comparative ease with which we crossed it.'

Filmer continued: 'I saw Sergt. Higgins jump down into the trench and bombing became general'. Filmer then 'left the direction of affairs in Lt. Nairn's hands and returned to the connecting post' according to his orders from the CO, 'in order to see that the assaulting party's retreat was assured'. A few minutes later Filmer heard the signal of three whistles for the general retirement of all the parties. As the centre party passed the connecting post, Nairn reported that he had left Ponsonby with a broken leg in charge of Private Sweetman. The right and left parties came back to the Guards' trench immediately after the centre party. Filmer stayed out with the connecting post until there was no possibility of any men of the attacking parties still being out before retiring the remaining forces and bringing up the rear himself.

Although noise from the German trench suggested it must have been strongly held, Filmer commented that no fire opened up until the retirement started, when heavy, but inaccurate fire was poured in from about 50 rifles. Higgins claimed, and this was supported by Nairn, that he silenced both the machine gun and its crew by throwing bombs into the emplacement through a wooden door at the back. 'This is further borne out by the fact that no machine gun fire was directed on us in our retirement or advance; the latter fact suggests that the MG crew must have been asleep or sheltering from the rain when we delivered the attack.' Higgins then tried to bring the gun back with him, but could not prise it from the covered emplacement, and so destroyed it in situ with another bomb. Filmer also confirmed that Higgins' party bombed several dug outs along the trench where lights were shining.

22 TNA: WO 95/1190, Guards Division HQ; 'Copy of Report on Bombing Attack carried out by Battalion Bombers and Volunteers from my Company the night of 11/12 December, 1915'. R. Filmer.

Apparently, Higgins' name had been submitted on several occasions for gallantry and Filmer now recommended him for a DCM. Filmer also recommended Private Sweetman who 'carried Lt. Ponsonby for some distance, and remained with him under heavy fire, until Lt. Nairn went and brought him in with a stretcher party under instructions from the CO as he was the last to see him'. Filmer's report finishes with this simple statement: 'Sergt. Higgins when he heard that Lieut. Ponsonby was out wounded went over the parapet again to find him without any orders.'

Despite the remarkable bravery of those involved and the apparent success of a raid planned in the greatest of detail, Seymour saw room for improvement! He concluded that not enough time had been spent in the German trenches and that it should be 30 minutes at least which would give 'time for enemy who have run away to be assembled and attempt a counter attack which can be dispersed with bombs. In our case enemy returned to the trench, bombed it, found we had gone, and opened a hot fire on our retreat.' In the future, Seymour recommended that it would be better to transport the bombs in covered carriers or buckets. Further: 'Life preservers would prove effective, and do not interfere with bomb throwing' and importantly, he noted that the 'enemy's sentries were not alert – night was dark, cold and stormy – their wire, which at point struck was low wire entanglement, proved no effective obstacle to keen men provided with nippers, and though the enemy were holding the trench in considerable strength, the sudden surprise and bombing attack completely destroyed their nerve, and the same operation could have been done with less men'. Finally, he argued for the issue of more revolvers.[23]

Cavan was clearly delighted with the raid which was 'only considered when patrols of December and especially of December 11th reported great slackness' with sentries in the German front lines. 'I consider the Officer Commanding 4th Battalion Grenadier Guards was quite right to seize his opportunity on this information, although some risk was taken perhaps in the necessarily hurried preparations.' The raid was the very epitome of Cavan's desire for the Guards Division to set the agenda during the winter period. He quickly forwarded the names of Filmer, Higgins and Sweetman for 'immediate reward' and the request was personally annotated by Douglas Haig who noted that the raid was: 'A well planned and well executed operation reflecting the highest credit on all concerned from Colonel Seymour commanding 4th Battn. Grenadier Guards downwards. The immediate rewards asked for have been well earned, and I shall a very great pleasure in recommending the names put forward.'[24]

Filmer was awarded the MC, Higgins and Sweetman the DCM. Tragically, however, on 25 January 1916, just two days after he was awarded his MC, Filmer was severely wounded by shrapnel and his horse was killed after he returned to retrieve his pince-nez spectacles at first light having left them behind whilst on duty the previous night.

23 TNA: WO95/1190, Guards Division HQ; 'Report on Surprise Attack, by O.C. 4th Bn. Grenadier Guards, by party of 4th Bn. Grenadier Guards on December 11th 1915'.
24 TNA: WO95/1190, Guards Division HQ: XIth Corps G.D. No. 453/G 13 December 1915.

According to press reports, he was advised that it was folly to go out into the open but ignored the advice. He died on 27 January.[25] He was aged just 37 and had never married. In the east window of East Sutton church is a memorial to the men of the parish who fell in the Great War. Sir Robert Marcus Filmer MC is depicted in Guards uniform. He is buried in Merville Communal Cemetery, 12 miles southwest of Armentieres.

There is an interesting postscript to Filmer's story. His servant, Private Frederick James Lillywhite, had been with him for some years before the war and, according to research carried out by the family, there was a strong bond between them. Apparently, Filmer had promised Fred that he would not be expected to travel abroad because Fred had made it clear that he did not wish to be apart from his wife. However, Filmer's doctor had suggested that it would benefit his health to do so and Fred had complied. When Filmer re-joined the army in 1915, Fred went with him, having been told by Filmer that if he died, Fred and his family would be provided for to the sum of £1,000. Unfortunately, there was nothing to this effect in Filmer's will. His heir, Arthur Stanley Wilson, Filmer's brother-in-law, did help Fred to start a grocer's business after the war but the business failed. In the mid-1920s Fred was bound over to keep the peace twice following two incidents in which he threatened Wilson with a revolver, and he also sent Wilson a letter threatening to burn the family mansion down if he did not honour the promise Fred claimed that Filmer had made to him before he died. In press reports of the case Wilson appeared to be sympathetic towards Fred, despite the threats, and acknowledged his faithful service to Filmer, particularly in caring for him during his final days.[26]

Filmer's raid was not the only raid of note during these weeks along the Guards front. In mid-December, the 2/Grenadier Guards mounted a raid to reconnoitre the state of the German trenches opposite and, in particular, to find evidence of mining activity which were an ongoing concern.[27] At 12:30 a.m. on 14 December a patrol of three NCOs and nine men under Lieutenant the Honourable W. Parnell went out from Red Lamp and got into the German trench. The war diary reports that the German wire at the point of entry 'was found to be much knocked about, though not entirely destroyed, and the patrol got through it without much difficulty'. The party worked southwest along the trench without finding any Germans. They found the trench to be 'deserted everywhere and knee deep in water, or deeper throughout. The patrol was never challenged, and no sound of the enemy could be heard. Several disused dugouts were entered without anything being found. At the suspected shaft head opposite our mines Nos. 1 and 2, a wooden hut was found … but no signs of a mine could be found'. Evidence of a telephone installation in the form of a china insulator together with a hand bell which was 'attached outside what looked like an Officer' dug out' were brought back.[28]

25 *Whitstable Times and Herne Bay Herald*, 26 February 1916.
26 The Great War Forum 1914-1918, < https://www.greatwarforum.org>, accessed 20 November 2020. See also: *Sheffield Daily Telegraph* 19 May 1925, *Sheffield Independent* 20 October 1926.
27 Headlam, *History of the Guards Division*, p.104.
28 Anthony Saunders, *Raiding on the Western Front* (Barnsley: Pen & Sword, 2012), pp.27–28: TNA: WO95/1212, 1 Guards Brigade HQ.

At a similar time on the following night, Parnell returned with the same party with the addition of a machine gunner together with one officer and one other rank from the RE Mining Company. They entered the German lines at the same point before proceeding in an easterly direction for about 400 yards. On this occasion, however, the party met with German resistance. They surprised a German post that was occupied by three German soldiers. Two were killed silently with trench clubs whilst one was taken prisoner. However, a German party arrived in an attempt to effect a rescue but were driven away. Private C.R. Maiden was mortally wounded and had to be left behind as the party started their return to safety. The mining engineers could find no evidence of mining activity in the vicinity. Meanwhile, a second party from the 2/Coldstream Guards had entered the German lines at the same point and proceeded for a distance of 700 yards in the opposite direction without finding any Germans. Wiliam Parnell deservedly received the MC for his efforts. He died aged 22 on 25 September 1916 and lies in the Guards Cemetery at Lesboeufs. Another member of the party, Sergeant J. Lyons, received the DCM.

Christmas Fraternisation and Two Courts Martial

On 22 December, Cavan was deservedly selected to command the newly created XIV Corps; an 'early promotion that had been anticipated for some time'.[29] However, his mood was very different just a few days later. Angry and with an undoubted sense of wounded pride, he sent this report to Haking of Christmas Day fraternisation on the Guards front:

> I much regret to report that in spite of special orders – there was some communication held between the lines occupied by the Guards Division and the 13th Bavarian Reserve Regt. This morning. I have seen the Brigadiers concerned who were on the spot within 20 minutes of learning of the episode, and our own men were back in the trenches within 30 to 40 minutes after first going out. I have ordered a full and searching enquiry to be made tomorrow as to how my implicit orders came to be disobeyed, which I will forward in due course. Large parties of unarmed Germans were the first to appear, but this is no excuse, and I regret the incident more than I can say.[30]

It is strange that Cavan used the phrase 'implicit orders'. It would appear his orders did not work their way down the chain of command as he had envisaged. The fraternisation involved the 1/Coldstream Guards, the 2/Scots Guards and the 1/Scots Guards.

Guards Division HQ had received a message only the day before from XI Corps HQ, pointing out that 'it is thought possible that the Germans may try to take advantage

29 Headlam, *History of the Guards Division*, p.113.
30 TNA: WO95/1190, Guards Division HQ XI Corps 25 December 1915. App 283.

of the period of Xmas and new year's day to make surprise attacks on the assumption that British troops may be off their guard. All commanders of troops should therefore be warned against any relaxation of vigilance or measure of defence.'[31] The war diary confirms that the message was 'passed on to C.R.A. and Brigadiers'. Consequently, the German trenches in the vicinity of Sign Post Lane and the Sunken Road were bombarded intermittently between 8:00 p.m. and 11:00 p.m. on 24 December and then in the early hours of Christmas Day between 1:00 a.m. and 5:00 a.m. in order to discourage fraternisation. A total of 1,000 rounds of machine gun fire added to the demonstration.[32]

Despite such acts designed to stop any repetition of the fraternisation witnessed on Christmas Day in 1914, Captain William Ewart of the 2/Scots Guards described what happened on 25 December 1915 in *Scots Guard on the Western Front*:

> So soon as it grows light this morning, we start peeping at each other over the top of the parapet … calling across to each other. And presently, at about 7.50, a German stands up openly on the parapet and waves his arms. He is followed by two in field-grey overcoats and pill-box caps. Then they come out all down the line, stand on the parapet, wave, shout, and finally swarm forth from their trenches on either side.
>
> A British sergeant is shot dead almost at the outset, as he stands on the parapet. But this makes no difference. It must be an accident. The supreme craving of humanity, the irresistible, spontaneous impulse born of a common faith and a common fear, fully triumph.
>
> And so the grey and khaki figures surge towards each other as one man. The movement has started on the right. It spreads like contagion. Only we officers, the sentries and a few non-commissioned officers remain in our trench. The men meet at the willow-lined stream; they even cross it and mingle together in a haphazard throng. They talk and gesticulate, and shake hands over and over again. They pat each other on the shoulder and laugh like schoolboys, and leap across the little stream for fun. And when an Englishman falls in and a Boche helps him out there is a shout of laughter that echoes back to the trenches. The Germans exchange cigars and pieces of sausage, and sauerkraut and concentrated coffee for cigarettes and bully beef and ration biscuits and tobacco. They express mutual admiration by pointing and signs. It is our leather waistcoats and trench coats that attract attention. We shout 'Hullo, Fritz', 'Good Morning Fritz', 'Merry Christmas', 'Happy Christmas' 'How's your father?', 'Come over and call', 'Come and have breakfast', and the like, amid roars of laughter … So for ten brief – all too brief-minutes there is peace and goodwill among the trenches on Christmas Day. Then from the trenches of the Ninety-fifth Bavarian Reserve Infantry Regiment two officers in black accoutrements and shiny field boots come out, wishing to take photographs

31 TNA: WO95/1190, Guards Division HQ, App. 281 Guards HQ, 24 December 1915.
32 TNA: WO95/1190, Guards Division HQ, 'Summary of Information No.52', 25 December 1915. App. 282.

> of our Tommies, and offering them cigars. Their request is refused, and presently they say: 'You will have five minutes to get back to your trenches before our artillery will open fire.'
>
> And it does. And two or three men are wounded almost at once. But for twenty-four hours not a shot is fired on either side. A common brotherhood of suffering – or is it an act of God, or just human activity? – has united Englishman and Bavarian in fraternity on this battlefield this grey Christmas morning which no one on either side who has taken part in this quaint scene will ever forget.[33]

Meanwhile, there was fraternisation on the front opposite 1/Coldstream Guards. Private Bertie Felstead served in the 15/Royal Welch Fusiliers who had temporarily been assigned to work alongside the 1/Coldstream. After the night's carol singing, Felstead recalled that 'feelings of goodwill had so swelled up that at dawn, Bavarian and British soldiers clambered spontaneously out of their trenches. Shouting such greetings as 'Hello Tommy' and 'Hello Fritz' they at first shook hands in no-man's-land, and then presented one another with gifts. German beer, sausages and spiked helmets were given, or bartered, in return for bully beef, biscuits and tunic buttons.' Felstead also recalled some football of sorts: 'It wasn't a game as such, more a kick-around and a free-for-all. There could have been 50 on each side for all I know. I played because I really liked football. I don't know how long it lasted, probably half an hour.'[34] More evidence of fraternisation can be found in the diary of Captain Carlos 'Pip' Blacker of the 1/Coldstream Guards:

> Loudening noises of shouts and singing came across no-man's-land, and when there was enough daylight figures could be seen moving about between their breastworks and wire. Our people followed suit. The Germans then came out in front of their wire. Our people did the same. No shooting anywhere. Both sides then gained in boldness until there was quite a crowd in no-man's-land … The two sides exchanged cigarettes and other souvenirs, including buttons and badges … The conversation, which was amiable, went on for about five minutes. It was brought to an end by a burst of shrapnel overhead.[35]

However, the weight of the full-scale Court of Inquiry was soon to bear down exclusively on just one battalion: the 1/Scots Guards and, in particular, two of its officers. Captain Miles Barne who was the acting battalion commander together with Captain Sir Iain Colquhoun,[36] a company commander in the same battalion were both court-martialled

33 William Ewart, *Scots Guard on the Western Front* (Stevenage: Strong Oak Press, 2001 [1934]), pp.77–79.
34 Jonathan Riley, *The Second Christmas Truce, 1915*, <http://generalship.org/royal-welch-fusiliers-articles/2nd-christmas-truce-1915.html>, accessed 18 December 2023.
35 John Blackler (ed.), *Have You Forgotten Yet? The First World War Memoirs of C. P. Blacker MC GM,* (Barnsley: Pen & Sword, 2000), pp.75–76.
36 Sir Iain Colquhoun, 7th Baronet, 29th Laird of Luss and often referred to as 'Luss'.

for their alleged failure to deal effectively with the fraternisation. The evidence suggests that they were scapegoated to cover the embarrassment of those above them in the chain of command. The actual fraternisation was relatively short-lived according to Barne:

> About 8.30 a.m. a large number of Germans walked over the parapet – and an Officer came forward to ask Colquhoun for a truce till 1 p.m. He would not grant this, but granted ¾ hr to bury dead – both sides. Some of the companies on the left saw this, and also came out -& there was some handshaking and exchange of cigarettes and 'souvenirs' … I went down about 10 a.m. with the Brigadier (Ponsonby), and we agreed that we could not have ordered our men to fire on the defenceless Germans who came over trusting us … However, the Divisional Commander is much annoyed at the whole thing and no difference should have been made, all should have been 'as usual'.[37]

Captain Sir Iain Colquhoun.

Colquhoun in his diary recorded that:

> Stand to at 6.30. Germans very quiet. Remained in Firing Trenches until 8.30. No sign of anything unusual. When having breakfast about 9 am a sentry reported to me that the Germans were standing up on their parapets and walking towards our barbed wire. I ran out to our firing trenches and saw our men looking over the parapet and the Germans outside our barbed wire. A German officer came forward and asked me for a truce for Xmas. I replied that this was impossible. He then asked for ¾ hour to bury his dead. I agreed. The Germans then started burying their dead and we did the same. This was finished in ½ hrs time. Our men and the Germans then talked and exchanged cigars, cigarettes etc for ¼ of an hour and when the time was up I blew a whistle and both sides returned to their trenches. For the rest of the day the Germans walked about and sat on their parapets. Our men did much the same but remained in their trenches. Not a shot was fired. At night the Germans

37 Randall Nicol, *Miles Barne's Diary: A Suffolk Countryman at War 1915–1917* (Solihull: Helion, 2018), p.83.

> put up Fairy lights on their parapets and their trenches were outlined for miles on either side.[38]

Within hours, Cavan was demanding a 'full and concise enquiry immediately' wanting to know 'why men left their parapets and on whose orders'. The Guards HQ war diary contains a report sent to XI Corps HQ on 26 December but this only details some observations 'brought back by men of 2nd Bn Scots Guards yesterday after the meeting with the Germans'. Apparently, the Germans were from the *15/16/17th Bavarian Regiments* and were 'all either very old or mere boys'. The Germans confirmed that the British shell fire overnight had been effective, causing several casualties. A German sniper's post had been identified which 'had been sought for some time'. Observations were also made about where the German lines were weaker or strong. A strong garrison was identified 'each side of the FAUQUISSART road in TRIVOLET'. Whilst 'some of their clothing was in a bad state of repair; some were covered with mud, and others were spotlessly clean'. Interestingly, the point was made that 'it is though(t) that these latter had been brought down specially from their rest billets, in order to deceive us as to the strength of their garrisons'. Whether this information was being presented as useful intelligence gained in the fraternisation to partly justify the actions of those who fraternised cannot be known.[39]

However, we do know that, whether this report or an additional report was sent on to 1st Army HQ at 10:15 pm on 26 December, it was not satisfactory as First Army responded with a request to the XI Corps HQ on 28 December for further information. Specifically: What exactly were the orders issued by Lord Cavan? Beyond that, how were they known to the Brigades? What exactly were the orders issued by the brigadiers of the 2nd and 3rd Guards Brigades and how were they known to the battalions? What exactly were the orders issued by the those commanding the three battalions involved in fraternisation? Finally, how were they made known to the companies and so to the men? Whilst the document does say that a formal Court of Inquiry was not necessary, statements from the relevant officers were urgently required. There was particular concern that: 'As the orders appear to have been verbal, some corroboration of the orders is desirable'. A concern perhaps, that, on Cavan's own admission, his orders had been 'implicit' and, therefore passed on verbally. Clearly, these events on Christmas Day were now having significant consequences that could affect the professional standing of those involved. The request from First Army HQ was passed on to the Guards Division HQ on 29 December with the additional handwritten annotation stating, 'Please forward *at once* the information required'.[40]

38 Diary of Sir Iain Colquhoun, http://www.valeofleven.org.uk/contributions/iaincolquhoundiary.html, accessed 23 November 2023.
39 TNA: WO95/1190, Guards Division HQ, 538/G, App 286, 26 December 1915.
40 TNA: WO95/1190, Guards Division HQ, HQ X1th Corps, 1st Army, No.C/497, App 297. 28 December 1915.

In fact, Cavan had already decided to hold a Court of Inquiry which met in the morning of 26 December. Barne's Diary for the day expresses his astonishment that a neighbouring division, the 19th (Western Division) had spread rumours that the Guards regiments involved had been deserting. Ominously he says that: 'The fat is in the fire and the higher authorities are in a great state of mind about it all ... I am evidently in disgrace & not allowed to command the Battalion any more!'[41] His entry for 27 December is even more troubled and worth recounting in some detail:

> Roger Tempest arrives about 9 a.m., from being Brigade Major to 3rd Guards Brigade – & throws some light on the whole subject. Apparently he had seen Cavan, who was very much annoyed because I did not issue orders to shoot the Germans showing themselves. As the Brigadier (Ponsonby) was with me, and he never said anything was wrong, nor gave orders to shoot the unarmed Germans, but he stood himself on the firestep taking immense interest in everything, I concluded that nothing very wrong was being done. No hint was ever given me that a great point was made of 'no truce' in high quarters or of course I would have issued very special orders. On 24th I issued orders all was to be 'as usual'. The orders I issued on 25th were not to shooting Germans walking about unarmed, not to leave our trenches and on no account to allow the Germans into our own except to surrender. This after hearing they were out. I issued these orders off my own bat, and not because I received any special orders. I did not dare say I had received no orders in giving my evidence before the Court of Inquiry, as I might have carted Genl. Ponsonby, who they said ought to have given orders himself on the subject.[42]

Barne was required to attend a meeting at the Scots Guards Brigade HQ on 29 December for more investigation. Brigadier Ponsonby made his own statement and according to Barne, he seems to have taken a less than serious approach to the requirement. 'The Brigadier treats the whole matter rather lightly, makes out a statement himself which he tries to read over, but fails to read his own handwriting, then we all have to criticise it – jokes fly about.' Barne however reflects his growing concern once again that 'in high places they seem to dislike ... my having told the Company Commanders not to shoot unarmed Germans out in the open who might be confidingly coming over'.[43] Nonetheless, the next development clearly comes as a great shock to Barne. Nearly a week passes before this entry in his diary on 4 January: 'A bombshell in the shape of the C.O. walking into my bedroom at 8 a.m. and placing me under arrest ... I am to be tried by General Court Martial'.[44]

41 Nicol, *Barne's Diary*, p.85.
42 Nicol, *Barne's Diary*, pp.85–86
43 Nicol, *Barne's Diary*, p.86.
44 Nicol, *Barne's Diary*, p.88.

Unsurprisingly, the summary of evidence presented in Barne's case failed to suggest that Barne had done anything wrong. Captain G. Rasch, Brigade Major 2nd Guards Brigade confirmed that he had told Barne when asked that 'Xmas Day is to be the same as any other day'. Captain Sir John Dyer of the 1/Scots Guards confirmed that Barne's 'direct verbal orders' to company commanders was to be as normal and 'if anything greater vigilance was to be observed in case the Germans made a surprise attack'. When the news had emerged that the Germans were coming out of their trenches, Barne notified the Brigade HQ and whilst waiting for a reply, had issued clear orders that the men should not leave their trenches under any circumstances and if any Germans approached they would only be allowed entry as prisoners of war. Dyer added that: 'In order to give them a chance of surrendering Germans leaving their trenches would not be fired upon.' Captain L. Norman, also of the 1/Scots, confirmed the same. Brigadier Ponsonby and Lieutenant Colonel Lord E. Gordon Lennox, commanding the 1/Scots Guards, both provided glowing character references.[45]

Despite this supportive testimony and his release from arrest on 5 January, Barne realised that he and Colquhoun would need to arrange for a counsel in their defence. Defiantly, after remarking that Ponsonby believed that the 'people at the top had got the wrong end of the stick', he stated that 'if they expect me or any other Officer to give an order to shoot down unarmed Germans in cold blood, they are very much mistaken'. As Colquhoun said: '... the men would not obey adding 'if they want it done, let them do it themselves'.[46] Clearly as the case against them had gathered momentum, they had, not unreasonably, became increasingly frustrated and angry but also, certainly on Barne's part, fearful of the outcome. On the following day, 6 January, Barne reported that Ponsonby advised him not to appoint a counsel because the authorities would do so in response. However, a 'prisoner's friend', he felt would be a good idea and he suggested that Barne should approach Lieutenant Raymond Asquith of the 3/Grenadier Guards, the eldest son of Henry Asquith the Prime Minister and a commercial barrister before the war to act on both his and Colquhoun's part. Coincidentally Asquith's niece, Dinah Tennent, had become Colquhoun's wife on 10 February 1915.

On 9 January, Barne complained of: 'Yet another summary of evidence has been taken in! It really seems that they are trying to 'cook' the evidence to suit the charge!'[47] This new demand for evidence led to Captain Sir John Swinnerton Dyer, a company commander of the 1/Scots Guards being asked: 'Did you or did you not receive from Captain Barne any orders about not shooting unarmed Germans on December 24th?' His reply was 'I did not'.[48] This strongly suggests that, as Randall Nicol has said: 'The prosecution line until the very last moment was to try to make out that Miles Barne had given this order on Christmas Eve'.[49] Barne's mood would not have been helped by Ponsonby's visit on

45 Nicol, *Barne's Diary*, p.89–90.
46 Nicol, *Barne's Diary*, pp.91.
47 Nicol, *Barne's Diary*, p.94.
48 Nicol, *Barne's Diary*, pp.94–95.
49 Nicol, *Barne's Diary*, p.95.

10 January; clearly Barne's misfortune had become the focus of ridiculously exaggerated falsehoods. 'The Brigadier ... says he is trying to get one of the Divisional Staff sent home to tell the truth of my story – as every sort of wild rumour is being concocted – that the 2nd Guards Brigade had a regular beano on Xmas Day with the Germans, I arranged it, Luss (Colquhoun) carried it out and the Brigadier sanctioned it all.'[50]

Meanwhile Ponsonby had approached Asquith on 10 January to ask for his help. Asquith, writing to his wife, Katharine, was apparently 'washing in that rather naked style' that she found amusing, when Ponsonby arrived at 9.00 a.m. having got past Asquith's servant.

> Needham did his best, but the gallant fellow was not to be denied, and burst into my room in a paroxysm of inarticulate enthusiasm. It appears that G.H.Q. has decided to Court Martial Iain Colquhoun and another Captain in the 1st Scots Guards for allowing their men to fraternise with the Germans on Xmas Day. There is a great to-do about it all, both on personal and regimental grounds and they want me to act as a 'Prisoner's Friend' – i.e. counsel for the defence…it seems a rottenish sort of case, but I said I would do my best. [51]

Writing on 12 January, again to his wife, Asquith says that Colquhoun has not returned from leave 'and nothing serious can happen until he does, as they might have known. They took some more evidence yesterday, which turned out to be favourable to the other officer concerned, and I should not be surprised if they stop the Court Martial in his case, though I imagine they mean to proceed in the other.' Clearly, Asquith had formed the view that Barne's position was far more secure than Colquhoun's. Asquith continued that:

> There is a good deal of excitement about it here, and I am regarded as such an important life now that yesterday morning the Brigadier issued a special order that I was not to accompany my battalion into the trenches ... but to remain here in billets. I am accordingly living in comfort at the H.Q. of the 1st Scots Guards, who kindly offered me bed and board.

By 15 January, Asquith had already had enough. The court martial had been scheduled for the 17 January. Clearly frustrated and increasingly impatient, he comments To Katharine that:

> On Monday there is this idiotic Court Martial, which has now begun to get rather on my nerves, because John Ponsonby is so excited about it and one of my two clients so terribly depressed. Ian Colquhoun, on the other hand, is perfectly haughty and

50 Nicol, *Barne's Diary*, p.96.
51 John Jolliffe (ed.), *Raymond Asquith, Life and Letters* (London: Collins, 1980), p.232.

> indifferent, and impresses me more and more as being a man of great individuality and charm, so far as one can have those things without a brain. [52]

The Court Martial proved to be rather an anti-climax despite the fact that the charge was changed:

> To my – & Asquith's- great astonishment we find a new charge- instead of 'Conduct to prejudice of good order and military discipline in that he at the trenches just N. of NEUVE CHAPELLE on Dec.24th although he had been warned by the Brigade Major, Capt Rasch, that everything was to be done as usual on Xmas Day, issued orders that unarmed Germans shewing themselves on or near their trenches were not to be shot at', which I had seen & Asquith too & had prepared to refute, the charge appeared 'Conduct ... Germans coming towards us were not to be shot at with a view to getting them to surrender'. So that now we had to prove that this order that I practically admitted issuing, was a right and proper order to give.[53]

Asquith was able to summon Ponsonby as a character witness who said that 'he would have given the same orders himself & every other C.O. in his Brigade would have done the same.' Adding to the surreal nature of events, Barne adds that 'Nor did Asquith cross examine the witnesses for the prosecution, for the simple reason that I admitted all they said' but made a clear and well argued statement lasting 14 minutes in Barne's defence.[54] The prosecutor, Captain Reginald Playfair Hills of the King's Own Scottish borderers was 'a well known barrister' who 'made a feeble effort but had not a leg to stand on' and Barne was acquitted and exonerated from all blame.[55]

However, Colquhoun's experience on the day was far less positive as his case followed on from Barne's and the charges were more serious. As he recorded in his diary: 'I am accused of Conduct to the prejudice of good order of military discipline in that on 25th Dec I (1) approved of a truce with the enemy (2) Permitted a cessation of hostilities.' Asquith cross examined Captain Harrison 'with the object of learning that when I went up to the trenches on Xmas morning, I found a very advanced situation which I did my best to regularise by having a definite agreement as to how long the situation was to last.' Ponsonby gave a very positive character reference before Asquith:

> ... then makes a splendid speech for the accused and Capt. Hill makes quite a fair speech for the prosecution. The court is then closed to consider its verdict. I sat there from 3 pm to 8 pm. At 8.20 I go in again having been found guilty. They ask me if I wish to make an address. I do not. The Court is then closed to consider its sentence.

52 Jolliffe (ed.), *Raymond Asquith*, p.235.
53 Nicol, *Barne's Diary*, p.97–98.
54 Nicol, *Barne's Diary*, p.98.
55 Nicol, *Barne's Diary*, p.98.

Asquith felt that he had done all that he could but regrettably 'the facts were sadly against us all the time.' He anticipated a light sentence or reprimand. Admitting that: 'I think there was no doubt that he committed a technical defence, but in reality he showed a good deal of decision and common sense, and his military character is so first rate that they ought to take a lenient view of the case.'[56] In an addition to the diary entry for 17 January, Colquhoun added: 'Three days later the result comes out. The sentence which is "Reprimanded" has been quashed by G.H.Q., but the conviction remains which nearly means that the whole thing is washed out. The whole Guards Division and everyone who knows the facts of the case all say that it was a monstrous thing that the court martial ever took place.'[57]

Douglas Haig fully understood the harm that had been done by what had become a damaging and ultimately unnecessary process and Colquhoun's sentence was remitted in view of his 'distinguished conduct in the field'.[58] By selecting two officers from just one Guards battalion, the Court of Inquiry had attempted through the full process of the law to distract attention from the extent of the fraternisation across the division whilst laying specific blame and responsibility away from more senior figures. Cavan had fully deserved his promotion to corps command, but this affair was undoubtedly bad for morale in the Guards Division. His period of divisional leadership had been an impressive one indeed but on this occasion his approach had been heavy handed, insensitive and ultimately counterproductive.

Feilding Replaces Cavan

Meanwhile, with Cavan taking command of the newly created XIV Corps, Feilding replaced him on 3 January 1916 as the GOC of the Guards Division. He was determined to press on with the offensive spirit that Cavan had been so keen to inculcate and regain the initiative after the Division's reputation had been tarnished by the ongoing furore created by the events of 25 December. In doing so, Feilding would be able to bolster his own credentials as a worthy successor to Cavan who had set such high standards. During a 48-hour period in mid-January, the Guards Division was able, once again to set the military agenda on its section of the front.

For example, a party from the 1/Coldstream Guards raided the German front lines on the night of 10/11 January. Wire cutting had begun at 11:00 p.m. and the raiding party went over at 3:00 a.m. The German trenches were empty, and the raiders proceeded 400 yards laterally and a further 150 yards up various communication trenches.[59] However,

56 Diary of Sir Ian Colquhoun, <http://www.valeofleven.org.uk/contributions/iaincolquhoundiary.html>.
57 Diary of Sir Ian Colquhoun, <http://www.valeofleven.org.uk/contributions/iaincolquhoundiary.html>.
58 Blake, *The Private Papers of Douglas Haig*, pp.124–126.
59 Nicol, *Barne's Diary*, p. 95.

whilst the raid was unopposed, the intelligence information brought back was considered to be very useful. The raiders confirmed that the Germans could be heard in what appeared to be their second line trench about 250 to 300 yards behind the first line. The raid also found that the trench mapping of the German trenches was inaccurate. Very precise details about a machine gun emplacement that 'is made of sandbags and forms the end of the trench' were outlined in the post-raid report. 'It is about 8 ft. high from the floor, but had a second wood flooring about 4 ft. from the ground, thus forming two stories. It contained 3 loopholes for a machine gun, one looking out towards our lines, one enfilading our lines, and the other enfilading the front of a communication trench running back towards their second line'. The raiders were able to provide significant detail about the physical condition of the German trenches, the manner of their construction and drainage and clear evidence that suggested 'the Germans do not hold their front line … but send a few snipers along the line to send up flares at intervals and fire occasional shots'.[60] Barne wrote of an amusing sequel to the raid:

> The Germans appear to have thought that they had come there and remained so organized an attack on them with bombers, from each side, in the same trench – as the moment arrived when they thought they would be approaching the English, one lot heard the other talking, and, imagining the talking was the English, began bombing, with the result that they had a bomb battle royal with each other![61]

On 12/13 January, a 'demonstration' was carried out in the form of an elaborate ruse to continue the momentum of pressure on the German lines. According to the 'Summary of Operations' report, the objective was 'to cause the Germans to man their parapets and then to inflict loss on them by artillery fire'.[62] In the morning of 12 January, the artillery cut the wire opposite Sign Post Lane. At 4:35 p.m. the front-line infantry:

> … made a demonstration with 200 dummies as if getting over the parapet, especially opposite the places where the German wire had been cut. Immediately after this a heavy rifle file and machine gun fire was delivered on the left of the dummies, and at the same time our artillery opened fire on the German front line, while our Howitzers formed a barrage in rear. During this the dummies simulated a second line going over the parapet. It was thought by this time (owing to hostile rifle fire) that [the] enemy had maned his trenches, so our batteries then enfiladed the German front line, and at the same time simulated a third line topping the parapet.[63]

60 TNA: WO95/119,1Guards HQ, App. 346, 'Summary of Information 11/12 January 1916'.
61 Nicol, *Barne's Diary*, p.96
62 TNA: WO95/1191Guards HQ, App 348.
63 TNA: WO95/1191Guards HQ, App 348.

The German response was evidently a weak one with red rockets as alarm signals 'followed by fire directed at NO MANS LAND, and on our parapets just behind' but confirming the details of the previous night's raid the report continues that 'The enemy's front line did not appear to have enough guns to make an effective barrage' and it concluded that 'The object of the demonstration appeared to be successfully achieved, as after the first three or four minutes, the enemy's rifle fire increased in intensity, as if supports had reinforced the front line … after dark, patrols reported enemy repairing his wires … Lewis guns and machine guns opened fire on them.' At 10:15 p.m. a reconnaissance patrol of one NCO and three men went out and found German sentries positioned every 10 to 15 yards and heard continuous conversation along the German front lines. The report concludes that 'it is very evident … that the result of our raid on the night of the 10/11 inst. has been that the Germans now hold their front line in this part much more strongly'.[64]

General Sir Henry Rawlinson, who now commanded First Army, was clearly impressed by what had been achieved, not just in these 48 hours but in previous weeks. He sent his congratulations to Feilding on 14 January. He noted that there had been six different 'raiding expeditions' in the previous four weeks. The raids, he observed were 'the result of carefully laid plans 'well and boldly executed' that had succeeded in establishing 'a moral ascendancy, which is of the highest value'. Holding the Guards up as an exemplar of good practice he concluded that: 'similar enterprises should be carried out by all Divisions in the future'.[65]

The Move to the Ypres Salient

Whilst the division continued with the ordinary routines of life in their trenches, Cavan's newly created XIV Corps was being established and it was not surprising that the Guards were moved across to it. Brigadier General C.E. Pereira, who had taken command of 1st Guards Brigade when Feilding was promoted commented in a letter to his wife on 16 February: 'I met Cavan lately and am delighted to be with him again.'[66] Without doubt, Cavan would have been equally delighted to have his old division in his newly created corps. Haking, for his part was sorry to see the Guards leave. Pereira, who was in temporary command of the division whilst Feilding was on leave, continued to his wife: 'I went to see Haking today and said goodbye for the Division. He was most kind and complimentary about us and full of regrets at our leaving.'[67]

64 TNA: WO95/1191Guards HQ, App 348.
65 TNA: WO95/1191, App 370, 14 January 1916.
66 Edward Pereira, Spencer Jones and Michael Locicero (eds.), *Catholic General: The Private Wartime Correspondence of Major-General Sir Cecil Edward Pereira, 1914–19.* (Warwick: Helion, 2020), p.179.
67 Pereira, Jones and Locicero (eds.), *Catholic General*, p.179.

The relief of the division began on 14 February. By the 17 February the Guards Divisional headquarters had been opened at Hazebrouck. Then from March until the move southwards to the Somme in July, the Guards were based on the Ypres Salient responsible for a front of approximately 3,700 yards from the Bellewaarde stream just north of the Menin Road to a point north of Wieltje Farm. This was 'incomparably the most unpleasant part of the whole British Front'. Another water-logged area but this time 'overlooked on three sides by the enemy's artillery' faced the Guards.[68] Fortunately, during these months things were relatively calm but not without risk. A German trench raid during the evening of 19 April succeeded in penetrating trenches held by the 2/ Scots Guards but was repulsed at the expense of 49 casualties in the Scots Guards and 27 in the 4/Grenadiers. Indeed, total casualties in the division for April were close to 400 in all ranks.[69] On 9 May, Brigadier General Heyworth, commanding 3rd Brigade was killed by a German sniper. Pereira was both saddened by his loss but clearly thought he had taken too grave a risk:

> Poor Pa Heyworth was killed this morning. Curiously enough I had argued with him about the safety of the very place where he was shot, and I maintained that it was dangerous in day light and I always refused to go there except at night. Unfortunately, he differed with me. People may think me fussy, but I don't see the point of running needless risks.[70]

In mid-June, the Guards Division moved a short distance to a new sector at Boesinghe. As the beginning of the Somme offensive grew closer, the Second Army's front saw an adjustment to a more aggressive posture with a notable artillery bombardment of the German lines opposite the Guards front on 24 June and increased raiding activity such as that carried out by the 1/Grenadiers on the night of the 25/26 June which succeeded in advancing the line of the 3rd Guards Brigade by about 200 yards or that at Krupp Farm which was carried out by the 2/Irish Guards plus attached Royal Engineers on 2/3 July 1916. Lieutenant F. Pym led a party of 40 other ranks together with an unspecified number of RE detachments under Lieutenant Penfold. The Krupps Raid's objectives were four-fold: to bluff the Germans into thinking that operations were being carried out on a large scale, to obtain prisoners, to locate and destroy machine gun or trench mortar emplacements and to obtain as much information as possible.

It was a clear evening and, at the last moment, the men were told to keep their jackets on to avoid their shirts being visible to the German defenders. Kipling observed that the men said later that the raid should have been postponed at this point. Supported by a preliminary bombardment of 20 minutes, the raiding party went over the top

68 Headlam, *History of the Guards Division*, pp.118–119.
69 TNA: WO95/1191, Guards Division HQ, 'Report on Attack at Wieltje 20 April 1916', App. 624.
70 Pereira, Jones and Locicero (eds.), *Catholic General*, p.190.

and immediately drew fire from several machine guns in the German second line. For Kipling, this was: 'a bad kick off, for, with our leading raiders out in the open, it would have been murder to have held the rest back'.[71] The whole attack reached the German front line and remained in their trench for 10 minutes. Apparently, 'Pym rushed through the leading men, jumped into the trench, landed in an empty German bay, shouting to them to follow, turned left with a few men, reached the door of a machine-gun dug-out with its gun in full blast, broke in, found two men at work, knocked one of them off the gun and … made him a prisoner.'[72] Three gas experts had been attached to the raid. Two had been wounded on the outward run and the other grabbed some potentially useful documentation but did not survive the return. Five prisoners were taken but three were killed. Most of the casualties suffered on the raid fell on or close to the British parapet as they returned under very heavy German fire.[73] The casualties were heavy indeed: four other ranks killed; one officer and 37 other ranks wounded and one officer and nine others missing. Lieutenant Pym himself was one of the missing and was later awarded the DSO for his outstanding leadership and bravery. Kipling's judgement is generous in the circumstances: 'The raid had been a fair, flat, but heroic failure, due, as most men said, to its being loosed in broad daylight at a fully prepared enemy'. Outside the two prisoners, nothing, not even a scrap of paper, was gained.'[74] In reality, this raid had been a disaster.

Major Miles Barne. (Courtesy of Miles Barne)

At 4:00 p.m. on 27 July, Major General Feilding handed over control of the Boesinghe sector to the 4th Division. The Guards now began their move south to the Somme to play what became a critical role in the Battles of Flers-Courcelette and Morval but they would be back at Boesinghe once again in July 1917.

71 Kipling, *The Irish Guards in the Great War: The Second Battalion*, p.85.
72 Kipling, *The Irish Guards in the Great War: The Second Battalion*, p.85.
73 Kipling, *The Irish Guards in the Great War: The Second Battalion*, p.85.
74 Ibid. p.87.

5

The Somme: 8 August–9 September 1916

Military Context

The Anglo-French relationship during the First World War was never an easy one. We have seen how the decision to fight at Loos in September 1915 in far from ideal conditions was influenced by Britain's desire to show greater military commitment to the alliance with the French. The same pressures now meant that the British Army would have to fight in a large battle somewhere along the Western Front in 1916. Douglas Haig had no objections to co-operating with the French but as William Philpott has argued he 'harboured a deep-seated grudge after French forces had seemingly abandoned him during the retreat in August 1914. He remained intensely suspicious and mistrustful of French intentions and promises.'[1] Haig's meetings with his French counterpart, Joffre, were difficult and tense occasions. At Chantilly from 8 December to 12 December 1915, the Allied strategy for the following year was decided upon. There would be co-ordinated offensives by the Franco-British, Italian and Russian forces in March but only an Anglo-French offensive looked a realistic proposition. It was important to act by the spring to forestall or nullify any German attack on the Russians by tying them down on the Western Front. On the BEF's front, there were two options: an attack in the Ypres area or on the Somme. On 20 January, Joffre agreed that the major British offensive of 1916 would take place in Flanders in the summer but before that there would be a subsidiary attack on the Somme in the spring. However, behind the scenes, Haig was under considerable pressure. David Lloyd George, now responsible for munitions supply, argued for a delay until the summer before any military action took place to allow for shortages to be made good.

However, the German attack on Verdun on 21 February changed everything. Verdun soon became a symbol of French national resistance that drew in increasing numbers of French forces. Unsurprisingly, the French now hoped that the British would launch a

1 William Philpott, *Bloody Victory: The Sacrifice on the Somme and the Making of the Twentieth Century* (London: Little, Brown, 2009), p.69.

premature offensive to take some pressure off them. Anglo-French discussions continued into the Spring before the military and strategic reality forced a decision. Haig met both Lord Kitchener and Sir William Robertson, Chief of the Imperial General Staff on 14 April:

> I saw Lord Kitchener at the War Office … Sir William Robertson was present at the first part of my interview. I asked them definitively, 'Did His Majesty's Government approve of my combining with the French in a general offensive in the summer'? They both agreed that all the Cabinet had come to the conclusion that the war could only end by fighting, and several were most anxious for a definite victory over German arms, viz. the Secretary for Foreign Affairs (Grey) and the Chancellor of the Exchequer (McKenna).[2]

Yet despite a decision having been made, uncertainty as to the exact date of the Somme offensive continued. On 25 May, Robertson visited GHQ. Haig later wrote:

> After dinner, we discussed whether the British Army should comply with the French Generalissimo's request to attack in the month of July, or wait till August 15th when we would be much stronger. I had gone fully into the various aspects of the question and what might be the results if we did not support the French. I came to the conclusion we *must* march to the support of the French. Robertson entirely agreed.[3]

On the following day, 26 May, Haig met Joffre. Despite his conversation the day before with Robertson, Haig still told him that he 'would like to indicate the state of preparedness of the British Army on certain dates and compare its condition. I took 1 and 15 July and 1 and 15 August. The moment I mentioned 15 August. Joffre at once got very excited and shouted that 'The French would cease to exist, if we did nothing till then! … They are, indeed, difficult Allies to deal with!'[4]

Despite this apparent prevarication, planning had been going on to prepare for the Somme offensive. Haig ordered General Rawlinson, who had been appointed GOC of the newly created Fourth Army in January, to drop preparations for an attack in Flanders. Instead, he moved his headquarters south to the Somme. With French reserves departing for Verdun in February, the British Third Army took over the sector that had been occupied by the French Tenth Army. The Fourth Army took responsibility for the area between the Third Army and the Somme.[5]

2 Sheffield and Bourne, *Haig: War Diaries*, p.186.
3 Sheffield and Bourne, *Haig: War Diaries*, p.187.
4 Sheffield and Bourne, *Haig: War Diaries*, p.188.
5 Robin Prior and Trevor Wilson, *Command on the Western Front: The Military Career of Sir Henry Rawlinson 1914–1918* (Oxford: Blackwell, 1992), p.139.

The defences opposite Fourth Army dominated the higher ground and were truly formidable. There were two main trench systems incorporated into a front line that consisted of several fortified villages: Fricourt, la Boiselle, Ovillers, Thiepval and Beaumont Hamel. This system was well protected by two belts of wire whilst the second line was on a reverse slope. The second line system was 2,000 to 4,000 yards further back. It was also well-wired and beyond the range of range of the main wire-cutting guns. In between the two main trench system there were a number of intermediate positions covering villages such as Montauban, Mametz and Beaucourt.[6]

By 5 April, Rawlinson was able to present his plan for the Somme offensive. He anticipated an attack by 10 divisions along a front of 20,000 yards following an artillery bombardment lasting four to five days. Essentially it would be a 'bite and hold' operation in stages whereby a section of the German defences would be taken, then consolidated before a resumption of the attack. Haig believed the plan was far too cautious, lacked the element of surprise and failed to consider the actions of the French to the south of the river Somme. Haig favoured a shorter, more intensive bombardment immediately prior to the attack and larger steps with shorter intervals. Haig believed that Rawlinson's plan simply lacked ambition; he wanted the German first and second lines captured in a single operation. A hurricane bombardment of a few hours would enable the infantry to seize the German front line and then, taking advantage of the now disorientated defences, quickly move on to the German second line. If the Germans could be dislodged from their defences into the open, success would follow, and the cavalry could then make a significant contribution.[7]

Rawlinson backed down despite aerial reconnaissance on 25 April confirming that a third line of German defence was being created which would almost be complete by 1 July. He was in no doubt that the Germans would not be rushed out of their well-constructed defences. On 16 May, Haig informed Rawlinson that the 'Serre-Mira(u) mont spur; Pozieres; Contalmaison, and Montauban be the objectives to be attained during the first day's operations … it is understood that you concur in the view'.[8] Whilst obviously Rawlinson did not, he complied. For him, the saving grace, at least, was that Haig backed down over the nature of the artillery attack. Probably now knowing that there were not enough guns to have the required impact in a short offensive, a longer preliminary bombardment would now take place even if that would mean any element of surprise would be lost.[9] The final detailed plans now took place within this agreed framework.

The first day of the Somme Offensive on 1 July 1916 saw the British Army sustain over 57,000 casualties and it occupies, of course, a unique place in British military history and popular memory epitomised by, for example, the experiences of the Pals battalions

6 Prior and Wilson, *Command on the Western Front*, pp.139–141
7 Prior and Wilson, *Command on the Western Front*, pp.146–147.
8 Prior and Wilson, *Command on the Western Front*, GHQ to Rawlinson, p.152.
9 Prior and Wilson, *Command on the Western Front*, pp.152–153.

at Serre, or the 29th Division at Hawthorn Ridge. Yet, despite the lack of progress on 1 July from Gommecourt to the north, through Serre, Beaumont-Hamel, the Thiepval Spur and at La Boiselle, there were some achievements south of the Albert-Bapaume Road at Fricourt, Mametz and Montauban. For example, by 1:00 p.m. 30th Division had captured all of its objectives, including Montauban and the 18th Division followed suit within a couple of hours. Casualty figures had, however been heavy with over 3,000 in each division. Undoubtedly, the comparatively weaker German opposition, the use of a creeping barrage and the accurate support of the adjacent French artillery were significant factors in British success here.[10] Over the next couple of weeks, British forces carried out several piecemeal attacks. For example, on 7 July 17th (Northern) and 38th (Welsh) attacked in the Contalmaison-Mametz Wood area without success and the 12th and 25th Divisions made ground at Ovillers. On July 10, the 23rd captured Contalmaison and the 38th took Mametz Wood.

This now provided a springboard for an ambitious attack on the Bazentin Ridge at Longueval on 14 July which was a stunning success. XV Corps and XIII Corps attacked in darkness after a five-minute bombardment. Surprise was achieved and by mid-morning 6,000 yards of the German second position had been taken. The British artillery had, this time, been very effective. Rawlinson had two thirds of the guns used on the first day on the Somme, but they were used to shell just over five per cent of the ground.[11] The difficulties of exploiting this apparent breakthrough were to dominate fighting in the coming weeks as progress ground to a halt in the fighting to secure High and Delville Woods. The pattern of piecemeal fighting then returned with little result; between 15 July and 14 September, 'the Fourth Army suffered 82,000 casualties while advancing only 1,000 yards on a 5 mile front. That is, while capturing a somewhat smaller area than in the massed offensive of I July, the Fourth Army, during six weeks of small-scale attacks sustained casualties that were 40 per cent higher'.[12] However, on the Fourth Army's front, things began to improve in early September. On 3 September, Guillemont fell to the British forces followed by Ginchy six days later. British forces had edged forward to provide a jumping off point, if not necessarily an ideal one, for the largest assault since 1 July in which the Guards would play a major role. The Battle of Flers-Courcelette would involve nine Fourth Army divisions on a very wide frontage plus the two Canadian divisions of the Reserve Army at Courcelette together with the French 6th Army to the south of the River Somme.

10 Sheffield, *The Somme*, p.64.
11 Sheffield, *The Somme*, pp.82–83.
12 Prior and Wilson, *Command on the Western Front*, pp.204–205.

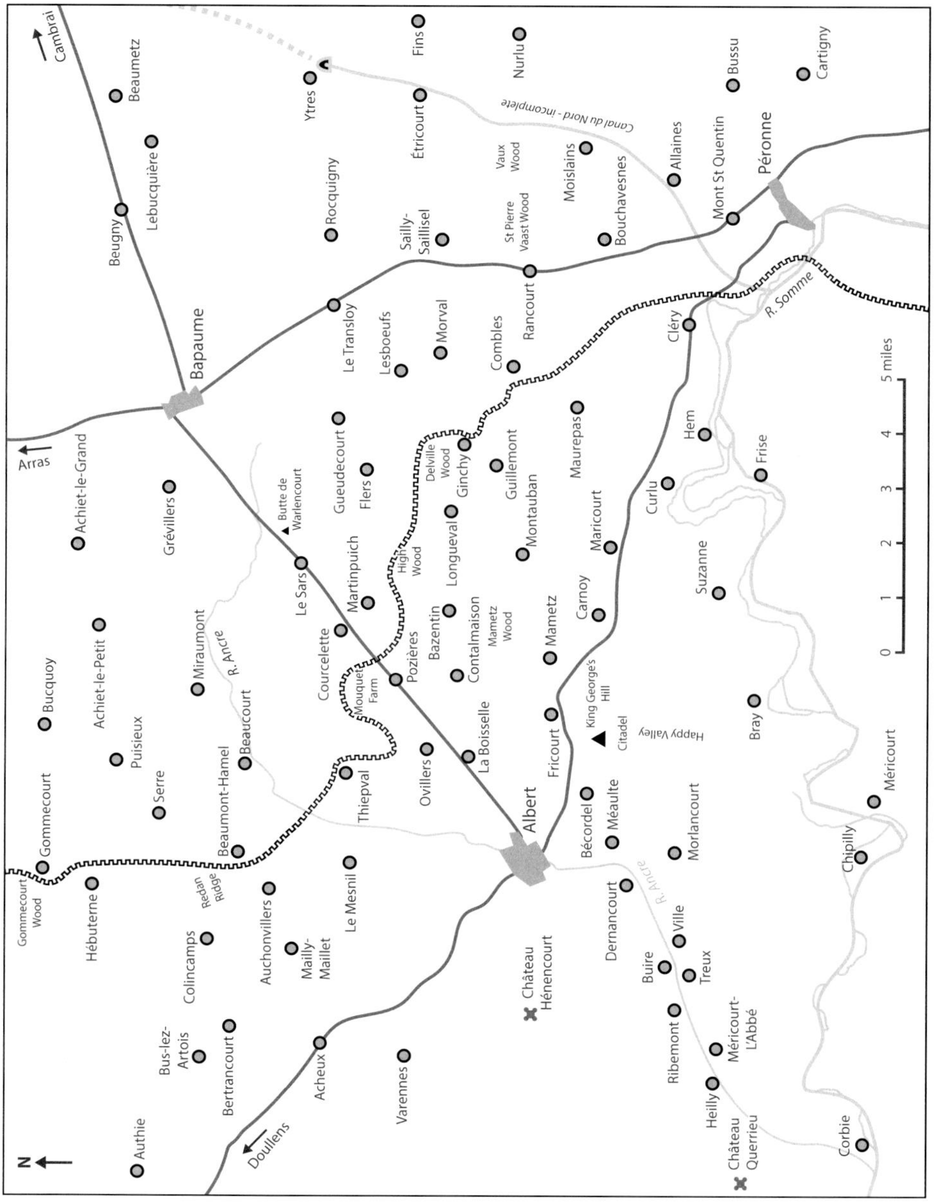

The Battle of the Somme, the line before 15 September 1916.

The Guards Arrive on the Somme

When the Guards Division arrived on the Somme, they initially found themselves in the exact sector fought over by the 29th Division on 1 July. They were placed in XIV corps reserve which held the front of the Reserve Army from the River Ancre to the Puisieux–Hebuterne Road. The 6th Division occupied the right of the line, the 25th Division the centre and the 20th the left. Feilding established the Guard divisional headquarters at Bus-les-Artois.[13]

It is interesting to note at this point the more collegiate approach to corps command that Cavan was taking prior to the Battle of Flers-Courcelette than that of Haking at Loos. Andy Simpson has noted that:

> On 3rd August he issued a document which clearly revealed in its first paragraph the command style favoured by the BEF, its attachment to established principles and its willingness to learn within their framework ... The need to attack in depth was stressed, with the responsibilities of divisional, brigade and lower commanders briefly outlined. The use of heavy artillery for destructive fire was mentioned, as was the need for infantry to stick as close as possible to the barrage. Consolidation of captured positions was dealt with, as well as the leapfrogging of successive waves of attackers through the first, the experience of 'many Brigadiers' being invoked to back this up, while also providing a good example of the upward dissemination of information in the BEF. In keeping with the tenor of his first paragraph, he did not order them, but made an 'appeal to all divisional commanders' to ensure that they got troops across no-man's land as soon as possible since the German counter-bombardment could render it almost impassable. Most important, however, was his stress on: 'Communications by runners, pigeons, visual and signal to the air'.[14]

In this way, Cavan 'let his immediate subordinates know that he respected their judgement and ability and understood the pressures they were under'.[15] Unfortunately, Cavan developed dysentery from mid-August, and he was hospitalised at Wimereux until 10 September so much of the corps level planning for Flers-Courcelette was the responsibility of Lieutenant General Morland of X Corps who took temporary command of XIV Corps.[16]

On 8 August, Feilding held a conference to consider the Guards immediate priorities as they moved into the line. Feilding was anxious that his troops had an immediate sense of purpose and direction as they moved closer to the front. The Guards Division had seen no combat since the events at the Hohenzollern Redoubt back in October 1915

13 Headlam, *History of the Guards Division*, p.128.
14 Simpson, *Directing Operations*, pp. 38–39.
15 Senior, *Haking: A Dutiful Soldier*, p.142.
16 Senior, *Haking: A Dutiful Soldier*, pp.142–143.

but that situation was likely to change soon enough as plans took shape and the Guards would have to be on their mettle. He stated that the division to be relieved (the 25th) had already started some important work that could be pushed on with: to 'approach' the front line nearer to the German front lines; the construction of deep dugouts; to improve the flooring of the main communication trenches as many lacked duck boards; the improvement of the wire; and finally, the construction of a new front line trench in the 3rd Guards Brigade sector. Feilding told the conference that future operations were still being planned but it was 'probable that the Division will be required to attack in conjunction with 6th Division on our right at some future date but not in the near future'. Feilding expected no complacency from his officers. Their reconnaissance was vital 'so that it can be decided what strong points in the enemy's lines require special attention from heavy artillery prior to the attack'.[17]

The Guards found a very different looking battlefield to the one that they had left behind on the Ypres Salient. Evidently, the more senior officers of the 1/Scots Guards would go riding in the afternoons. On 5 August Sir Iain Colquhoun rode over with Lieutenant Orr Erwing to lunch with the 2/Scots Guards before proceeding to the Brigade HQ:

> … in front of Albert and facing Pozieres. Had most interesting time, saw all going on behind the Line and the huge numbers of guns they have. Was very much struck by the small amount of shelling that there had been behind the Line. Nearly all the billets are standing and even Albert is scarcely touched – people walk all about in full view of the German line about 1,500 yards away, in perfect safety. It is extraordinary after coming from the Salient where everything is in ruins.[18]

The next day, 9 August, was a busy one with the King and the Prince of Wales visiting Feilding before going on to the individual brigade headquarters while the Guards began their relief of a brigade of the 6th Division and the whole of the 25th Division. Miles Barne wrote that there was:

> Such a scramble all the morning, receiving instructions & making arrangements firstly for the King's visit, and secondly for moving into the line. The King appeared about noon and shook hands with all the C.O.s, 2nds in Command, Adjts and Quartermasters of the Brigade. He then motored off & was cheered by the men as he went-but looked very ill & white & nervous. I thought he seemed to want to say something to us each, but did not know what to say.[19]

17 TNA: WO95/1217, 2 Guards Brigade HQ, 'Conference held at Divisional Headquarters', G.D. No. 2018/G, 8 August 1916.
18 Randall Nicol. *Till the Trumpet Sounds Again: The Scots Guards 1914–1919 in Their Own Words, Volume 2* (Solihull: Helion, 2016), p.13.
19 Nicol, *Barne's Diary*, p.174.

The new divisional headquarters were moved to Bertrancourt with the relief as a whole completed by 11 August. The Guards Division now held the centre of the XIV Corps front. Their 'Summary of Operations' confirms that the nights of 12/13 August and 14/15 saw a heavy artillery bombardment of the German lines supplemented by indirect machine gun fire which brought only 'slight' enemy retaliation. There were plans to discharge gas across the divisional front on both nights. Miles Barne mentions that on the afternoon of the 12 August, he went round the line:

> …visiting the 'White City', to arrange about this evening when gas is to be discharged in conjunction with the attack on our right all round THIEPVAL and MOUQUET FARM. We make elaborate arrangements for getting the men under cover during our bombardment etc, but the wind proves wrong, and no gas is let off–however we bombard heavily, which does provoke some retaliation, but they do no serious damage to our trenches & we have no serious casualties.[20]

Indeed, the divisional artillery carried out several bombardments in retaliation for German trench mortar activity. Patrols were sent out every night but there were no signs of any German ones.

In mid-August XIV Corps was moved to the area of Fourth Army south of the river Ancre replacing XIII Corps on the front between Longueval and Combles. Cavan established his new headquarters at Etinghem near Bray-sur-Somme on 16 August. The Guards Division began their move southwards on 19 August by road and rail to a pre-determined timetable. Re-joining XIV Corps on 25 August, the new divisional headquarters was opened at Treux with the 1st Guards Brigade at Meaulte, the 2nd at Morlancourt and the 3rd at Vignacourt.[21] Pereira, writing home from Meaulte on 26 August observed that:

> Our present billets are by no means luxurious, fly and rat-infested, but we are likely to be here a little while and will continue what we have been doing for two years, scavenging. The Brigade is very fit, and one has a great feeling of pride as one sees the whole lot swinging through the villages and along the roads. They are as big as ever and it is the finest brigade in the army. When regularly in the trenches one sees nothing of one's brigade, as a whole, and 10 and 12 mile marches are a pleasant change.[22]

Lyttelton also expressed his pride in the Guards at this juncture:

> At the end of this unexpected pause it would have been difficult to match the Guards division in any army, in peace or in war. Once when I was watching a

20 Nicol, *Barne's Diary*, p.174.
21 Headlam, *History of the Guards Division*, pp.139–140.
22 Pereira, *Catholic General*, p.200.

> battalion of the Grenadiers on the line of March, we passed and saluted a French general. He beckoned me and said, '*Alors, ce regiment vient d'arriver en France? Non, mon General, c'est un bataillon de la Garde qui se bat depuis dix-neuf cent quinze.*' A proud moment. The troops were sunburnt and looked as fresh and professional as you could have wished. Their equipment and turn-out were perfect.[23]

On 28 August, a conference was called for the various commanding officers at Guards Division HQ. Although clearly the attack that the Guards Division would be undertaking was getter closer, but its precise date was contingent on events elsewhere. Nonetheless some details of the attack were considered at this meeting. The war diary of the 1st Guards Brigade noted that:

> Such points as the dress and equipment of troops in the assault; distinguishing badges for carriers; runners and clearing-up parties; the frontage to be allotted to a Company in the assault; the number of waves and the interval between them; the method of advance; consolidation of ground gained and the bold handling of patrols and Lewis guns to gain ground after the capture of the final objective, were all discussed and laid down.[24]

A further conference was held at Guards Division HQ on 3 September where it was now possible to outline in general terms the task that would be allocated to the individual brigades. The attendees were left in no doubt that that the task would be a very ambitious one that would put great demands upon the Guards Division. However, the exact details of the attack still depended upon success in the attacks on Guillemont and Ginchy – the capture of the line Ginchy Telegraph to the western edge of Leuze Wood. That would then establish a 'jumping off' point for the Guards in the next stage of the offensive when a more detailed plan of attack would be made available. However, the likely key objectives were made clear at the meeting. The Guards would be expected to press forward to a distance of 3,000 yards from the departure trenches. Part of the main German reserve line between Morval and Flers was to be the first objective for the Guards and the second objective would be part of the switch line around Morval. The third objective would involve pressing forward another 1,000 yards into an area in which the Germans had no organised defensive line to include the northern portion of Lesboeufs. The whole operation would take place in a single day.

Feilding said that there were certain likely factors which those present should be mindful of in their immediate preparations. The divisional front would be narrow and probably not more than 1,000 yards meaning the front of each attacking brigade could be expected to be around one half of this. Two brigades would probably be employed in

23 Chandos, *Memoirs*, p.58.
24 TNA: WO95/1213, I Guards Brigade HQ, 'Operations Carried Out by 1st Guards Brigade during August and September 1916'.

the attack with one brigade in immediate support. It would be necessary, he continued, to move forward the reserve brigade in immediate support of the attack. The initial advance would require the troops to keep close to the barrage and it would be important to avoid the German barrage on the front-line trenches. Consequently, this would 'necessitate the advance of the maximum number of troops at zero, formed up in the minimum of depth'. It would then be possible to move forward the attacking brigades in five 'thick' lines in the first advance to escape the barrage. Some points for particular attention were highlighted:

1. The maintenance of direction in the attack.
2. More consideration of the most effective attack formations.
3. Appropriate and effective arrangements for the flanks.
4. The supply of rations, water and ammunition over a 3,000 yard advance.
5. Issues created by the need to dig in on a position which had not already been entrenched by the Germans.

Feilding asked for the brigadiers to discuss these points with their commanding officers, but caution should be taken so that no details were communicated below the level of battalion commanders. The conference concluded with measures that should be implemented to avoid 'sick wastage' to counter a potential outbreak of dysentery which was already affecting troops in the forward areas of XIV Corps and some of the German forces.[25]

Training

The 1st Guards Brigade remained at billets in Meaulte throughout this period, as they trained and prepared for the forthcoming attack. Pereira remarked that: 'We have fine training facilities here, a lot of ready-made trenches for practising the assault and for bombing, also a large tract of land for battalion field days.'[26] The brigade's war diary gives a detailed account of these preparations which were being mirrored of course by the other Guards brigades at the same time. The training area allotted to the brigade was sub-allotted to the 1st Brigade's four battalions. There was a very suitable bombing ground where the brigade bombing officer took two different companies each day to receive training in the best use of bombs and rifle grenades. In the training area, live bombing was carried out by individual battalions and there was also a trench system which was allotted to battalions so that the companies could be given assault practice. An area to practice open fighting was also available.

25 TNA: WO95/1192, Guards Division HQ, 'Conference held on 3 September, 1916.'
26 Pereira, *Catholic General*, p.203.

Loos: Dud Corner Cemetery looking towards the lines of attack of the 2nd Guards Brigade from left to right. (Author's Photo)

Loos: Hill 70 from the North-West. (Author's Photo)

Loos: Looking down the D. 943 towards Vermelles from Dud Corner Cemetery. The advance of 3rd Guards Brigade towards Loos came alongside this road. (Author's Photo)

Robert Filmer: Stained glass, East Sutton Parish Church, Kent. (Photograph by Mark Turner Hellfire Pictures Ltd)

Miles Barne, memorial cross, St Margaret's Church, Sotterley, Suffolk. (Author's Photo)

The Somme: From the position of the Quadrilateral towards Ginchy. (Author's Photo)

The Somme: The Guards' Memorial (Author's Photo)

The Somme: The Guards' Cemetery, Lesboeufs. (Photo Stephen Kerr)

The Somme: Along Straight Trench towards the Guards' Memorial (Author's Photo)

The Somme: From the Guards' Memorial down Straight Trench. Location of Fred McNess' VC action is across the road and to the right. (Author's Photo)

The Somme: Looking towards Ginchy from the Guards' Memorial showing the line of advance taken by the Guards on 15 September, 1916. (Author's Photo)

Above left: Grave of Lieutenant W. Parnell, Guards' Cemetery. Died 25 September 1916. (Author's Photo)

Above right: Grave of Captain A.K.S. Cunninghame. Died 25 September 1916, Citadel New Military Cemetery, Fricourt. (Author's Photo)

Left: Grave of Lieutenant G.A. Arbuthnot. Died 25 September 1916 Citadel New Military Cemetery, Fricourt. (Author's Photo)

Grave of Lieutenant Raymond Asquith. Died 15 September 1916, Guillemont Road Cemetery. (Author's Photo)

Memorial Plaque to Raymond Asquith, Amiens Cathedral. (Author's Photo)

HRH The Prince of Wales. (Author's Collection)

UP GUARDS AND AT'EM. (Author's Collection)

Up until 4 September, training was carried out primarily in companies although on one occasion the 3/Coldstream carried out a practice attack that incorporated the use of at least one contact aeroplane. This provided a useful training opportunity for the battalion's signallers and indicated the level of accuracy with which a contact patrol could follow the movement of troops. From 5 September, battalions practiced the assault on a first objective from an imaginary line of trenches before then moving on for around 1,000 yards to a second objective. 'Although the exact task of the Brigade in the near future had not yet been indicated', it was becoming clear that 'the task which the Brigade would have to carry out would be an ambitious one, and for this reason great attention was paid during the whole of this period to training in open fighting. The pushing forward of patrols, moving in artillery formation, deploying from artillery formation were practised freely every day.'[27]

The Grenadiers' history praised the preparation of the 2/Grenadiers who: 'received a thorough course of training, something in the nature of a dress rehearsal ... Careful consideration was given to the difficult task of getting the men across No Man's Land, and every detail was rehearsed. Later the whole Brigade was practised in the attack, and in maintaining constant communication during an advance.'[28] Clearly attempts were being made to improve the effectiveness of signalling in anticipation of the forthcoming attack. The Brigade Signalling Officer ran a training class for the signallers where there was an emphasis on visual signalling with every form being practiced apart from heliograph and extra runners, up to eight per battalion, were given specialist training. Consideration was given to trying to establish one main trunk line to a point as far forward as possible, rather than attempting to get a number of 'bad' lines to each unit. This trunk line was to be by either telephone, visual or relay posts and, if possible, all three.[29]

Work platoons of 30 men under an officer were formed in each battalion and were trained each day under the 75th Company RE and extra men from each battalion were trained by the Trench Mortar Battery which would be available to replace casualties in the battery if there were heavy casualties. From 4 September, all training efforts were centred on battalion training. Particular attention was now paid on how best to get the men across no man's land in the shortest time, how to keep the infantry close under the barrage, the formation for attacking various objectives and on effective communications. Training culminated on 8 September with a brigade field day.[30]

Headlam pointed out that Feilding and his brigadiers were normally present at the practice attacks and 'exercised a close supervision over all the work done. In this way a

27 TNA: WO95/1213, I Guards Brigade HQ, 'Operations Carried Out by 1st Guards Brigade During August and September 1916'.

28 Frederick Ponsonby, *The Grenadier Guards in the Great War Volume 2* (London: Macmillan, 1920), pp.42–43.

29 Ponsonby, *The Grenadier Guards*, pp.42–43.

30 TNA: WO95/1213, I Guards Brigade HQ, 'Operations Carried Out by 1st Guards Brigade During August and September 1916.'

uniformity of tactical doctrine was established.'[31] Certainly, the need to establish such uniformity was now seen as a priority but it should be seen as 'a work in progress' at this stage of the war rather than something that had been established. As such, the Guards Division was clearly engaged in learning how to adapt to battlefield expectations. However, some training events were perhaps less successful. The 2nd Guards Brigade naturally undertook a similar programme of preparation but Robert Asquith's description of their brigade field day was typically irreverent. Writing to his wife on 7 September he explained that:

> Yesterday we had a Brigade Field Day under John Ponsonby illustrating all the newest and most elaborate methods of capturing German trenches with the minimum of casualties. It involved getting up at 5 a.m. but in other respects was funny enough. The 'creeping barrage' i.e. the curtain of shell fire which moves on about 50 yards in front of the advancing infantry, was represented by drummers. The spectacle of the whole four battalions moving in lines across the cornfields at a funeral pace headed by a line of rolling drums, produced the effect of some absurd religious ceremony conducted by a tribe of Maoris rather than a brigade of Guards in the attack.[32]

Nonetheless Roger Wood's study of the evolution of brigade command between 1916 and 1918, is right to praise the work done by the Guards brigadiers in the training, planning and implementation of the September attacks in the hectic days beforehand. 'The transformation of staff responsibilities at this stage in the evolution of brigade command demanded a more responsive approach to combat conditions and more professionalism and better teamwork'. As we have seen, progress had been made towards developing a unified tactical doctrine and attention had been paid to finding new methods to obtain intelligence and maintenance of communications such as the use of contact aircraft and the implementation of signalling courses in order to assist in planning command and control.[33]

Despite the increasing intensity of this training in this period, there was only one casualty in the Guards Division: Second Lieutenant Grey de Leche Leach, aged 22, who was the bombing officer of the 1/Scots Guards in the Second Guards Brigade. On 9 September, he was working alongside two NCOs inserting detonators and fuses into Mills bombs at Morlancourt when a fuse ignited. It was probable that the pin fell out and the striker then sprang up thereby hitting the detonator. Leach received the Albert Medal (Gold) for a remarkable act of bravery as can be seen in his citation:

31 Headlam, *History of the Guards Division*, p.140.
32 Raymond Asquith, *Life and Letters*, p.293.
33 Wood, Roger, 'The Evolution of Infantry Brigade Command in the British Army on the Western Front, 1916-1918', PhD thesis, University of Wolverhampton, (2020). p.115.

> Shouting a warning he made for the door, carrying the bomb pressed close to his body, but on reaching the door he found a party of men assembling for a church parade, so that he could not throw the bomb away without exposing them to grave danger. He continued therefore, to press the bomb to his body till it exploded and mortally wounded him. Second Lieutenant Leach might easily have saved his life by throwing the bomb away, or dropping it on the ground, and seeking shelter, but either course would have endangered the lives of those in or around the building. He sacrificed his own life to save the lives of others.[34]

A fellow officer, Captain Rowland Feilding of the 1/Coldstream recounted that he and a fellow officer were outside when there was a sudden loud explosion:

> Leach lay on his back, in a pool of blood, his arms outstretched and both his hands blown off … I can only suppose that seeing Cecil (Lieutenant Cecil Trafford) and myself in the middle of the yard he came to the conclusion that his one chance of throwing it away safely was gone. So he turned his back to us, faced the wall, and hugging the bomb in his hands, allowed it to explode between his body and the wall. It is impossible to speak of such courage and self-sacrifice.[35]

The Introduction of Tanks and the Problem of the Quadrilateral

As training progressed, Haig's big hope that he believed could be the game changer in this forthcoming battle was the tank. Back on 16 August, Haig had asked Rawlinson to submit plans to 'seize the last line of the prepared (German) defences between Morval and Le Sars with a view to opening the way for the Cavalry'.[36] Just three days later Rawlinson saw a tank for the first time when he visited the tank training ground at St Riquier. He was impressed, to an extent, but had doubts about their reliability and the inexperience of the crews. His instinct was to use them cautiously and not too ambitiously; an approach that he knew Haig would not welcome. Rawlinson's first plan of 28 August involved six divisions and would lead to the capture of the German front line. Thereafter, the use of tanks could make it possible to take locations such as Flers before they were withdrawn. The second line would be attacked within 24 hours but nothing beyond that point. Unsurprisingly, Haig who was buoyed by British intelligence reports of the deterioration of German morale, demanded that Rawlinson come back with something far more ambitious.

Rawlinson wrestled with the problem of how to incorporate the use of a large and heavy machine that had obvious attributes but only moved at a maximum speed in these

34 Headlam, *History of the Guards Division*, p.141.
35 Nicol, *Till the Trumpet Sounds again, Volume 2*, p.25.
36 Robin Prior and Trevor Wilson, *The Somme* (London: Yale University Press, 2005), p.216.

battlefield conditions of two miles an hour, which was actually slower than the pace of an infantryman. His plan was to introduce gaps in the creeping barrage so that it would fall in the areas where the infantry were advancing but not in the areas where the tanks were operating. As the tanks were being utilised to attack the German strong points, it would mean that the artillery barrage could not be against them. Consequently, the infantry close to the tanks would lose the support of the creeping barrage. The tanks would be brought up to the starting line under darkness to be ready for zero at 6:20 a.m. and, in the advance, they would be used in groups of three in line so that all of their guns could be utilised. To put so much faith in an untried and inadequately tested new weapon alongside infantry who had absolutely no training in such combined operations at such a critical point in the Somme offensive seems quite incredible in retrospect. Exactly how the cavalry would be utilised was not resolved despite such concerns as to whether they and the infantry might impede each other suggesting that perhaps Rawlinson did not expect them to be called upon.

The German defensive work known as the Quadrilateral or *Sydow-Hohe* was opposite the front of XIV Corps and would prove a significant barrier for the Guards on 15 September. Situated approximately 1,000 yards to the east of Ginchy, it was 'a four-sided trench in the form of a parallelogram of some 300 yards by 150 yards'.[37] Duffy describes the location as 'not so much a hill in the conventional sense, but a huge and open swell of ground that was located in an enfilading position and commanded an excellent field of grazing fire'. He continues, however, to suggest that there was a degree of exaggeration taken by the British histories 'as the 'German sketch maps show nothing beyond an ordinary trench with a couple of pieces of fragmentary trenches behind. On 15 September, at least, the strength of the position derived from the lie of the ground and the front.'[38] Later, Germans claims that: 'It was no fortress at all' but a series of 'rifle trenches which were repeatedly ploughed into heaps of rubble … and in shell holes, where thirsty men with hollow cheeks, blackened with dust, crouched with burning eyes … determined to defend the position entrusted to them with their last breath' may have sought to portray its defenders, quite fairly, in heroic terms. Yet the reality was that the Quadrilateral was a very significant obstacle to the attacking forces on 15 September.[39] Moreover, the German sketch maps that Duffy alludes to may have been inaccurate and Peter Hodgkinson has rightly concluded that aerial photographs suggest that it was much stronger than these maps suggest.[40] It could not be observed from any point behind the British front line and neither could the German wire in the Combles Valley. As Prior and Wilson pointed out, the requirement to bombard unobservable defences was not a new one and neither was Rawlinson's solution; aerial

37 T.O. Marden, *A Short History of the Sixth Division* (London: Hugh Rees, 1920) p.20. Quoted in Hodgkinson, *Complete Orchestra of War*, p.134.
38 Christopher Duffy, *Through German Eyes: The British and the Somme 1916* (London: Phoenix, 2007), p.228.
39 Duffy, *Through German Eyes*, p.235.
40 Hodgkinson, *Complete Orchestra of War*, p.149.

observation would be used to confirm if the artillery had destroyed the German defences. This, they argue, might have worked in the case of the Quadrilateral which was a relatively large target close to the British front line but would have no chance against small targets such as wire. Ominously, just as on 1 July, Rawlinson appears to have assembled as many guns and shells as possible rather than considering what kind of weight was necessary to suppress the German defences.[41]

Nonetheless Haig remained optimistic that this attack would bring the long-hoped for breakthrough that would lead to more mobile operations. On 9 September he entertained Lieutenant General Charles Kavanagh, who he had recently appointed to command the Cavalry Corps, to lunch:

> I explained that the Enemy seemed to have exhausted his reserves, and that I thought that after the next attack the crisis of the battle is likely to be reached, and the moment might possibly be favourable for cavalry action. Circumstances seemed to require the cavalry to operate, to start with, in three main groups. *Everyone* must put forth the greatest effort and be ready to suffer privation for several days in order to reap the fruits of victory.[42]

On exactly the same day, Miles Barne had his first encounter with a tank:

> Marched to …HAPPY VALLEY, a camp on the way up to the line, where we saw a lot of 'Tanks', or sort of creeping forts on caterpillar wheels – otherwise known as 'Land Dreadnoughts' or 'Willies'. We saw them climbing up banks and over trenches etc, we also went on board some of them – there are cocks and hens – the former have 6lb guns, the latter only machine guns. It remains to be seen what use they are … they say they will revolutionize the war. I can't help thinking that just at first they will terrify the Hun until he finds out how to meet them.[43]

Others were far more enthused with the prospects for these new machines. Corporal Jack Critchley, who was attached to the Guards Division, remembered:

> One day, we were in the wagon line – quite a few of us – and somebody came along and said, 'The war is finished. Just go half a mile down the road, look in a field, and you will see!' He wouldn't tell us why. So we went down and there was quite a crowd there. We saw these 'tank' things that we had never seen or heard of, and the tank men were full of it. 'Oh this is it, boy!' and they were describing the tanks to us in full. 'This is a female tank, it has nothing but machine guns, but this is a male tank, it has cannon, and can fire this many shells, and these slots at the bottom of

41 Prior & Wilson, *The Somme*, pp.216–226.
42 Sheffield and Bourne, *Haig's War Diaries*, pp.228–229.
43 Nicol, *Barne's Diary*, p.185.

the door are where we point the revolvers through when we are going over trenches, and we kill them that way!'

After that, we thought, 'When we get a few of these lads over, the war is finished! We are going to be home by Christmas!' That was a feeling a lot of us had.[44]

44 Joshua Levine, *Forgotten Voices of the Somme* (London: Ebury, 2008), p.221.

6

The Somme: The Battle of Flers-Courcelette, 15–16 September 1916

Preliminary Actions, 9–13 September

With the 'Operation Order' to proceed with the attack now imminent, work still needed to be done in minimising as much of the German threat posed to the attackers and to provide the best foundations for the main attack to succeed but unfortunately, they were far from successful. These actions between 9 and 13 September were characterised by their sheer brutality and considerable loss of life.

The 3rd Guards Brigade had moved into the front line during the night of 9/10 September as part of relief of the 48th Infantry Brigade of the 16th Division. The whole of the 16th was engaged in attacking Ginchy but had no supporting troops. Definite information had reached 3rd Guards Brigade HQ that Ginchy had been captured but that the right of the attack had been held up. The Welsh Guards immediately began their relief at 8:30 p.m. and the 4/Grenadiers two hours later. The Grenadiers were to relieve the 47th Brigade although it was not clear what the exact position held by the 47th was but they were believed to be about their original line on the Guillemont-Leuze Wood Road. Unfortunately, all communication between the Brigade HQ and the 4/Grenadiers was lost.[1]

By 1:00 a.m. the 1/Welsh Guards had completed their relief of the 48th Infantry Brigade and were digging in on a line from 200 yards east of the southeast corner of Delville Wood to 100 yards north of Ginchy on the Flers Road and 250 yards east to the Lesboeufs Road. Their left was in touch with the 164th Brigade but their right was in the air. Meanwhile the 4/Grenadiers relieved the 47th Brigade but found themselves under frequent artillery fire in shattered trenches. Orders were sent to them to push up north to gain touch with the 1/Welsh Guards. Regrettably, the order did not reach the

1 TNA: WO95/1224, 1/Welsh Guards War Diary, 'Report on the taking over and holding Ginchy from midnight of 9/10 Sept. 1916 to 11 p.m. night of 11/12 Sept. 1916'. 13 September 1916.

4/Grenadiers until 6:00 a.m. and so could not be complied with. The 1/Welsh Guards were, therefore, in a weak and exposed position.[2] During the night, Major Bromfield of the Prince of Wales Company made repeated efforts to gain touch with the 4/Grenadiers but reported that he found 'nothing but Germans, who fired and disappeared in the darkness, though a few were caught'. Conditions the next morning were not ideal with 'a misty dawn, and at 7 o'clock there was very little light'. Broomfield remained concerned about his flank and sent out a patrol under Sergeant Ashford which succeeded in finding a mixed company of around 70 men from the 48th Brigade 'under a gallant officer who had been shot through the neck but, although he couldn't talk, was still active and eager'. Ashford returned to brief Major Bromfield when the Germans attacked from the northeast in what became a serious confrontation. Bromfield feared that he would be surrounded and ordered the right of his company to fall back into a nearby wood but they then met the German's left which had swept into the wood and this led to desperate hand to hand fighting in the most difficult of circumstances as the Welsh Guards' history confirms:

> It must be understood that this wood was a mass of deep shell-holes. It had been bombarded by the British heavy guns for some weeks and there were heaps of brick from the demolished houses by the side of the road, and large heaps of earth from German dugouts; there were fallen trees, too, and a great number of standing ones. It was a confused jumble, and the men taking cover in one shell-hole could not possibly tell if anyone was in the next, or if it was friend or foe.[3]

In such conditions, there was no question of artillery support for the Welsh Guards. Lieutenant Colonel Murray Thriepland identified Captain Ashworth, who on his own initiative took on the leadership of a large mixed force, as the hero of the day. Leading his own Company, No. 2 Prince of Wales together with three platoons of No. 4 Company, 50 men of the 1/Grenadier Guards and 50 of the 2/Scots Guards whose officers had become casualties including Bromfield who had now been killed, the combined force managed to regroup and take back a considerable amount of the ground that had been lost.[4] In total there were 205 casualties. The Welsh Guards' history highlights two soldiers, amongst many, who fought heroically. Firstly, Lance Corporal C.L. Glover, 'who was blown up and sent to the dressing-station apparently stone deaf and terribly shaken; but when he arrived at the dressing-station he found his hearing returning, although his nerves were still twitching so that he could not keep his hands quiet', but, nonetheless, after a brief stay, 'still twitching and shaky, returned to the Prince of Wales's Company and carried on as acting company sergeant-major'. Secondly, Private William Williams who 'was

2 Ibid.
3 Ward, *History of the Welsh Guards*, pp.116–117.
4 TNA: WO95/1224, 1/Welsh Guards, 'Report on the taking over and holding Ginchy from midnight of 9/10 Sept. 1916 to 11 p.m. night of 11/12 Sept. 1916'. 13 September 1916.

seen to dispose of several of the enemy, until with a furious thrust he completely transfixed a German and was unable to free his bayonet. He knocked another down with his fists, and seized yet another by the throat, when they both fell into a shell-hole. More Germans rushed up, and the gallant Williams did not rise again.'[5]

Inevitably, most attention focussed on eliminating the threat posed by the Quadrilateral. At 2:00 a.m. on 12 September, No. 2 Company of the 1/Grenadiers under Captain A.C. Graham, was ordered to bomb along a trench running east from the right of No. 3 Company along the south side of the Ginchy Telegraph Road, and attack the southern end of the Quadrilateral. Although the exact strength of the German defences at the Quadrilateral were not known, it was felt that the attacking force made available would be sufficient. According to the Grenadiers' history:

> There were three bombing parties, two blocking parties and a Lewis gun. Each bombing party was composed of the following:
> 2 bayonet men carrying 6 bombs each.
> 1 thrower carrying 6 bombs.
> 2 carriers carrying 12 bombs each.
> 1 N.C.O. carrying 6 bombs.
> 1 Mills adapter firer carrying 6 Mills adapters.
> 2 Mills adapter carriers carrying 10 Mills adapters.
> 2 bomb carriers carrying 12 bombs each.
> Each blocking party was composed of four privates and one N.C.O., carrying 25 sandbags and 1 shovel each. Every man in the Company carried 4 Mills bombs, 4 sand-bags, and 225 rounds of S.A.A., while every alternate man carried a shovel. Six men and 1 N.C.O. were left in the old line, with a Lewis gun to cover the right flank, while No. 3 found the Lewis gun to cover the left.[6]

All of the ground had been obliterated by shells and No. 2 Company struggled to find its direction getting to a point within 100 yards of the Quadrilateral before being held up by machine gun fire. Captain Graham was killed by a shell during the advance and was replaced by Captain Fisher-Rowe. The party were unable to get any closer and so Fisher-Rowe took the decision to block the trench as far as they had got and consolidated the line. At 6:00 a.m. the whole battalion made another attack and attempted to seize the Quadrilateral in conjunction with units from the 56th Division, but the German stronghold continued to resist and heavy casualties were suffered.

The 2/Irish Guards relieved the 4/Grenadiers on the evening of 12 September in what were only recently dug but shallow trenches.[7] During the relief, Second Lieutenant Zigomala and 10 men had been wounded and on the following day, the Irish took a

5 Ward, *History of the Welsh Guards*, p.119.
6 Ponsonby, *History of the Grenadiers*, vol.2, pp.113–114.
7 Ponsonby, *History of the Grenadiers*, vol.2, pp.113–114.

further 40 casualties from the hands of snipers and the effects of artillery including Second Lieutenant Vaughan and several men from No. 1 Company who were killed by a single shell. Kipling described the situation facing the Irish eloquently:

> The enemy, well aware of what was intended, did all they could to cripple, delay and confuse, and waste the men and material on our side. Their chief reliance was their 'pocketed' machine guns with which the whole ground was peppered; and their gunners instructions, most gallantly obeyed, were, on the withdrawal of any force, to remain and continue killing till they themselves were killed. Consequently it was necessary at frequent intervals to hunt up these pests by hand rather as one digs out wasps nests after dark.[8]

A trench east of Ginchy, which was part of the Quadrilateral, was a particular concern with its machine gun emplacements and the 2/Irish Guards together with troops of the 71st Infantry Brigade were ordered to attack on the night of 13 September. Earlier in the day, the 71st Brigade had attacked the Quadrilateral from the southwest. They gained control of the line of the Leuze Wood–Ginchy road but were then held back by German machine gun fire. A fresh effort involving the 9/Suffolks and 2/Sherwood Foresters resulted in the total loss of 21 officers and 500 other ranks.[9]

On the night of 13 September, 6th Division organised an artillery bombardment which was designed to cut the wire before No. 2 Company of the 2/Irish Guards filed across a section of the open Ginchy to Morval road. At this point, they were enfiladed by machine gun fire before dropping into cramped trenches. It soon became apparent that not enough of the wire had been cut. Kipling, clearly angered by what ensued wrote that: 'When the attack was launched, in waves of two platoons each, undisturbed machine guns in a few dreadful minutes accounted for more than three-quarters of the little host … That wiped out No. 2 Company, and next day, its thirty survivors were sent back to first-line Transport – a bleak prelude to the battle ahead.'[10] The attack by the 71st Infantry Brigade also failed. Major C.A. Rocke, writing in his after-action report was bitter: 'I attribute the failure of the attack to the feebleness of the barrage that preceded it. The trench which No. 2 Company had to attack was full of the enemy, who shot at their ease over the parapet supported by machine guns. The men behaved with great gallantry, and only stopped when ordered to do so'.[11]

Despite the heroic efforts that had been made, Cavan had already decided that if this final operation should fail, the situation would have to be accepted and the attack on the 15th would be launched from the existing line.[12]

8 Kipling, *The Irish Guards in the Great War: The Second Battalion*, p.92.
9 Wilfrid Miles, *Military Operations, France and Belgium, 1916 Volume 2* (Tennessee: Battery Press, 1995 [1938]), pp. 277–278.
10 Kipling, *The Irish Guards in the Great War: The Second Battalion*, pp.91–92.
11 Headlam, *History of the Guards Division*, p.149.
12 Miles, *Military Operations, France and Belgium, 1916 Volume 2*, p.278.

Final Operation Orders

Meanwhile, on 12 September, Guards Division HQ had received the much anticipated 'Operation Order No. 76':

1. The Fourth Army will attack the enemy's defences between Combles Ravine and Martinpuich on Z day with the object of seizing Morval, Lesboeufs, Gueudecourt, and Flers, and to break through the enemy's system of defence. The French are undertaking an offensive simultaneously on the South and the Reserve Army on the North.
2. The attack will be pushed with the utmost vigour all along the line until the most distant objectives are reached. The failure of one unit on the flank is not to prevent other units pushing on to their final objective, as it is by such means that those units who have failed will be assisted to advance.[13]

The 1st Guards Brigade and 2nd Guards Brigades were to carry out the attack on the Gueudecourt–Lesboeufs–Morval line. The 2nd Guards with its HQ in Dummy trench west of Trones Wood held the right, 1st Guards Brigade with its HQ in Bernafay Wood held the left of the line. XIV Corps was to advance with three divisions in the line: 56th Division on the right, 6th in the centre and the Guards on the left. The 14th (Light) Division of XV Corps were to the left of the Guards.

The Guards Division had four objectives each identified as a coloured line:

1. The 'green line' which was approximately 1,000 yards to the north and north-east of Ginchy. Beginning from a point just southeast of the Ginchy–Gueudecourt Road, it continued in a south-easterly direction towards and beyond a German defensive position, the 'Triangle'.
2. The 'brown line' ran in a northerly direction from the 'green line' before swinging westwards towards the Ginchy–Gueudecourt Road. This objective was to be taken by the 1st Guards Brigade which would be attacking on the left.
3. The 'blue line' was 800 to 1,000 yards to the east of the 'brown line'. It ran from a point on the Flers–Lesboeufs road about 800 yards north-west of Lesboeufs in a southerly direction in front of the village.
4. The 'red line' was just to the east of Lesboeufs.[14]

Each Guards Brigade was expected to advance on a narrow front of around 500 yards with full artillery support. An artillery barrage would begin on 12 September and was to

13 TNA: WO95/1192, Guards Division HQ, Guards Division Order No.73. App. 1093, 12 September 1916.
14 Headlam, *History of the Guards Division*, pp.146–147.

be carried out daily from 6:00 a.m. to 6:00 p.m. until zero on 15 September. Half of the available artillery was to be utilised in firing a creeping barrage to cover the advancing infantry with the other half putting down a stationary barrage which would be lifted back as soon as the 'creeper' got level with it.[15] This was the first creeping barrage in history to support a combined infantry and tank assault. In detail, the instructions were that:

> At zero the creeping barrage will open 100 yards in front of our front trenches and will advance at the rate of 50 yards per minute until it is 200 yards beyond the first objective, when it will become stationary.
>
> At zero + 1 hour the creeping barrage will become intense on the line 200 yards in front of first objective and will creep forward at the rate of 50 yards per minute in front of that portion of the 1st Guards Brigade which is to advance to the second objective.
>
> At zero + 1 hour and 10 minutes the creeping barrage will become intense on a line 200 yards in front of the first objective … thence on a line 200 yards in front of the second objective and will advance at the rate of 50 yards per minute until it has passed 200 yards beyond the third objective, when it will become stationary.
>
> This barrage is to cover the advance of the tanks. There will be no creeping barrage in front of infantry during their advance to third objective, which commences at zero + 2 hours.
>
> At zero + 3 hours and 30 minutes the creeping barrage will become intense on a line 200 yards in front of third objective and will advance at the rate of 30 yards per minute until it has passed 200 yards beyond fourth objective, when it will become stationary. This barrage is to cover the advance of the tanks. There will be no creeping barrage in front of the infantry during the advance on the fourth objective, which commences at zero + 4 hours and 30 minutes. In the attack on the first and second objectives gaps of 100 yards wide will be left in the creeping barrage for the routes of the tanks.[16]

On 13 September Feilding held a conference at Guards Division HQ when he gave his final instructions to his brigadiers and commanding officers. Seeking to capture the enormity of the occasion as he saw it, he observed that: 'This is perhaps the greatest battle that has ever been fought. The Guards Division has been specially selected for the operation – the eyes of the whole of England will be watching us and I have absolute confidence that we shall live up to our reputation.'[17] Certainly, this was a critical moment in the Somme campaign and a major breakthrough of the German defences was sorely

15 Headlam, *History of the Guards Division*, p.147.
16 TNA: WO95/1192, Guards Division HQ, Guards Division Order No.73. App. 1093, 12 September 1916.
17 Headlam, *History of the Guards Division*, p.148. Footnote.

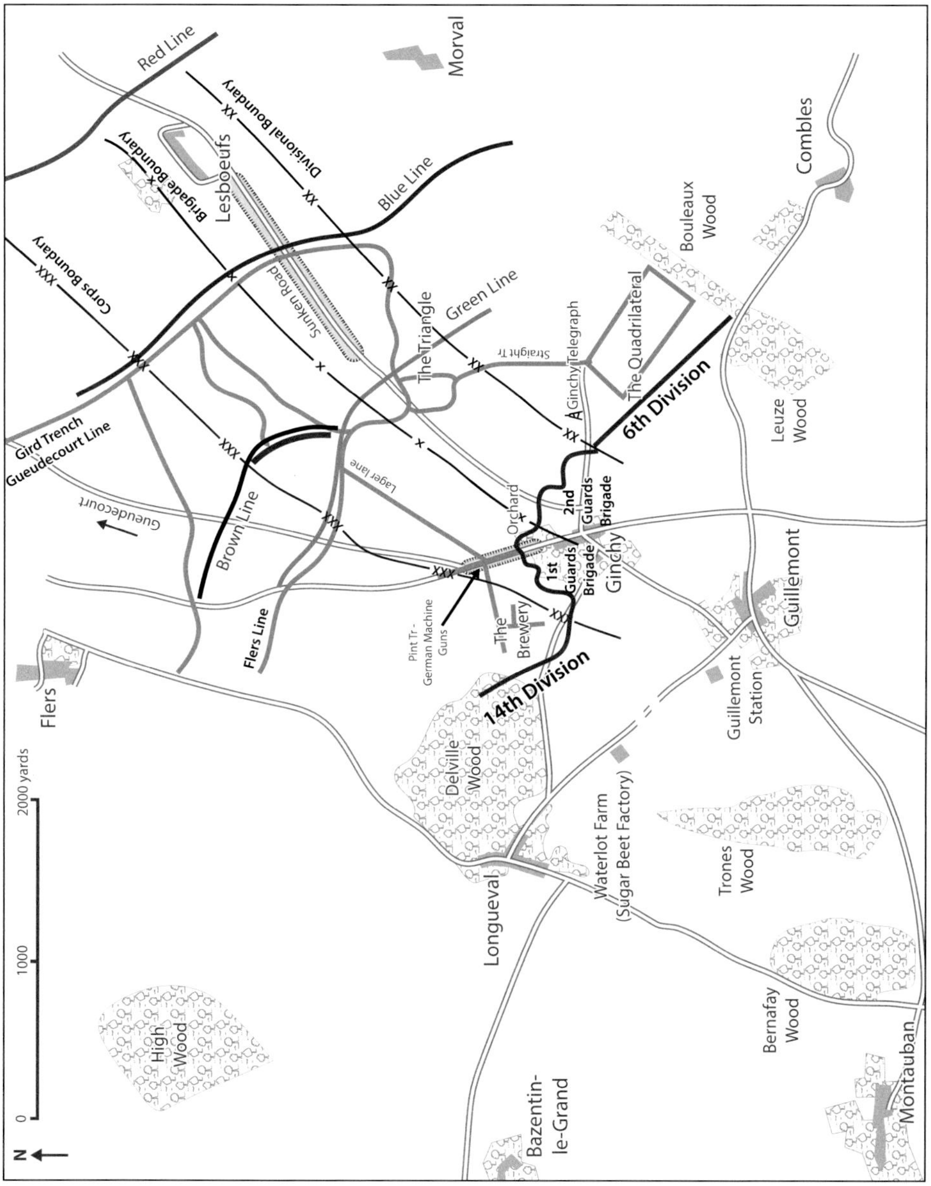

The Battle of the Somme, the attack from Ginchy towards Lesboeufs, 15 September 1916.

needed. In this context, it is not difficult to see why Feilding believed that the Guards had an historic opportunity to change the direction of the war.

There was no doubt that heavy casualties were anticipated. It was felt that so great was the danger of battalions being 'practically annihilated in an attack' that orders were issued 'for a certain nucleus of officers and N.C.O.'s to be left behind … to make sure of a sufficient number surviving to carry on beyond the immediate requirements of the attack'. This meant that 'the Second in Command, the junior Captains of companies, the Battalion and Company Sergeant-Majors and Quartermaster-Sergeants in each battalion were left behind.'[18] To many, this was a great disappointment. Miles Barne wrote that 12 September was a 'very dismal day for me … I never had a bigger wrench than leaving the Battn after nearly months with them, and then to be left behind, while they take part in the biggest battle of the war, in a few days time'.[19]

Battle Joined: 15 September

On 14 September the Guards Divisional HQ moved to Bernafay Wood. During the night of 14/15 September, the troops went to their assembly points. The divisional front was about 1,200 yards in length. As Headlam observed, 'There was no front trench system to accommodate this assembly of troops and the various positions were indicated by means of tapes and signposts provided by the R.E.' In reality these cramped and crowded positions were no more than a mass of shell craters as far away as possible from the ruins of Ginchy which was always a target for German gunners. It was a cold night with some men suffering from exposure.[20]

Ultimately, after much debate at brigade level, it had been decided that 'the assaulting battalions should advance in four successive waves with a frontage of four platoons, the men being in single file columns of half companies and the platoons 500 yards apart. On the right, the 2nd Guards Brigade under Ponsonby consisted of the 1/Coldstream and the 3/Grenadiers in the front with the 1/Scots and the 2/Irish in the second line. It assembled south-east of the Ginchy–Lesboueufs road which was under a frequent barrage. The plan was for the whole brigade to pass right through to the final objective. On the left, the 1st Guards Brigade under Pereira occupied a frontage of similar dimension but with the flanks bending backwards. The left flank was well inside the corps boundary with the 3/Coldstream and the 2/Coldstream in front, the 1/Irish Guards in the second line and the 2/Grenadiers in the rear. The Coldstream were expected to advance to the third objective, after which the 1/Irish Guards would go through to the final objective. The 2/Grenadiers would protect the left flank and provide general support in the later stages of the attack. Two machine guns were to accompany each of the leading battalions and

18 Ponsonby, *History of the Grenadiers*, vol.2, p.35.
19 Nicol, *Barne's Diary*, p.187.
20 Headlam, *History of the Guards Division* pp.149–150.

four were to move forward with each supporting battalion. Three more machine guns were to follow to the rear with a Stokes mortar on each flank. Meanwhile, 3rd Brigade was in divisional reserve and moved forwards into Trones Wood and Guillemont during the night.[21] Facing the Guards Division was *7th Bavarian Regiment* of the *5th Bavarian Division*. This was a competent and experienced division that had performed well in the Battle of the Frontiers in 1914. It was seen as 'not amongst the best Bavarian divisions' but 'it was a good combat unit'.[22]

Any success that the Guards might achieve was of course dependant on the ability of the 14th Division on the left located between Ginchy and Delville Wood and the 6th Division to the right who faced the Quadrilateral to clear their flanks. The two attacking Guards Brigades would immediately be exposed to fire from the Quadrilateral to their right and from the German positions between Ginchy and Delville Wood on the left as they jumped off. Whilst the 14th Division controlled the eastern edge of Delville Wood, unfortunately there were German troops still occupying some of the trenches located between the 14th and the Guards Division.[23]

As we have seen, much was expected from the tanks.[24] The Guards' attack was to be supported by 10 tanks from C Company placed into three groups or columns. Each column consisted of three tanks with a single female tank on their Western flank. In the east, No. 1 Column would begin on the Ginchy to Lesboeufs road. It consisted of two male tanks and one female. The male 741 (tank A) was commanded by Lieutenant Jethro Tull, *Campania* (tank B) was commanded by Second Lieutenant Jack Clarke, and the female (tank C) *Casa* was commanded by Second Lieutenant Victor Smith. The tanks from this column would advance north of the road to Lesboeufs between the 1/Grenadier Guards and the 3/Coldstream Guards along the inter-brigade boundary. The tanks' first objective was the southeast part of the Triangle, the strongpoint on the enemy frontline which was to the south of that road. The allocation of two male tanks shows that No. 1 Column's chief targets were German machine-gun positions at this strongly defended location.[25]

In the centre of the Guards' attack was No. 2 Column. It had two female and one male tank. Their primary role was to suppress German troops in the trenches as the 2/Coldstream attacked the Serpentine Trench/Flers Line to the northwest of the Triangle. No. 2 Column was required to start from a position northeast of Ginchy and advance on the right-hand flank of the 2/Coldstream. On the western side of the Guards front, the No.3 Column consisted of two males and a female to deal with the machine-gun emplacements in that area. The three tanks were required to advance on the left flank of

21 Headlam, *History of the Guards Division*, pp.149–151.
22 Anon: *Histories of 251 Divisions*, p.122.
23 Headlam, *History of the Guards Division*, p.151.
24 Much of our understanding of their role in this operation is a result of the pioneering research carried out by Trevor Pidgeon and more recently by Stephen Pope.
25 Stephen Pope, *The Tanks Corps in the Great War: Volume 1. Conception, Birth and Baptism of Fire, November 1914–November 1916* (Warwick: Helion, 2022), pp.144–145.

the 3/Coldstream. These machine-guns also posed a significant threat to the advance of 14th Division. The first female tank was 507 (tank D) commanded by Captain Herbert Hiscocks, the second female 513 (tank F) by Second Lieutenant Tom Murphy and the final 722 (tank E) by Second Lieutenant Alec Arnaud. The single tank was a female variant, *Clan Cameron* and it carried an 'L' designation. It was required to operate on the west flank undertaking a preliminary operation against the Brewery Salient between Ginchy and Delville Wood.[26]

Guards Division HQ provided precise timings for the tanks' deployment and start times. For example, the second stage of the Guards attack would commence at Z+ 90 minutes (7:50 a.m.). At this point No. 1 Column was ordered to pass through into the 6th Divisional in map square T9 Central. This particular as area contained a group of six parallel trenches which posed a significant barrier unless they were dealt with. However, the instructions for 'L' were remarkably vague by comparison being required 'to report to Brigade Major, Left Guards Brigade and ask him for any information which may aid you' just prior to Zero.[27]

The day before the attack, 14 September, was a demanding day for the tank crews. The skippers supporting the Guards Division had to meet their guides at 6:00 a.m. to check the route to Ginchy which had been decided upon the day before. It soon became apparent that several of the tanks were short of petrol and urgent requests for fresh supplies were sent back to their base at the Loop which was C Company's HQ. Urgent attention was required during the day by the crews as they topped up the lubricants in their engines, transmissions and running gears as well as tightening their tracks.[28]

At 7:00 p.m., with dusk approaching, the tanks set out towards their differing starting positions. The Guards Division's tanks had an especially demanding route:

> A great deal of difficulty was experienced in getting the tanks from their position of assembly southwest of Trones Wood to the forward positions during the night. Tapes had been laid on the ground from a point southwest of Guillemont to the forward position on the outskirts of Ginchy. The ground over which the tanks had to travel was as bad as possible and, without the existence of tapes, the tanks would have been unable to reach their forward positions.[29]

Despite having the furthest to travel, all three tanks in No. 1 Column successfully reached he starting point to the east of Ginchy on time. Regrettably only Hiscocks' female tank in No. 2. Column reached the starting position. Of the other two tanks, one had suffered a mechanical breakdown before departure and the other became ditched in a

26 Pope, *The Tanks Corps in the Great War: Volume 1*, pp.144–145.
27 Pope, *The Tanks Corps in the Great War: Volume 1*, pp.144–145.
28 Pope, *The Tanks Corps in the Great War: Volume 1*, p.146.
29 Report by GOC Guards Division quoted in Trevor Pidgeon, *The Tanks at Flers: An Account of the First Use of Tanks in War at the Battle of Flers–Courcelette, the Somme, 15 September 1916* (Cobham: Fairmile. 1995), p.92 and Pope, *Tank Corps in the Great War: Volume 1*, p.148.

shell hole on the outskirts of Ginchy. Regrettably, Hiscocks' tank ditched as it proceeded towards the front line. This meant that there were no tanks to lead the 2/Coldstream to their first objective or counter the German machine-guns coming from the Triangle and Serpentine trench. Fortunately, all three tanks from No.3 column arrived safely to their starting point west of Ginchy as did Cole in 'L' who had been briefed along the way by 1st Guards Brigade HQ at Waterlot Farm.[30] It remained to be seen how effective the seven surviving tanks would be as the Guards attack got underway.

During the night of 14/15 September, there was a continuous heavy bombardment of the German positions opposite Fourth Army. Lieutenant Oliver Lyttelton of the 3/ Grenadiers waited nervously to move up to the jumping off point. He anticipated heavy losses: 'some of us knew what it would be like and that we couldn't get out under twelve officers, and two hundred and fifty men. Some of the young fellows were looking forward to it but I think on everyone else there was that aching load of anticipation'. Reassuringly, he read that 'Kits of deceased officers will be returned to railhead packed in canvas and labelled 'Cox's Shipping Agency'. When the time came to move forward, the Irish Guardsman who acted as his battalion's guide lost his way in ground where 'there is not one square foot without a shell-hole, they all overlap and stretch drearily into the half-darkness'. Eventually, using a compass, they reached the jumping off point over five hours before zero. 'This meant that we join up shell holes as best we can and get into them'. At 5:30 a.m. the light began to break, and the commanding officer was becoming anxious stating that, 'I wish we were going now. It is very quiet and they will probably spot us on the bank'. The British barrage began at 6:00 a.m. eliciting a German response targeting Ginchy. Fortunately, 'we were not there and so escaped'. The countdown to zero began and tension mounted still further. At 6:10 a.m. Lyttelton destroyed 'all the orders, papers etc. except for one map'. Now 'nothing could be altered, no more orders given.' Anxious about the barrage, he commented that 'I hope sincerely … if it does not come down at the right time, will be late and not early'. At 6:20 a.m. the attack began. Lyttelton continued:

> Our 'creeping barrage did not seem to me to be very clearly defined. The smoke was terrific but one could see and indeed feel the whole brigade pressing on…then we killed, I have only a blurred image of slaughter. I saw about ten Germans writhing like trout in a creel at the bottom of a shell-hole and our fellows firing at them from the hip. One or two red bayonets.[31]

The events that were to follow as the Guards attack got underway were violent, intense, frenzied and confused. As the regimental history of the Coldstream Guards pointed out:

> A detailed description of the course of a struggle such as that which took place on the Ginchy-Lesboeufs plateau on the 15th September, must always be a matter of

30 Pope, *Tanks Corps in the Great War: Volume 1*, pp.148–149.
31 Lyttelton, *From Peace to War*, pp.164–166.

> some difficulty; for the confusion caused by the conflict makes many of the incidents connected with it obscure, and a full story of what really happened can hardly be compiled … When troops are launched forward in attack, the control over them is necessarily weakened, and to some extent they get out of hand. The line can scarcely ever maintain its original formation; parties of men become separated from their comrades; they get mixed up with other units; and they instinctively collect into groups, and have to act on their own initiative without guidance, or under an officer or other leader who may chance to be on the spot. It is impossible to follow the fortunes of all these groups, or to know for certain at what time some of their deeds were done; and thus the account to be given is sure to be imperfect.[32]

Whilst these circumstances are, of course, not unique to other actions in the Great War, they are especially apposite to the events of 15/16 September.

Before looking in detail at the Guards' attack, it is important to be aware of the dire situation that was about to confront the 6th Division. The heavy artillery bombardment that had lasted for the best part of three days had barely affected the Quadrilateral. The weather had made observed shooting difficult but amazingly, the gunners had not identified the location accurately. Their fire had been on the reverse slope of the ridge rather than the summit and forward slope; a calamitous situation confirmed from an aerial photograph before the 6th Division attacked. Apparently, the error was due to 'an incorrect spot height on the map, suggesting that the fire plan may have been based upon inaccurate information'.[33] To make matters even worse, two of the three tanks that had been planned to deal with any remaining German defenders broke down and the third was withdrawn unable to deal with the German armour-piercing ammunition. When the 6th Division attack began, there was no creeping barrage to protect it as the barrage began beyond the Quadrilateral itself. Meanwhile, the German machine-gunners were able to man their parapets with disastrous consequences for the attackers. On the left of the 6th Division's front, further mistakes were made by the artillery. The 6th Division's barrage 'was placed on an arbitrary line on the ground to match the barrage fired on behalf of the Guards. So while the Guards' barrage coincided with an actual German trench, that in front of the left of 6th Division did not.'[34] Major General Charles Ross, commanding the 6th Division was to complain that: 'The stationary barrage was put on this line, where there was not a single German, instead of on the trench which was full of Germans, as one well knew for we had already been repelled from it [on the 12 September]'.[35] Within just 10 minutes, the 6th Division's attack lay in ruins and the Guards' attack itself lay exposed to murderous fire from the Quadrilateral.

32 John Foster Ross-of-Bladensburg, *The Coldstream Guards 1914-18 Volume 1* (London: Oxford University Press, 1928), p.486.
33 Wood, 'Evolution of Infantry Brigade Command', p.116.
34 Prior and Wilson, *The Somme*, p.232.
35 Prior and Wilson, *The Somme*, p.232.

When the two Guards brigades began their advance, it was the first time in the history of the regiment that three battalions of the Coldstream Guards attacked in the line together.[36] As the right of the 2nd Guards Brigade, moving in a north-easterly direction, reached the crest of the higher ground, it received intense fire from the direction of Straight Trench and the Quadrilateral. They suffered heavy losses including Lieutenant Colonel B.N. Sergison-Brooke of the 3/Grenadiers who was amongst the wounded. The Grenadiers and Coldstream pressed on however although tending to drift to the left of their intended course. The rear battalions were close behind. Some distance beyond the crest, Germans were discovered occupying a previously undetected advanced position in a series of shell holes. Brigadier Ponsonby, commanding the 2nd Guards Brigade, reported afterwards that 'the existence of unknown lines between the starting-place and the first objective' led to a 'loss of momentum in the attack, owing to lack of strength, at the moment when its chance of complete success was greatest.' Aerial reconnaissance had failed to identify these shell holes which were strongly held by, according to captured documents, the *2nd Battalion* of *IR14* whereas it was discovered that there were only two companies in the 'green line' itself. Apparently, 'the garrison in them escaped all preliminary bombardment except the rapid passage of the creeping barrage.' This newly detected German defensive position was in the form of a switch line 'running back diagonally from a parallel. The strength of this system was that 'while the parallel line can be rushed, the switch line is only reached piecemeal, and in the interval is bringing flanking fire to bear on the rest of the attack.' Consequently, 'the delay, mixes up the attacking waves, and tends to confuse the direction of the attack.'[37] Nonetheless, with all four battalions mixed together, the Guards pressed on into the northern part of the Triangle and part of Serpentine Trench, further to the left. They found that the three belts of wire in front of this position had been well cut by the artillery and the Guards were able to stifle any resistance and take a number of German prisoners. By 7:15 a.m. the 2nd Guards Brigade, now significantly reduced in numbers, and with just a few officers remaining, had reached part of their first objective.[38]

However, there was frustration within the 2nd Guards Brigade about what might have been achieved thereafter:

> Considerable parties advanced from the Green Line, cleared the switch line which ran from it into the Blue Line, and established themselves in positions varying from 400 to 200 yards from the Blue Line itself. These parties saw the enemy entirely disorganised, and were themselves prepared for anything, but they had not the strength by themselves to take the Blue Line and LES BOEUFS. On this account senior officers all attach great importance to the presence close up and

36 Headlam, *History of the Guards Division*, p.15.
37 TNA: WO 95/1217, 2nd Guards Brigade HQ, 'Report of Experience Gained in the Attack of Sept. 15.'
38 Miles, *Military Operations, 1916 Volume 2*, p.312.

> the prompt use of strong reserves … There is a universal belief amongst the officers who survived that had it been possible to throw in strong reserves at any time between 9 a.m. and 2 p.m. on the 15th the enemy would have been too shaken to resist another determined blow and a decisive advantage would have been secured on a big front.[39]

Lance Sergeant Frederick McNess VC.

Lance Sergeant Frederick McNess of the 1/ Scots Guards was awarded the VC for his part in this fighting. He had led his men forward with great courage in the initial attack before personally leading an attack against German bombers. The fight went on for 90 minutes as the Germans were gradually pushed back. Despite being wounded, McNess continued to throw bombs and organised the establishment of a block.[40]

In a quite remarkable and very detailed account, McNess described these events:

> One of the men in my platoon was shot through the lungs, or some such place. He gasped terribly for breath, and fell behind me. Easing his head with my left hand, I threw bombs with my right, also saying a few cheering words to the boys. Presently I felt his head drop back – his fight was over. I was just preparing another bomb, with the upper part of my head and chest well above the parapet, when a German bomb burst near my neck, blowing away the left side of the same and part of my jaw, lower teeth and gum and upper teeth. Left arm was blown round my neck and the biceps muscle was contracted like a ball on the top of the left shoulder. Jugular vein, windpipe and carotid artery were fully exposed, and shoulder blade badly out of place. My head lay helplessly on my arm, and sometimes almost rolled on my back. For a moment I was dazed, as I had already been hit three times with shrapnel in the early part of the morning while organizing men of some other unit, who had lost their officers and their NCOs, but I was soon clear again; still what with loss of blood and almost blinded with it, I had to leave the boys, but I did not go far, only to the first line, where I lay in a shell

39 TNA: WO 95/1217, 2nd Guards Brigade HQ, 'Report of Experience Gained in the Attack of Sept. 15.'

40 Paul Oldfield, *Victoria Crosses on the Western Front: Somme 1916, 1 July-13 November* (Barnsley: Pen & Sword, 2016), pp.108–109.

> hole and watched how things progressed. But feeling myself becoming weaker and weaker, I set off to find a doctor. I had not gone far when I found the remnants of a carrying party. I wrote on a piece of paper asking for a dressing station, and they asked for the direction the boys had advanced. They were carrying bombs and the boys wanted them, so, staggering away, I took them up through the barrage. Five parties I led back, but the last one never got there, for a shell came over, killed three of them, and broke my jaw in another two places, so, almost blinded with blood and falling at every three or four steps, I left the field.[41]

Unsurprisingly, McNess suffered from the most terrible wounds and had to have part of a rib used to reconstruct his jaw. His treatment and convalescence lasted 18 months. He later married one of the nurses who looked after him and started a shoe repair business with £400 gifted to him by a grateful local community in Leeds and his hometown of Bramley. He attempted to enlist again in during the Second World War but was turned down. Shortly after retiring to Bournemouth in 1956, he tragically committed suicide by cutting his throat. It would take the intervention of the Scots Guards before his war pension payments were reinstated two years after his suicide.[42]

The 1st Guards began their assault on the left at zero hour with 'the left of the 3/Coldstream having to wheel into its proper alignment'.[43] Critically, however, both Coldstream battalions suffered heavy casualties as they were caught by German machine gun fire from the junction of Pint Trench with the sunken portion of the Flers Road before they had reached just 100 yards. Major Vaughan, second in command of the 3/Coldstream, was killed as well as his adjutant. The infantry attempted to deal with this task without the tank that had been allocated to the task. Lieutenant Colonel J.V. Campbell realised that no progress could be made until the sunken road was cleared before enabling the attack on the left flank to be pressed home. He carried a hunting horn from his days with the Shropshire Harriers and, 'A few notes from the hunting horn which he carried were sufficient to restore the confidence of the leading waves and the attack went forward in one headlong and irresistible rush'.[44] Some German prisoners, four machine guns and a trench mortar were the reward for this courageous but vital action. In the confusion of battle, however, the two Coldstream battalions and the 1/Irish Guards (already mixing with the Coldstream) became further mixed up with a portion of the 1/Coldstream from the left of the 2nd Guards and a few from the 3/Grenadiers who had strayed from the extreme right of the divisional front. The 1st Guards Brigade found itself, therefore, being pushed in a northerly direction by this sequence of events, instead of its planned north-easterly direction. As they pressed on, an enemy shell hole was overrun, and the first objective was reached and stormed at about the same

41 Nicol, *Till the Trumpet Sounds*, vol.2, pp.39–40.
42 Oldfield, *Victoria Crosses on the Somme*, pp.427–428.
43 Miles, *Military Operations, 1916 Volume 2*, p.313.
44 Headlam, *History of the Guards Division*, p.154.

time as the 2nd Guards reached theirs. But unfortunately, the 1st Guards were now occupying a portion of the trench beyond the corps boundary whilst, to the right, the Germans still occupied Serpentine Trench at both sides where it joined Calf Alley.[45]

Lieutenant Colonel John Campbell VC.

This was a precarious moment in the battle. The various battalions were all crowded together, many officers had been lost and the respective battalion commanders led from the front. As if to emphasise this, when the men of the 1/Coldstream were being moved to the right, their CO, Lieutenant Colonel the Honourable G.V. Baring was killed. The three remaining battalion commanders held a brief conference (R.B.J. Crawford of the 2/Coldstream, R.C.A. McCalmont of the 1/Irish and Campbell). In the confusion and chaos, they were convinced that they must have reached the third objective but unfortunately, unknown to them, this was still 1,300 yards ahead of their present position. A pigeon message was sent back with their conclusion. But as the *Official History* states: 'The mistake is understandable, for no part of the objectives had been visible from the forming up positions of the brigade, and few landmarks could be distinguished in the shell-shattered landscape. Moreover, that part of the second objective assigned to the brigade faced almost due east, and did not coincide with any German trench.'[46] This example of three battalion commanders working together in extremis as men on the spot was enshrined, of course, in the *Field Service Regulations* of 1909 which encouraged them to use their initiative.[47] In trying to maintain command and control, difficult decisions were necessary in the most challenging of circumstances and mistakes were inevitable on occasions.

Unsurprisingly, for XIV Corps HQ command and control became a huge challenge especially with the lingering mist and heavy smoke resulting from the bombardment. Contact aeroplanes were sent up but could not report with any great certainty what

45 Miles, *Military Operations, 1916 Volume 2*, p.313.
46 Miles, *Military Operations, 1916 Volume 2*, pp.313–314.
47 Peter Hodgkinson, 'Infantry Battalion Command on the Somme 1 July–18 November 1916', in Spencer Jones (ed.), *At All Costs: The British Army on the Western Front 1916* (Warwick: Helion, 2018), pp.448–449.

progress was being made by the three assaulting divisions. So heavy was the German barrage that communications from the front lines were erratic at best and non-existent at the worst. A good example of the operational complexities facing Cavan at Corps HQ can be seen in an attack which was planned for 1:30 pm; the 6th Division's 16th and 71st Brigades were to attack the Quadrilateral from the north, west and south. Meanwhile, the 18th Brigade would be brought up from reserve to move through the area of the Guards Division and advance to Morval. The *Official History* explains that this:

> ... latter movement was decided upon owing to erroneous reports of the great progress made by the Guards – at one time they were said to be in Lesboeufs – and the whole operation was calculated to carry out the intention of the corps order, received by the 6th Division about noon, to pass the reserve brigade through the Guards area whilst the 56th Division 'cleared up the situation' on the other flank.[48]

However, air reports came in that provided Cavan with a more accurate idea of the situation up on the right front of the Guards where very few troops had penetrated from the first objective. He called off the attack immediately and so a disaster was averted.

The Guards Division continued to face stubborn German resistance as they continued their attack beyond their first objective. To the right, the 2nd Guards Brigade formed a defensive flank and was then immediately committed to taking control of the Triangle's trench system which was finally cleared by around noon. Further progress was now problematic with significantly depleted forces and the continuing check of the 6th Division to the right. However, a mixed party of around 100 men (Scots, Irish and Grenadiers) did succeed in pushing forward for around half a mile to reach a point in front of the third objective.[49]

Meanwhile the 2/Grenadier Guards (1st Guards Brigade) commanded by Lieutenant Colonel de Crespigny had entered the battlefield. They had been ordered to follow in the rear of the 2/Coldstream and fulfil a vital role in the attack:

> The 2nd Bn. Grenadier Guards will move in rear of the 2nd and 3rd Battalions Coldstream Guards. When the latter advance to the assault of the second objective the 2nd Bn. Grenadier Guards will occupy the first objective until the 1st Battalion Irish Guards have passed through them; they will then follow and support them in their attack on the fourth objective.[50]

The battalion emerged from the ruins of Ginchy where it had been under heavy artillery fire, with its right on the Ginchy–Lesboeufs Road. Unfortunately, there was

48 Miles, *Military Operations, 1916 Volume 2*, p.315.
49 Miles, *Military Operations, 1916 Volume 2*, p.316.
50 TNA: WO95/1213, 1 Guards Brigade HQ, 1 Guards Brigade Order No.73, 13 September 1916.

absolutely no sign of the 2/Coldstream. De Crespigny knew that his own men were in their correct positions and so decided to continue to follow his orders. He assumed that the Coldstream had carried their objective and were continuing to the 'brown line'. His task, therefore, was to occupy the captured position. As the battalion pushed on north-eastwards it came under heavy fire from the section of Serpentine Trench still occupied by the Germans. The Grenadiers lost heavily as they deployed from their artillery formation, but a bayonet charge secured a hold on the line which was successfully consolidated by bombing parties who were able to gain touch on the right with some of the 3/Grenadiers (2nd Guard Brigade) and had almost joined up with the Coldstream of the 1st Guards Brigade on the left. Thus, the gap had been filled in the divisional line and the first objective for the Guards Division had been secured.[51]

Harold Macmillan, now a captain, took part in the attack by the 2/Grenadiers and was wounded twice; indeed, he was very fortunate to survive. There is a detailed account of his experiences in his memoir. Whilst being led in artillery formation by de Crespigny 'in his usual smart but irregular dress', Macmillan recounted how he was hit by 'a piece of shell in the right knee, just below the knee cap … but managed to continue and did not feel much inconvenience until later'. The 'two Coldstream battalions were nowhere to be seen' because 'the whole of the leading attack had swerved to the left, and the Coldstream battalions were no longer in front of us. We were supposed to be in support of them but they had mysteriously disappeared.' As the battalion advanced to what they believed was their first objective which was expected to be 'in the hands of our friends', the 2/Grenadiers found that it was still occupied by the Germans. Without any artillery support, the battalion had no option other than to deploy and attack. The ensuing fighting proved to be heavy but the German line was taken. However, 'there was some tiresome machine-gun fire annoying us from a position on our left flank' and Macmillan together with small party went out to deal with it. Macmillan continued that:

> Unluckily, although the enemy gunners were successfully dealt with, I was shot at short range while half crawling, half-crouching. The machine-gun bullets penetrated my left thigh just above my pelvis. Quite unlike the far less dangerous wound in my hand which I had received at Loos and which was excruciatingly painful, this body blow knocked me out, but did not hurt. I rolled down into a large shell-hole, where I lay dazed, but not – at first – unconscious.

In effect, Macmillan was in no-man's land with the trench that his battalion had taken behind him and the next objective in front and no further advance was possible by his battalion 'partly owing to the failure of the attack of the 6th Division on our right, and partly because of the heavy casualties suffered by the two Coldstream battalions and ourselves'. With heavy fighting close by, Macmillan described how, 'I lay in my hole.

51 Miles, *Military Operations, 1916 Volume 2*, p.316, Headlam, *History of the Guards Division*, pp.155–156.

Even if I had known of a "better 'ole" I could not have gone to it. I had in my pocket Aeschylus's *Prometheus* in Greek. It was a play that I knew very well, and seemed not inappropriate to my position. So, as there seemed nothing better to do, and I could not move in any direction, I read it intermittently.' He reasoned that the only threat to his position might come from a 'short' shell despite the fact that 'shelling went on from both sides with tremendous uproar'. German soldiers came close in 'two or three' counter-attacks. When German soldiers 'ran round the lip of my shell-hole … I lay "doggo" and feigned to be dead.' Macmillan lay there for more than 12 hours. His 'chief worry was the fear that I had been hit in a vital place, for everything seemed numbed' and he had no water because his water bottle had been destroyed by machine-gun bullets. He lay there hoping that he would either be found if there was an advance or, if the battalion was able to consolidate its position, a party would come out to look for him.

Fortunately, Sergeant Norton went out with a search party under darkness and he was found and brought in. His right knee was 'stiff and unusable', and his thigh wound had knocked out his left leg too. Clearly very concerned, de Crespigny decided that MacMillan 'better be off' but that process proved to be equally hazardous. Two four-men stretcher parties got him and another wounded officer as far as Ginchy only to find that the dressing-station there had been abandoned because of a heavy bombardment. Believing there was too much danger to the lives of the stretcher-bearers, Macmillan and his colleague sent them back. In the ensuing chaos and confusion, the two men became separated. Macmillan managed to stumble out of the village fearing for his life before rolling into a ditch and was very fortunate to be picked up by the transport of a battalion of the Sherwood Foresters. 'Whether it was that day or the next, I am not sure.' Macmillan's war was now, not unsurprisingly, over. A series of operations followed, and his hip took several years to heal. For the rest of his life, he walked with a slight shuffle and a suffered from a limp grip in his right hand from his hand wound at Loos.[52]

Harry Crookshank was also a casualty. A somewhat reluctant Lewis gun officer in the same No.3 Company of the 2/Grenadiers as Macmillan, his own war diary records that he was just about to push forward at around 7:00 a.m. when a shell burst a few yards in front of him. 'I felt a great knock in the stomach and saw a stream of blood and gently subsided into a shell hole.' Unfortunately, this particular shell hole was not deep enough to provide sufficient cover and if another shell was to land nearby then he would probably not have survived. Fortunately, his orderly and a wounded corporal were able to move him to a better hole where there were 'rather fewer shells dropping'.[53] Here he was able to dose himself with morphine and after an hour's wait the stretcher-bearers arrived. 'Crookshank was conscious but mutilated: the shell had castrated him.'[54]

The troops of the 1st Guards Brigade, now reorganised, were in the first objective further along to the north-west. Lieutenant Colonel J.V. Campbell of the 3/Coldstream

52 Macmillan, *Winds of Change*, pp.87–90.
53 Crookshank's War Diary quoted in Ball, *The Guardsmen*, p.60.
54 Ball, *The Guardsmen*, p.60.

was determined to seize the moment and make a further advance. The men of the 2/Coldstream and 3/Coldstream soon encountered a heavy German barrage but they pushed on to the sound of Campbell's hunting horn. Campbell led his men through a small opening in the wire and he was one of the first to enter the German trench. Fighting their way forward, they captured part of the 'brown line' by 11:15 a.m. although the exact point that they had captured was outside the corps boundary.

Oliver Lyttelton found himself right at the centre of this action. He recounts how, in the confusion and mingling of units, he came across Captain Mylne of the 2/Irish Guards, a 'most gallant fellow'. Lyttelton was caught up the sheer exhilaration of the attack's momentum: 'We all fairly had our tails up and the men simply itching to go on.' Mylne urged the need for reorganisation but whilst Lyttelton agreed with the basic principle, he wanted to 'push on beyond this German line and make a line in the open.' Then on hearing the sound of Campbell's hunting horn, Lyttelton realised that Campbell was shouting for him to return to receive orders.

> 'This is great fun I must say' was all the report I could give. 'Fun be damned,' he said. 'We have taken everything in sight but, you blasted idiot, if you go on you will be in our own barrage. Don't you know this is the second objective? Dig! Where's my map? Where's my adjutant? Damn, he's been killed. Sharpe, where are those pigeons?' 'Here they are, Sir'. 'Oliver give me your map.' I expressed the opinion that it was the first objective, owing to the contours. He and Longueville laughed at this and wagged their fingers at Ginchy, which did certainly look the hell of a way off. Anyway a pigeon message was sent off by J.C. to say that he had reached the second objective.[55]

Lyttelton dug in as ordered but it soon became apparent that 'we were not in touch with anyone on our right and the Germans had a trench running at right angles to the one we were in and on slightly higher ground'. The German force there numbered approximately 40 men and it was ideally placed to pour enfilade machine gun fire into the Guardsmen. After an initial attempt to take the German position failed despite the covering fire provided by three Lewis guns, Campbell ordered Lyttelton 'to bomb the Hun out'.

> This was not easy to organise as we have very few bombs. However, with the aid of Mylne I slowly got something like a party together and after receiving an order from Rocke to start bombing at 11.20 a.m. all was ready. We proposed to cover our bombing party with a few rifle grenades. Meanwhile our situation in the trench was becoming most precarious. A lot of men had been knocked out – nearly all shot through the head – and in addition to this enfilade rifle fire we were also getting shelled from both flanks by field artillery. [56]

55 Lyttelton, *From Peace to War*, p.167. D.F. Longueville later Lt. Col. Coldstream Guards.
56 Lyttelton, *From Peace to War*, p.168. Afterwards Lt. Col. C.E.A.S. Rocke DSO.

Despite such unfavourable circumstances, the attack was a success and Lyttelton found himself in what appeared to be a redoubt or headquarters. The situation had suddenly changed for the better:

> The contrast to our previous situation was extraordinary. All resistance seemed to have snapped. We had just been getting it in the neck and had been looking back on a sea of desolation. Now we were complete masters of the position and were looking forward towards as perfect a bit of 'partridge country' as you could wish to see. Germans were retreating towards Bapaume and field guns were withdrawing from the neighbourhood of Flers. Here I met up with Luss of the bloody club and Hugh Ross wounded over the eye and seeming weak and shaken. We all looked at the map and decided to push on towards Lesboeufs.[57]

The combined strength of these patrols was around 120 men, and they moved forwards for about another 600 to 800 yards before it was decided to call a halt 'although we deemed it likely that we could actually get into Lesboeufs, so demoralised did the enemy appear to be'. But this force was clearly small in numbers and its flanks were exposed. Moreover, there was only a relatively small field of fire to the front, the standing crops were an obstacle and 'the scratch nature of the party', whilst it had done remarkably well to get to this position, was inadequate to press on any further.[58] Lyttelton noted that the time was about 1:00 p.m. Runners were then dispatched to brigade headquarters asking for further orders. Whilst waiting for a response 'we got rather sniped from the standing crops in front and had to watch how we moved about.' Mylne was badly wounded. With commanding views from their position, he was able to observe German troop movements. 'At about 5 p.m. we had the chagrin of seeing a whole battalion debouch from Bapaume and slowly make their way across the intervening ground towards our left flank.' Now very concerned, Lyttelton observed that: 'We had been promised support but it was clear to us that if it was not soon forthcoming, we should be enveloped.'[59]

We have already seen that Brigadier Ponsonby and his staff at 2nd Guards Brigade HQ had felt that an injection of reinforcements could have made a significant impact during the afternoon. Indeed, he had formally asked for the reserve to be committed but, as Kipling put it: 'As they were utterly detached from an already detached force, they might as well have indented for elephants.'[60] Feilding believed that that any further advance with the reserve (3rd Guards Brigade) would be too risky after receiving information from aerial observers that the Guards had not got so far as previous reports had suggested. Between them, the two assaulting brigades had lost approximately

57 Lyttelton, *From Peace to War*, pp.168–169. Luss/Sir Iain Colquhoun had fought some Germans with a club. Captain Hugh Ross Scots Guards.
58 Lyttelton, *From Peace to War*, pp.168–169.
59 Lyttelton, *From Peace to War*, pp.168–169.
60 Kipling, *The Irish Guards in the Great War: The Second Battalion*, p.96.

three-quarters of their officers and two thirds of their ranks. Finally, the 6th Division had not made progress and any forward thrust by the Guards might have left them dangerously exposed to a German counter-attack. However, some reinforcements were sent to certain positions: the 4/Grenadiers to strengthen the right flank of 2nd Guards Brigade and the 2/Scots to reinforce the 1st Guards Brigade.[61]

Unfortunately, Lyttelton's worst fears were confirmed:

> About 7 p.m., after we had had several casualties by bullets from the rear a strong party, 200-500 men, jumped up from the front and made for us with the bayonet. We were thus completely surrounded and had to retire, endeavouring to delay the enemy by fire from our refused flanks. However, the Hun was so close on top of us being considerably hidden by the standing crops that I personally shared a trench with them for a moment and was obliged to throw my empty revolver at a gentleman who evidently wished me dead. Fortunately he thought it was a Mills bomb and ducked, which allowed me to scramble up the parados and get away. The Huns lost their heads and instead of sitting down and shooting us, came on after us firing from the shoulder with an occasional man kneeling. Consequently we regained the main position with astonishingly light losses.[62]

Kipling commented that this German attack, 'should have killed or captured everyone in the position'. However, 'probably due to our controlled rapid fire-they failed. Our men fought their way out and back to the main body with surprisingly few casualties; and the enemy excitedly following them, came under a limited but well directed machine-gun fire from the main trench.'[63]

The Failure of the Tanks

During these critical hours, the tanks had failed to support the Guards effectively, and in the various Guards' after-battle reports, it is clear that they were considered a significant hindrance rather than an asset. The three tanks of No. 1 Column, in support of 2nd Guards Brigade, set off from their starting point on time but soon ran into problems. Their target was to the south-eastern corner of the Triangle but unlike other groups, No. 1 Column's tanks were not authorised to follow a specific track or trench. Instead, the skippers were ordered to use their tank compasses to reach their objective despite their concerns which proved well grounded. Unsurprisingly the bearing of 42 degrees proved impossible to follow as their compasses proved to be totally unreliable as the

61 Headlam, *History of the Guards Division*, pp.158–159.
62 Lyttelton, *From Peace to War*, p.170.
63 Kipling, *The Irish Guards in the Great War: The Second Battalion*, p.96.

tanks moved erratically over a cratered landscape. To make matters worse, the skippers had few landmarks to guide them.[64]

Setting off in a thick mist at 5:40 a.m., 40 minutes before zero, the No. 1 Column was led by male tank 741 commanded by Tull but their progress was immediately compromised when 741's steering wheels were damaged. Tull turned back towards the start point as did Clarke in *Campania* who elected to follow 741 before Hiscocks ensured that *Campania* and *Casa* drove in a north-easterly direction towards their original objective at the Triangle. In the general confusion, it is not known when they actually reached the German front line. *Campania* then 'turned north along Serpentine Trench where her crew engaged a number of machine-guns, firing 60 rounds of 6-pounder ammunition. Clarke claimed that he knocked out six machine guns. He waited until the Guards arrived and consolidated their position … Clarke, who was concerned about the lack of fuel even though he had not completed his mission.'[65]

Caisa reached the Triangle (its first objective) although Smith was unable to identify exactly where he had gone when he returned. There is some evidence that *Caisa* breached the German wire and front line at High Road trench and then worked its way eastwards into the 6th Division's area. Smith became concerned about his tank's engine bearings and he was faced with the decision to push onto the Blue Line (the third objective), wait until the infantry appeared or withdraw. He decided upon the latter and reached 1st Guards Brigade HQ some time after 9:00 a.m. Meanwhile Tull's tank returned with a damaged running gear and little petrol remaining.[66]

Because of the failures in No. 2 Column, 1st Guards Brigade had no tank support on their right flank. Ambrose in K tank of the No. 3 column failed early on because of engine and steering problems, probably only moving around 300 yards. The other two tanks in No.3 column skippered by Elliot and Bates started at 5:30 a.m., on time, and moved on the left flank of the brigade without attracting any German fire, possibly because they held their fire – not wishing to compromise their positions and encourage a direct attack. L tank or *Clan Cameron* failed to make any impact. It reached its first objective but got no further, conflicted perhaps by that it had been given four sets of orders! Certainly, it did not engage the machine guns along Pint Trench and the Germans did not engage it, again possibly to avoid giving away their position. It managed to get back to HQ 1st Guards Brigade at 9:04 a.m. with one tank track needing to be replaced.

The two male tanks in No. 3 Column (Bates in No. 714 and Elliot in *Centurion*) in support of 1st Guards Brigade on the left flank appeared to have moved along the road to Flers in line ahead. As they moved alongside Pint Trench, they did not engage any of the machine gun posts. In the poor light and misty conditions, it is perfectly likely they did not see the posts and/or the Germans chose not to give themselves away by engaging the tanks. Unfortunately, they appear to have made little, if any contribution to the brigade's

64 Pope, *Tanks Corps in the Great War*, pp.158–159.
65 Pope, *Tanks Corps in the Great War*, p.160.
66 Pope, *Tanks Corps in the Great War*, pp.160–161.

attack and ultimately drifted into 14th Division's area with Bates ditching just north of the Brown Line.[67] As Stephen Pope concluded: 'Regrettably, none of the ten tanks supporting the Guards Division could be considered as being effective as, although four did reach their initial objectives, the Bavarian machine-gunners were not deterred from firing on the enemy.'[68] Despite much thought beforehand and their incorporation into a final plan that exposed the advancing troops to increased risks, they had no real impact on the day. Rushed into service in such an important attack before their reliability had been established to work alongside troops who were totally unprepared in how best to fight alongside them and may not even have seen one before, was always likely to end in disappointment. Nonetheless the remarkable bravery of these pioneering tank crews and their skippers can be in no doubt.

A Day of Failure?

This had been an intense day of combat under the most trying of circumstances. The 2/Irish Guards alone had suffered 300 casualties in the ranks together with eight officers. The Coldstream had begun the day with 17 officers and 690 other ranks. They ended the day with just three officers (one was wounded) and 221 other ranks. The Grenadiers lost 17 officers either killed or wounded who entered the battle and suffered 395 casualties in the ranks.[69] Prior and Wilson looked at the casualty figures for nine of the assaulting divisions on 15 September and estimated that the Guards' losses of approximately 4,000 were the third heaviest and not far behind the 14th and 56th Divisions.[70]

Headlam argued that a great opportunity had been lost:

> The attack by the Guards Division on the 15th of September will rank for all time as a splendid military achievement, and, if it failed to obtain a full measure of success, the failure was due to causes over which the attacking troops themselves had no control. There is little doubt that, had the divisions on the flanks of the Guards been able to carry out their share in the advance, the 1st and 2nd Guards Bdes. would have reached their final objectives.[71]

Elements of the Guards had managed to push the German defenders well beyond the first objective before withdrawing, and along the whole of XIV Corps' front the Guards Division had been the only division to capture their first objective. As Prior and Wilson put it, this was 'quite a feat in the circumstances'.[72] The Guards' final position towards

67 Pope, *Tanks Corps in the Great War*, p.161.
68 Pope, *Tanks Corps in the Great War*, p.163.
69 Headlam, *History of the Guards Division*, p.153, footnotes.
70 Prior and Wilson, *Command on the Western Front*, p.243.
71 Headlam, *History of the Guards Division*, p.160.
72 Prior and Wilson, *The Somme*, p.233.

the end of the day's fighting, however, was far from ideal. Essentially, the two Guards brigades had established an less than ideal exposed line, in effect a small salient, which 'ran from a point on the Ginchy–Lesboeufs road a little to the north of the "Triangle" in a north-westerly direction to a point approx. 300 yards from the Ginchy–Gueudecourt road about three quarters of a mile north of Ginchy'.[73] To describe the attack as a 'splendid military achievement' was clearly inaccurate. The action on 15 September can best be regarded as a heroic failure despite the remarkable bravery and impressive leadership that had been displayed. Headlam's implied criticism of the battlefield performance of the neighbouring divisions would have reflected how the Guards saw things at the time and could be seen as an attempt to deflect responsibility away from themselves. It also illustrates the expectations put on the Guards as an elite formation. As we have seen, the 6th Division had been placed in an impossible position by artillery failures. At Loos, the Guards found that their own ambitions were checked by circumstances that were beyond their control, and this applied to Flers-Courcelette as well.

For Rawlinson, it was too easy to focus on XIV Corps as the culprits for the failure of 15 September describing it as being rather 'sticky': 'I have been rather disappointed at the push and drive of XIV Corps – I don't think Cavan has the initiative and go of [General Congreve] … but I must not complain for all have done their best'.[74] Peter Hodgkinson has argued responsibility for the failure on the day was actually much broader. Inadequate and inflexible planning blighted the 6th Division's attack and these factors, of course, applied to the Guards Division as well:

> The chain of command that operationalised Sir Douglas Haig's orders for the 15th, through Fourth Army and XIV Corps, allowed no wriggle room to take into account local tactical situations such as that which faced 6th Division. Fourth Army HQ had no understanding of the nature of the problem that the Quadrilateral would present. Indeed, they perhaps did not know it existed – it was too small in their scheme of things. Even at corps level it was simply too late to fine tune the motion of the juggernaut on 15 September.[75]

For individual Guardsmen, 15 September was inevitably a day of 'winners' and 'losers'. As Simon Ball has remarked: 'If it possible to talk of a day changing men's lives then 15 September 1916 was that day for Lyttelton, Macmillan and Crookshank. As night fell, Macmillan and Crookshank were cripples, Lyttelton was a hero.'[76] For Oliver Lyttelton, 'The 15th was the most wonderful day of my life. I drank every emotion to the dregs and I was drunk. It was superbly exhilarating.' Admitting that 'the show was not a complete success' because of the failure of the division to the right. Nonetheless 'we forced our

73 Headlam, *History of the Guards Division*, pp.161–162.
74 Quoted in Senior, *Cavan*, p.143.
75 Hodgkinson, *A Complete Orchestra of War*, p.168.
76 Ball, *The Guardsmen*, p.63.

way across 1,200 yards of ground and captured two trench systems and 500 prisoners'. Despite the heavy casualties that were suffered, 'that day we had a joy in battle and felt the passions of hate and fear and grief and anger and pain and fatigue – it can be a passion to wish to sleep – and gratitude and prayer and peace'.[77]

Conversely, for the Asquith family, 15 September was a day of tragedy. Almost as soon as the attack commenced, whilst leading the first half of No. 4 Company, Raymond took a bullet in his chest. Determined that his men should not be distracted, he lit a cigarette before being given morphine. He died before his stretcher bearers could reach the dressing station on the Montauban to Guillemont Road. His servant, Needham was present at his burial nearby and wrote to his wife later that 'such coolness under shell fire as Mr. Asquith displayed would be hard to equal'.[78] Cynthia Asquith recorded in her diary on 19 September: 'Heartbreaking day. Came downstairs in high spirits, opened newspaper, and saw in large print: LIEUTENANT ASQUITH KILLED IN ACTION. Darling, brilliant, magically charming Raymond – how much delight and laughter goes with him! It seems to take away one's last remains of courage. One might have known that nothing so brilliant and precious could escape'.[79] Brigadier Ponsonby wrote to Raymond's wife expressing his condolences.

> What I think struck most of us out here was the extreme modesty and the really entire unselfishness in the way he never thought of himself … I know he was one of the officers who really did work night all night and most of the day … He was always in such good spirits and saw the funny side of everything even when things got rather hot … Most of his friends in his battalion and the Brigade have now gone – either killed or wounded or sick but those of us who are left will always remember his charming personality and his very gallant conduct under fire.

In fact, 17 of the 22 officers of his battalion who went into action on 15 September were either killed or wounded.[80]

Unsurprisingly Campbell was awarded the VC for his remarkable bravery and leadership and the popular press were quick to call him 'The Tally-Ho VC'. His citation read:

> For most conspicuous bravery and able leading in an attack. Seeing that the first two waves of his battalion had been decimated by machine gun and rifle fire he took personal command of the third line, rallied his men with the utmost gallantry, and led them against the enemy machine guns, capturing the guns and killing the personnel. Later in the day, after consultation with unit commanders, he again rallied the survivors of his battalion, and at a critical moment led them through a

77 Lyttelton, *From Peace to War*, p.163.
78 Quoted in Asquith, *Life and Letters*, p.296.
79 Cynthia Asquith, *The Diaries of Lady Cynthia Asquith, 1915–18* (London: Century Hutchinson, 1968), p.217.
80 Asquith letters, *Life and letters*, pp.296–297.

> very heavy hostile fire barrage against the objective. He was one of the first to enter the enemy trench. His personal gallantry and initiative at a very critical moment turned the fortunes of the day and enabled the division to press on and capture objectives of the highest tactical importance.[81]

Pereira was later to write to his wife on 22 October that:

> We received an unofficial telephone message last night that John Campbell had been given the V.C. I feel as pleased as if I had won it myself. It is a great day for the Brigade and the Coldstream. It was most historically magnificent, and it was won under the most striking circumstances and there will always be a great glamour about it. The famous horn I am taking home as I insist on its being hung up in the Regimental H.Q. and when I go home I will order a replica for John with a suitable inscription as a small memento from his brigadier of the great event and the great day.[82]

Exactly 100 years later, on 15 September 2016, a member of the Coldstream Band played his original horn as a special memorial outside the Ministry of Defence in Westminster was unveiled in his memory.

16 September: Anti-climax

Planning now began to continue with the attack on the following day, 16 September. At 7:00 p.m. a preliminary order was received by Brigadier General Corkran by telephone for the 3rd Guards Brigade to attack the 'trench in front of LES BOEUFS at 9.30 a.m. tomorrow.' At 10.30 p.m. Guards Division Order No. 78 was received: 'The Brigade together with the 61st Brigade on the right and the 14th Division on the left is ordered to capture first the line south of GUEUDECOURT to west of LES BOEUFS, secondly GUEUDECOURT and LES BOEUFS and a line joining the two villages.'[83] There would be no troops attacking on the right of the 61st who had been put under Feilding's command from the 20th Division. In effect, the first objective was the third objective of the previous day, the 'blue line', and the second, the fourth objective of the previous day, the 'red line'. The troops of 61st Infantry Brigade would leave Trones Wood at midnight with the details of the guides and routes to be decided (at what was a very late stage) between the 61st Infantry Brigade and the 2nd Guards Brigade. The 3rd Guards Brigade were to advance from approximately the line held by the 1st Guards. Artillery cover would

81 Gliddon, Gerald, *VCs of the First World War: The Somme 1916* (Stroud: Alan Sutton 1995), pp.144–145.
82 Pereira, *Catholic General*, p.214.
83 TNA: WO95/1221, 3 Guards Brigade HQ, Order No.78, 15 September.

be provided with the standing barrages on the first and second objectives lifting back as the creeping barrages reached them. The troops of the 1st and 2nd Guards Brigades in the 'green line' were to be in divisional reserve and they would not move forward with the attack but would not be withdrawn that night. Zero was fixed for 9:25 a.m.[84]

Corkran reported to Feilding at midnight that conditions were highly unfavourable for the attack. 'The front line was packed with men of many units, there was 'nowhere to form', and he predicted failure'. Also, these troops were not fresh: 'Of the 3rd Guards Brigade, the 1/Grenadiers had been used for carrying parties; the 4/Grenadiers had supported the right attack, becoming involved in the fight; and the 2/Scots Guards, had suffered in supporting the left, losing its commander and second-in-command. The only unit of the brigade which was comparatively fresh was the Welsh Guards'.[85]

Unsurprisingly, with so little time to finalise arrangements, orders got delayed. For example, Operation Order No. 61, the final orders for the attack were issued at midnight but failed to reach some battalions until about 1:00 a.m. on the 16th. The 3rd Brigade war diary continues that 'at 2.30 a.m. O.C. 1st Bn. Welsh Guards reported that he had just received his patrol reports to the effect that his forming up area for the attack was already over-crowded with troops of the 1st and 2nd Guards Brigades and that he was doubtful if it would be possible to find an assembly position from which the attack could be launched as soon as 9:25 a.m.'[86]

At XIV Corps HQ Cavan, aware that the Guards' attack had to go ahead because it formed an integral part of an offensive along the Fourth Army front, became increasingly alarmed by the way things were developing. Corkran duly ordered the 1/Grenadiers (on the right) and 1/Welsh (on the left) to pass through the front held by the 1st Guards Brigade and to carry out the attack. The 4/Grenadiers were to follow in support while the 2/Scots would remain in reserve attached to 1st Guards Brigade. However, the target for zero at 9.25 a.m. slipped later and later and the actual assault finally did not get underway until 1.00 p.m. It had been a pouring wet night, the ground to the east of Ginchy was very challenging and 'much confusion ensued owing to the congestion caused by all 3 Brigades being in a very small area'. Several battalion war diaries described the chaotic situation that prevailed. For example, the war diary of the 1/Grenadier Guards records:

> At 3 a.m. the battalion moved up to be in readiness for an attack at 9.30 a.m. but our guides got lost, and, after three hours' wandering, the battalion returned to its old position when the order came at 9 a.m. to go up again so as to get in with the attack at 9.25 a.m. We arrived at a position just behind the starting point at 11.15 a.m.[87]

84 TNA: WO95/1221, 3 Guards Brigade HQ, Order No.78, 15 September, Headlam, *History of the Guards Division*, p.162.
85 Miles, *Military Operations, 1916 Volume 2*, pp.345–346.
86 TNA: WO95/1221, 3 Guards Brigade HQ War Diary, Dummy Trench, 15 September 1916. The actual entry was undoubtedly written on the following day.
87 Headlam, *History of the Guards Division,* p.168 footnote.

The experience of the Welsh Guards was not untypical of those in the 3rd Guards Brigade: 'Being warned that he would have to attack the next morning, Lieutenant Colonel Thriepland moved the battalion slightly nearer to Ginchy, and in the evening sent forward to find out if there was any forming-up ground with cover. Every trench, however, was occupied.' When orders arrived at 1:00 p.m. mounting any attack was challenging in the extreme with 'local conditions ... so bad they could not be surmounted so easily. Orders arrived in pulp, a solid sheet of rain fell all night, and communication was fearful'. With all available trenches already occupied, 'rather than have daylight find the battalion in this unenviable position, the Commanding Officer, having tramped about vainly in all directions seeking non-existing trenches, ordered the companies back to Ginchy'. This was only a temporary reprieve however as 3rd Brigade HQ confirmed the previous orders to attack.[88] The 3rd Brigade war diary concluded that: 'It is probable that the assault would never have been delivered at all but for the determination of all ranks to push forward and the able leading of Company and platoon commanders'.[89]

By 1:00 p.m, the 61st Infantry Brigade on the right had already reached its first objective and was consolidating but the 14th Division on the left by comparison was progressing slowly. Certainly, any element of surprise that there might have been in the Guards attack was now lost and when the attack did eventually get underway, the war diary of the 1/Grenadier Guards states that the 'Brigade, 1st Batt. on right, Welsh Guards on left and 4th Batt. in support, advanced to attack LESBOEUFS without artillery or other support'.[90] Headlam concluded that this was a clear inference that, whereas the 61st Infantry Brigade's attack had received artillery support the delayed Guards attack clearly had not. In effect 'a small infantry attack over heavy country unsupported by artillery had little or no chance of success'.[91] This was definitely the experience of the Welsh Guards who found that, 'the engagement was a repetition of the day before ... The advance had to be made in sectional rushes, and the assaulting troops got into standing crops, where they lost direction, and mistaking Gueudecourt for Lesboeufs, swung round to the left'.[92]

Regrettably, the 14th Division failed to clear the left flank of the 3rd Guards Brigade. The 1/Grenadiers succeeded in advancing to the high ground west of Lesboeufs but under heavy machine gun fire, was ordered to consolidate its position. On the left the 1/Welsh reached a line south of the Flers–Lesboeufs Road where it was ordered to dig in. Reinforcements were then sent forward: the 4/Grenadiers strengthened the right flank of the 3rd Guards Brigade front while the 3/Coldstream linked up the line of the 1/Grenadier Guards with that of the Welsh Guards. Because of the heavy casualties

88 Ward, *History of the Welsh Guards*, p.122.
89 TNA: WO95/1221, 3 Guards Brigade HQ War Diary, Guillemont Station, 16 September 1916. Brigade WD.
90 TNA: WO95/1223, 1/Grenadiers WD; Headlam, *History of the Guards Division*, p.164.
91 Headlam, *History of the Guards Division*, p.164.
92 Ward, *History of the Welsh Guards*, p.122.

suffered, Cavan stood the Guards down on the night of 16/17 September. The 1st Guards Brigade moved to Fricourt, the 2nd and 3rd Guards to Carnoy.[93]

The Guards Division was to perform much more effectively in the second stage of these operations; the Battle of Morval and this success was built on the patchy record of 15 and 16 September 1916. For this attack, the three tanks designated to support the Guards were held in reserve but remained unused.

It is worth noting at this point that, finally, the Quadrilateral fell on 18 August after another assault by the 6th Division. This achievement 'was undoubtedly down to the carefully observed, and hence successful, bombardment of the Quadrilateral for nine hours on the previous day. The wire had now effectively been destroyed, and many of the defenders annihilated. Proper preparation was the key.'[94]

93 Headlam, *History of the Guards Division*, pp.164–166.
94 Hodgkinson, *A Complete Orchestra of War*, pp. 149–150.

7

The Somme: Morval, 25 September 1916

The Battle of Morval was carried out by 10 divisions. Five (the 23rd, 1st, 55th, 21st, and 5th) were fresh having seen no action on 15 September. The main focus was on capturing Gueudecourt, Lesboeufs and Morval which was the responsibility of XIV and XV Corps. A particular feature of this battle was to be the more concentrated artillery fire of approximately 400 pounds of shell for every yard of trench that was attacked which amounted to a 40 per cent increase in intensity over 15 September.[1] However, for Prior and Wilson, the 'experience of the much-tried Guards Division would demonstrate that many things could go wrong even in a successful attack, and that the experience of battalions in the same attack could be quite different.'[2]

On 19 September, Feilding held a conference at 2nd Guards Brigade HQ at which he confirmed that the division would once again be required to mount an attack just days after the brutal encounter of 15/16 September. Feilding stated that:

> It is realised by all the higher authorities that it is a heavy call, but the Commander-in-Chief once more calls upon the Corps to attack the enemy in conjunction with the French on our right. Although we have had a severe time, the XV Corps on our left have had a more severe time and the 5th Division has had already very heavy fighting in this area since the battle of the Somme began.

However, the audience was reminded that, 'This Division is still the strongest in the Corps'. Headlam argued that new recruits were 'trained men imbued by their instructors with the methods, the tradition and the moral of the Brigade of Guards, fit and ready to take their places in the line.'[3]

Some of his men may, however, have had doubts about Feilding's claim and would certainly have challenged Headlam's conclusion. Lieutenant G.P.A. Fildes of the 2/ Coldstream Guards wrote that news of another attack seemed 'incredible'. He continued

1 Prior and Wilson, *The Somme*, p.244.
2 Prior and Wilson, *The Somme*, p.245.
3 Headlam, *History of the Guards Division*, p.165.

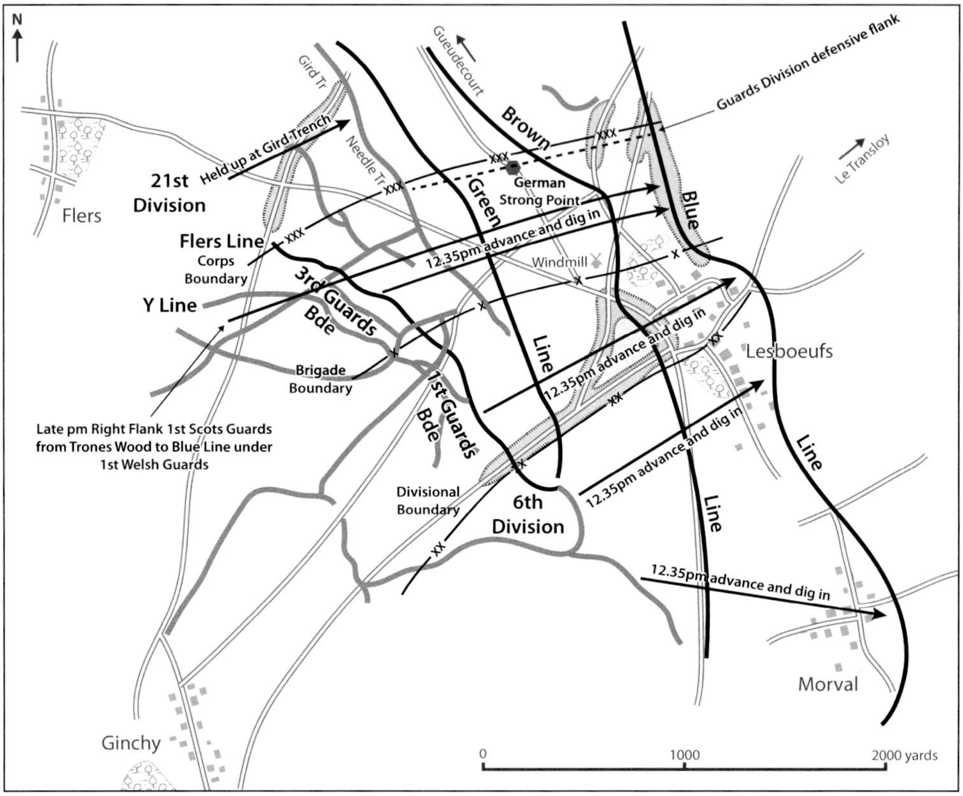

The Battle of the Somme, the capture of Lesboeufs, 25 September 1916.

that, 'the *cadres* of the units composing the division still existed, but there remained now only a third of those effectives which had travelled southwards so joyfully a few weeks before. True, we had just received reinforcements, but these were not either in quality or quantity all that we could have wished for in the circumstances.' The 2/Coldstream had received a draft from the Entrenching Battalion which had been camped nearby. Together with other reinforcements, the 2/Coldstream could now muster around 500 men. Yet 'it would be vain to try and assure ourselves that we were equal to our usual standard; we were not, and no account of self-delusion could alter that fact.' Gloomily, he continued that half of these men 'had never heard the whine of a bullet; many of our NCOs had only received their stripes within a day or so and had no experience of leadership whatever.' The same situation applied 'to almost all the Captains, while practically none of our junior officers had undergone their baptism of fire.'[4] For Fildes the reputa-

4 G.P.A. Fildes, *Iron Times with the Guards* (Uckfield: Naval &Military Press, 2016 [1918]). pp.271–272.

tion of the regiment itself was at stake. Interestingly, Pereira's wife wrote to her husband with similar worries to say that she was 'dumbfounded' to hear that he was 'going in for your second helping'. She continued that 'I was most perturbed as I thought of you with hastily reformed battalions as there was practically nothing left of the old ones.'[5]

Any similar doubts that Feilding may have had privately were not allowed, of course, to cloud his judgement as the meeting continued. Clearly, heavy German resistance was expected and discussions at the 19 September meeting reflected experiences learnt in the previous assault. For example, 'If the attack is held up on the whole or part of the front of the attack, Brigadiers should not order a fresh attack without calling on the Division to provide adequate artillery support' and the 'Maintenance of direction by subordinate commanders is of great importance'. The Guards were to take Lesboeufs, 'The danger is that if attacking troops rush straight through the village to the final objectives, enemy troops may issue from cellars and dugouts after our troops have passed.' However, it was agreed that 'arrangements would be made to have strong parties detailed to follow up the attacking line and clear the village in detail'.[6]

On the following day, 20 September, Feilding issued a brief memorandum to all of his brigadiers and the CRE in which he stressed the 'necessity of pushing on with the construction of assembly trenches for the attack. These trenches are of special importance owing to the probability that the attack will take place in the afternoon.' The distance that was to be covered in the attack was approximately 1,500 yards and there was 'the possibility of having to form a defensive flank if the attack to North or South of us were held up'. Strong reserves should be posted behind the starting off positions in case of a counter-attack from Lesboeufs. Also, all battalions entrusted with the launching of the attack should be well forward before zero. Specifically, the memorandum warned that. 'To attempt to bring up troops, after the attack has started … is not advisable. They may suffer heavy casualties on the way, and must be out of touch with operations at commencement of the attack.'[7]

At midday, 20 September, Operation Order No. 82 was issued. The Allied advance was to be directed across on the whole line between the Somme and Martinpuich. Specifically:

1. (a) The Fourth Army will renew the attack on Z day in combination with attacks by the French to the South and the Reserve Army to the North.
(b) The objectives of the Fourteenth Corps include Morval and Lesboeufs, and those of the Fifteenth Corps Gueudecourt.
(c) The attack of the Fourteenth Corps will be carried out by the Fifth Division on the right, the Sixth Division in the centre, and the Guards Division on the left. The Fifty-Sixth Division will form a defensive flank to the south of the Fifth Division. The Twenty-first Division will be attacking on our left.

5 Pereira: *Catholic General*, p.211.
6 TNA: WO95/1192, Guards Division HQ, Conference held at 2nd Guards Brigade HQ 19 September, Appendix 1099.
7 TNA: WO95/1213, 1 Guards Brigade HQ WD, G.D. No: 2288/G 20 September 1916.

2. The 1st Guards Brigade will attack on the right and the 3rd Guards Brigade on the left.
   The 2nd Guards Brigade (less one Battalion) will be in Divisional Reserve.
   1st Battalion 2nd Guards Brigade will be in Corps Reserve; 2nd Guards Brigade will notify Divisional Headquarters the name of the Battalion detailed.

3. Preliminary Bombardment. A steady bombardment of hostile positions will be commenced at 7 a.m. on Z day, and will be continued to 6.30 p.m.; it will recommence at 6.30 a.m. on Z day. The ground in front and rear of the German trenches Chapter which are being bombarded will be searched occasionally with 18-pdr. shrapnel and H.E. shell.
   There will be no intensive fire previous to the hour of zero. Night firing will be carried out nightly between the hours of 6.30 p.m. and 6.30 a.m.[8]

In effect this meant that the 56th Division would form the right flank guarding Combles, the 5th Division was expected to capture Morval, the 6th Division was to occupy the southern end of Lesboeufs, and the Guards Division to take Lesboeufs itself. Unfortunately, a period of bad weather then intervened resulting in the attack having to be postponed on two occasions until 25 September. However, during the night of 21/22 September, the 1st Guards Brigade passed the front to the south of the Ginchy–Lesboeufs road over to the 6th Division so each Guards Brigade was now in the line with a frontage of approximately 500 yards. The Guards were given three objectives represented as follows:

1. The 'green line' which was the first target running for about 1,500 yards in a northerly direction from a point about 500 yards west of Lesboeufs on the more southern of the two roads leading from Ginchy to Lesboeufs.
2. The 'brown line', the second target, ran from the cross roads south of Lesboeufs along the western outskirts of the village.
3. The 'blue line', the third and final target which incorporated Lesboeufs itself ran just east of Lesboeufs from the Lesboeufs–le Transoy road in a northerly direction along the Lesbooeufs–Gueudecourt road.[9]

The Guards' attack was to be entrusted to the 1st and 3rd Brigades. Great importance was given to creating and maintaining a momentum in the attack with troops being committed as needed. Artillery support would be critical to ensure success. To the right, 24th, 74th and 75th Brigades RFA under Lieutenant Colonel Bethell covered the front of

8 TNA: WO95/1192, Guards Division HQ, Guards Division Order No 82. App. 1118, 21 September 1916.
9 Headlam, *History of the Guards Division*, pp.167–168.

the 1st Guards Brigade whilst the 3rd Guards was to be covered by the 61st, 36th and 93rd Brigades under Lieutenant Colonel F.A. Buzzard. There would be a bombardment of the enemy's positions from 7:00 a.m. to 6:30 p.m. on the day before the attack. It would then recommence on Z day. To cover the attack itself, half of the artillery on the divisional front would fire standing barrages, while the remainder was to supply the creeping barrages as the advance was made. A standing barrage was to be placed on the 'green line' at zero and then lifted to the other two lines according to a timetable. The 'creeper' would be laid down 100 yards in front of the line occupied by the attacking troops at zero hour, and then was to be moved forward at a rate of 50 yards a minute until it reached a line 200 yards behind the 'green line' when it would be made stationary. The creeper would be resumed at zero plus one hour and at zero plus two hours in order to cover the advance of the infantry to their second and third objectives.[10] Three tanks were allotted to the Guards Division, assembling at Trones Wood by 5:00 p.m. on Y Day before proceeding forwards to await their orders from 1st Guards HQ.[11] However, they were not called on during the day itself. Bearing in mind the problems of integrating tanks into the attack on 15 September and the critical comments that were made in the after-battle reports, perhaps this is not surprising.

The 1st and 3rd Guards Brigades's front extended north-west to south-east crossing the Ginchy–Lesboeufs road. The 2/Grenadiers and the 1/Irish were on the left and right respectively. The 2/Coldstream and the 3/Coldstream were in support. The 3rd Guards Brigade was made up of the 4/Grenadiers on the left and the 2/Scots on the right who were in touch with the left of the 1st Guards. The 1/Grenadiers were in support and the 1/Welsh in reserve.

The orders of the two brigades differed. For the 1st Guards Brigade the leading battalions were to take all the objectives, and when they passed on, the battalions in support were to consolidate each line. In the 3rd Brigade, the two leading battalions were to take the first two objectives and then throw out a defensive flank; the battalions in support were then to advance through them and secure the third objective, one of these again throwing out a defensive flank.

Operation Order 82 also laid out the plans for when the objectives were reached and then consolidated:

> 9. (a) The task of the two leading Guards Brigades is to press the attack through to the Blue line. A sufficient flow of troops must be maintained by the 1st and 2nd Guards Brigades from zero onwards to ensure that the attack made from the Brown line is strong and well supported.
> (b) Special arrangements must be made to deal with resistance in Lesboeufs and thus prevent any possibility of the enemy getting round our troops who have gained the Blue line.

10 Headlam, *History of the Guards Division*, pp.168–169.
11 TNA: WO95/1192, Guards Division HQ, Instructions for Tanks, issues with Guards Divisional Order No. 82, 21 September 1916.

> (c) The 1st and 3rd Guards Brigades will garrison and consolidate the Brown line with a portion of their reserves when the attack goes forward to the Blue line.
> (d) On gaining the Blue line. Battalions will be sent forward to any ground from which observation can be gained ; such points will be consolidated and eventually joined up with our line.[12]

The weather on 25 September was much improved and the attacking troops benefitted from more favourable ground. Zero hour had been fixed for 12:35 p.m. The creeping barrage was put down effectively as the Guards battalions moved forwards in two waves 75 yards apart. Within one minute of the attack's launch, the German artillery response fell heavily both on the front of 1st Brigade and on the rear trenches but fortunately the leading waves advanced so quickly that they escaped it. They were close to the German lines by the time that barrage lifted. The Irish Guards soon took their objective but the 2/Grenadiers on the right had a torrid time. The battalion had moved up from Bernafay Wood to relieve the 2/Coldstream during the night of 24/25 September. Their commanding officer, de Crespigny, wrote vividly of his battalion's experiences:

> A good deal of shelling was going on during the relief but we only had a few casualties. The morning of Sept. 25th was a very bad one for us as the trenches were very narrow and the men shoulder to shoulder almost unable to sit down. It was quite impossible to lie down. At 12.35 our barrage opened, and we advanced in two waves of two Companies each. The Germans evidently knew that an attack was imminent as within one minute they began putting heavy shell into the waves and at the same time a terrific barrage was opened up on our front line … About 12.39 or 12.40 p.m. the first objective was gained with a certain amount of difficulty as our Artillery had entirely failed to cut a single strand of the wire'. In fact, the wire was not cut well anywhere but the section of unbroken wire facing the 2/Grenadiers was 'three lines deep which the artillery had not been able to observe. As soon as our barrage lifted the Germans lined the parapet and opened with rifle and machine gun fire … the co-operation of the Artillery was remarkable for its absence and a great deal of ammunition was uselessly expended on ground where no Germans were, and places where Germans could be seen were left untouched.[13]

The *Grenadier Guards History* recounts that this led to a remarkable act of bravery on the part of four officers:

12 TNA: WO95/1192, Guards Division HQ, Guards Division Order No 82, 21 September 1916.
13 TNA: WO95/1215, 1 Guards Brigade 2nd Battalion HQ. Narrative of Events 24–26 September. Written on 28 September 1916.

> There seemed no possibility of getting through it (the wire), with the Germans so close, and for the moment the whole advance of the Grenadiers was held up. Captain A. Cunninghame, Second Lieutenant G.A. Arbuthnot, Lieutenant W. Parnell, and Lieutenant Irvine at once ordered their men to lie down, and the four gallantly advancing by themselves proceeded with the utmost coolness to cut gaps in the wire. Their one thought seems to have been that the attack must not be checked on any account, and as the task of cutting the wire meant almost certain death, they never thought of sending on any of their men but decided to do it themselves.[14]

Only Irvine survived.

By about 1:15 p.m. the 'green line' had been secured by 1st Guards Brigade. Fortunately. the next two assaults at 1:35 p.m. on the west side of Lesboeufs and the second at 2:35 p.m. on the eastern side of the village were only lightly opposed. As planned, the 2/ and the 3/Coldstream began to move forward by the new communication trench dug the night before to the now vacant front and support lines and were in close support and touch with the leading battalions. The assault at 1:35 p.m. towards the second objective was supported by a 'creeper' and the position was secured in just 10 minutes. Remarkably, the 2/Grenadiers had only two company officers remaining as they mounted this assault, Lieutenant A. Lawson-Johnston and Second Lieutenant Layland-Barratts, so in effect, it was led by NCOs. German dug-outs in a sunken road to the right of the 2/Grenadiers were all searched, and a number of prisoners were taken. The 1st Brigade HQ responded: 'Prisoner you sent down states that the rest of his Company are in dug-outs or subterranean passages about 250 yards east of Lesboeufs and south of the sunken road. He appears to think they are anxious to surrender but gives no reasons. In thinking this he seems to be more talkative than reliable.'[15] However, the prisoner's claim was correct: 'By the time the search of these dug outs started, all their occupants had already run out, holding up their hands. During this second phase of the attack, the enemy appear to have offered little resistance, and many more were captured than killed.'[16] The 'blue line' was assaulted at 2:35 p.m. and by 3:30 p.m., the two leading battalions of 1st Guards had passed through Lesboeufs and were firmly established on the eastern outskirts of the village. Meanwhile the 2/Coldstream and the 3/Coldstream had followed successfully behind to consolidate the 'green' and 'brown lines' and were clearing Lesboeufs. Almost inevitably, however, there was a 'hitch' in the attack according to the *Grenadier Guards History*:

> Arrangements had been made for the artillery barrage to be put down 200 yards east of the final objective, but the position of the trench was marked differently on the artillery and infantry maps, and the shells fell short. This not only caused

14 Ponsonby, *Grenadier Guards History*, vol.2, p.80.
15 Ponsonby, *Grenadier Guards History*, vol.2, p.81.
16 Ponsonby, *Grenadier Guards History*, vol.2, p.82.

> a good many casualties amongst the men who were digging in, but also prevented the attacking force from pushing forward patrols and occupying the best ground for observation. A furious message was sent back by Captain Bailey: 'Our artillery are blowing us out. Please stop it at once,' but whether the messages miscarried or whether the maps were so inaccurate that the orders were not understood, the shelling continued for nearly two hours.[17]

In the attack by the 3rd Guards Brigade, the 2/Scots reached their first objective with few losses but the 4/Grenadiers came against a German trench which had escaped the British artillery. They took heavy casualties but were in possession of the first objective by 1:35 p.m. killing around 150 Germans in the process. Lord Henry Seymour said that: 'The Battalion did what they were told to do, and I don't think they could have done better. I know that there was not a single shirker in the lot. Our dead lay in front of the first German trench, but there were 100 to 150 German corpses there when I came up.'[18]

However, the left flank of 3rd Guards Brigade now found itself in an exposed position because the 64th Infantry Brigade had not reached Gird trench. It was necessary to react quickly and put down a defensive flank using the left flank company of the Grenadiers to ensure a smooth progression in the attack. The remainder of the company on the right of the line kept touch with the Scots Guards and advanced to the second objective gaining this with relative ease. At 2:35 p.m., after two companies of the 1/Welsh Guards had been sent forward to strengthen the left flank, the 1/Grenadiers passed smoothly through the leading battalions so that at approximately 3:30 p.m. the third objective was secure. Lesboeufs was now clear of Germans and the troops of 1st and 3rd Brigades were able to consolidate their new positions from the Lesboeufs – le Transloy road just north of the village of Lesboeufs to Windy trench. The Guards were now in touch with the 6th Division to the right but on the left flank there was a significant gap between the 3rd Guards Brigade and men from the 21st Division.[19]

Both Cavan and Feilding were concerned about the safety of this left flank and decided, wisely as it happened, not to carry on with the advance on the evening of the 25 September. Corkran had suggested the employment of cavalry to complete the rout of the apparently demoralised German forces. However, the light was fading and the failure to capture Gueudecourt meant that the front was too narrow for an effective cavalry manoeuvre and a local infantry advance would have been a risk. Early on the next day 64th Infantry Brigade, aided by a tank, captured Grid Trench. Between 300 and 400 Germans surrendered here. At 4:00 p.m., the 21st Division captured Gueudecourt to link up with the 3rd Guards Brigade midway between the village and Lesboeufs. The Germans were now visibly in retreat and were easy pray for the British artillery but

17 Ponsonby, *Grenadier Guards History*, vol.2, p.82. W.R. Bailey was the adjutant of the 2/ Grenadiers.

18 Headlam, *History of the Guards Division*, Letter to from Lord Henry Seymour to Sir Henry Streatfield, 27 September 1916, footnote, p.172.

19 Headlam, *History of the Guards Division*, pp.172–173.

enemy machine gun fire from a chain of posts on the high ground east of Lesboeufs northward to Le Transloy together with German artillery meant that the strengthening and deepening of the Guards' new defensive line was a more worthwhile activity. Reliefs began during the night of 26 September.[20]

With all of the objectives secured, congratulations flowed. For example, Lord Cavan sent the following message to Brigadier General Pereira: 'Hearty thanks and sincere congratulations to you all. A very fine achievement, splendidly executed.' To which Pereira replied: 'Your old Brigade very proud to be able to present you with Lesboeufs. All ranks most gratified by your kind congratulations.'[21] On 28 September, Pereira sent this message to his brigade:

> You have again maintained the high traditions of the 1st Guards Brigade when called upon a second time in the battle of the Somme. For five days previous to the assault the 2nd and 3rd Battalions Coldstream Guards held the trenches under constant heavy shell-fire and dug many hundred yards of assembly and communication trenches, this work being constantly interrupted by the enemy's artillery. The 2nd Battalion Grenadier Guards and 1st Battalion Irish Guards, though under shell-fire in their bivouacs, were kept clear of the trenches until the evening of 24th September, and were given the task of carrying by assault all the objectives to be carried by this Brigade. Nothing deterred them in this attack, not even the fact that in places the enemy wire was cut in the face of rifle and machine-gun fire, and in spite of all resistance and heavy losses the entire main enemy defensive line was captured.
>
> Every battalion in the Brigade carried out its task to the full.
>
> The German Reserve Division, which includes the 238th, 239th, and 240th Regiments, and which opposed you for many weeks at Ypres, left the salient on the 18th September. You have now met them in the open, a worthy foe, but you have filled their trenches with their dead and have driven them before you in headlong flight. I cannot say how proud I am to have had the honour of commanding the 1st Guards Brigade in this battle, a Brigade which has proved itself to be the finest in the British Army.[22]

Taking Stock: After the Battle Reports for the September Attacks

Feilding was able to draw on several 'after-battle' reports from 1st Guards Brigade in framing his final after-battle report to Cavan at XIV Corps HQ on 5 October. Taken together, they provide a comprehensive picture. Pereira's report from the brigade HQ confirmed the inadequacies of the initial jumping off point and the reasons for the loss of

20 Headlam, *History of the Guards Division*, pp.173–175.
21 Ponsonby, *Grenadier Guards History*, vol.2, pp.83–84.
22 Ponsonby, *Grenadier Guards History*, vol.2, pp. 85–86, Pereira, 28 September 1916.

momentum and direction on 15 September that have already been noted in the previous chapter. Unfortunately, casualties were increased because the tank designated to have passed over the northern end of the sunken lane had not materialised just before the attack. A gap of 100 yards in the barrage along the intended route of the tank meant that the barrage failed to deal with the point where German machine guns were known to be located. They were able to open fire immediately that the men left their trenches. Afterwards four machine guns were removed from this deadly position. Immediately to the north of the 1st Brigade's left flank there was a German salient that was meant to have been dealt with by a tank just before zero. The conditions for launching the attack could not have been more difficult and it would have been 'worth a small minor operation to ensure a straight run for the beginning of the assault and to make it possible to have a straight barrage in front, instead of the semi-circular barrage which had to be put down at the beginning of the attack on September 15'. Further comment was made about the artillery barrage on September 25. Referring to 'when the final objective is indefinite … the Artillery barrage must not be put down too close as thus suitable ground for the digging of trenches is denied to our troops. Also the question of the lifting of the barrage in order to allow patrols to go even further forward must be considered.' With regard to FOOs, it would be best if they were pushed forward to the newly won front line with a telephone wire to enable them to deal effectively at once with local circumstances. It was important that they could work with the artillery liaison officers as the battalion HQ moved forward. On both 15 September on and the 25th, it proved possible to lay and keep a wire going to battalion HQs as soon as they were established in a position. Whilst pigeons and runners proved themselves invaluable, visual communication was impractical because of the combination of shell fire, smoke and haze. Relay posts of runners proved to be very useful for providing guides to the front. With regard to machine guns, it was felt that they should only be sent forward from objective to objective with these teams choosing their own time and pace. Finally, the 1st Guards Brigade Report observed that when the final trench has been reached then it is best if all lines of trenches 'be thinned out and the garrison organised in depth in order to lessen the number of casualties. Commanding Officers must not be afraid of sending parties back to rear lines of defence'.[23]

The report of the 2/Grenadiers made some very specific and practical recommendations. There was a call for every NCO and man to be a trained bomber. Apparently, it was found that men would not throw bombs although they all knew how to; only those with appropriate badges 'came to the fore and took charge of the situation. It would also be beneficial if the NCOs and men understood German bombs. It was important that a Lewis gun should work with a bombing party. 'On Sept. 15th it was found that a Lewis Gun kept down enemy fire of covering party and also kept down the heads of the observers, while our observers were able to stand well up on the parapet and observe

23 TNA: WO95/1213, 1st Guards Brigade HQ, Lessons from the recent Attacks on Sept.15th and Sept., 25th by 1st Guards Brigade, 3 October 1916.

fire.' The men should understand that many German bombs have a very local effect' making 'a lot of noise but do very little damage'. With regard to close-artillery co-operation it was observed that: 'Many good chances were lost on 15th, 16th and 25th by the Artillery Observing Officer having no communication to their Batteries and apparently making no effort to do so'. On 25 September, the 'importance of keeping close to our own creeping barrage was again shown, also all waves should be got clear of our jumping off place as soon as possible. The Germans can and do drop their barrage within one minute of assaulting troops appearing. It is well worth risking packing troops into our own front line very tightly'. When an advancing, all ranks must understand that while certain men cut any uncut wire 'everyone else shoots at the enemy parapet and bombs it. This is bound to save many lives if everyone is prepared for it.' The report also suggested that the attack's objectives were communicated too late, the report stated: 'It makes all the difference if the objectives are made known two or three days beforehand, so that every man in the Battalion has a chance of knowing exactly what to do and where to make for.'[24]

The 2/Coldstream Guards also identified issues with the artillery barrage on 15 September. The attack had been held up by machine gun and rifle fire about 150 yards from the start so that the creeping barrage consequently advanced without the infantry. When the infantry were free to advance around 15 to 20 minutes later, there was no creeping barrage to offer them protection. Because there was no direct communication with the artillery, this could not be avoided. Once again, there was criticism of the tanks but in this account it is scathing in its tone. The sunken road to the left provided a strong point for enemy fire but was 'practically untouched by the barrage. This may be accounted for by the fact that this road was one of the routes of advance of the much vaunted "tanks".' The fact that the tanks failed to advance meant that at this point led to enormous casualties. 'Had the creeping barrage been used on the Sunken Road instead of relying on these Tanks, it is possible, or even probable', that the advance would not have been held up'. Communications during the attack had been unsatisfactory. For example, the report explains that after leaving the first objective, communication with Brigade HQ became challenging:

> What few pigeons survived the first 1st advance were used from the first objective and it was subsequently necessary to use runners over a long distance and frequently through heavy barrages. Messengers from Brigade HQ were unable to find their way to Battalion HQ and it was not until a late hour on 15th or early on the 16th than any messages from Brigade reached Battalion in Brown Line.

Something as straightforward as a brigade relay established at the point of the first objective would have been very useful to the battalion. Some dissatisfaction is expressed

24 TNA: WO95/1213, 1st Guards Brigade HQ, Report by W.R. Bailey i/c 2/Grenadiers, 4 October 1916.

with the men once a position was captured. They are accused, in both of the September attacks, of having a tendency 'to hang about in batches after the capture of a position instead of taking cover and getting to work with the consolidation'. It was claimed that for about 30 minutes after a position was captured there was little or no German fire and 'during this lull ... much valuable work could be done'.

One part of the report describes a practice that is not identified in the other after battle reports. Headed 'Robbing the Dead', it describes a macabre practice: 'I would suggest that more attention be given to the conduct and discipline of parties sent out to clear the Battle-field and bury the dead. I have made enquiry and without doubt an impression exists among the troops that all valuables viz. watches-rings-cash-etc., become the property and are the perquisites of these parties.'[25]

The brief report submitted by the 3/Coldstream Guards on both of the September attacks suggested some practical measures to improve the effectiveness of the infantry. Men had to carry either a box of bombs or SAA, rations or flares together with a tin of water, rum and charcoal which 'is a heavy night's work over such rough ground, especially if it is all wet before an attack'. A lighter tool with a definite arrangement for carrying it was suggested because everyman needed to carry a pick or shovel even though it was not known which men would survive to make and consolidate on the final objective. It was pointed out that the experience of the assault had showed that the pocket was unsuitable for carrying bombs as it was found to be impossible to get them out quickly enough as this process was impeded by their equipment. 'The best method', the report argued, 'seemed to be to carry 20 rounds of S.A.A. from the extra bandolier in the pouches, and then carry the bombs in the bandolier.' Once again, the men did not always behave sensibly when as position had been gained. Concealment does not seem to have been a priority: 'It should be impressed on all ranks not to walk about even if the enemy do not shoot at them, as men are very much inclined to walk about and give the position away'. Finally, the report made some recommendations regarding the use of the artillery which are worth recounting in full:

> There should be some form system of signal with Very Light or some such method, between the leading waves, of the Infantry and the Artillery, so that the Infantry can control our barrage. It is impossible to work to a definite time table as if things are very successful it is far better to push on immediately from one objective to another, which under the present system where halts are arranged necessitates our men running into their own barrage. If a system of Signals was arranged a halt could be had, if necessary, or the Infantry could advance if an opportunity occurred.[26]

25 TNA: WO95/1213, 1st Guards Brigade HQ, 2/Coldstream Guards: Lessons from the Attack, September 15th, 4 October 1916.
26 TNA: WO95/1213, 1st Guards Brigade HQ, 3/Coldstream Guards Notes and Suggestions on the recent operations, 4 October 1916.

The 1st Guards Brigade's machine gun company report of the September attacks lamented the lack of up-to-date maps which, it was recommended, should be issue a day or two before operations. The actual maps that they were given were issued had at least two lines of unmarked German trenches which had to be crossed which were all manned by Germans. This caused 'much confusion in the minds of Officers conducting the Operations and others who naturally could not properly distinguish when they reached their various objectives.' More significantly, this report reveals the reasons for a much-improved operational performance by the machine gun company between the two dates. On 15 September, one section of four guns went with each of the two flank companies. The idea behind this approach was that by doing so, they would escape the heavy barrage that was anticipated. Unfortunately, there was strong opposition to the attack and the distance to the first objective was so great that few of the guns of the attacking battalions reached it. The casualties experienced by the company were therefore relatively heavy at four officers and 90 other ranks.

On 25 September, a different approach was taken that ended in a much better outcome. On this occasion, the machine gun sections were not attached to battalions but were organised independently to target specific objectives: the brown line and the blue line. The company was organised into three sections of four guns each identified as the blue section, the brown section and the reserve section. Operation orders for the attack on Lesboeufs specified that one section would occupy the blue line after the village had been taken and two sections would occupy the brown line. The blue section dug themselves in just behind the jumping off line during the night of 24 September. The brown section did the same except that two guns were at either end of the brigade frontage. Their role was to form a defensive flank if necessary. The reserve section was held back and was not sent for until the blue line was occupied. The machine gun teams were kept in hand by their commanders and did not advance until the line in front of them was captured. They chose their own time and route to do this. All 12 guns reached their objectives and were withdrawn again on relief. On the 25 September, the casualties were very much lighter than on 15 September; four killed and seven wounded. Control throughout was exercised by the CO of the machine gun company who was based in the HQ of the supporting battalions. [27]

The report of the 1/Irish Guards expressed concerns about 'the question of Artillery co-operation, as having been hardly satisfactory'. This seems rather understated in light of the events described by their CO. For example, on 15 September, Lieutenant Colonel R. McCalmont was accompanied by a liaison officer who 'was, through no fault of his own, quite useless. He was never in touch by wire, and I doubt whether any of his messages by runner were of any use.' When the liaison officer was wounded in the afternoon, McCalmont had, for a short period, the assistance of an New Zealand R.F.A.

27 TNA: WO95/1213, 1st Guards Brigade HQ, Report on the actions of Sept.15th and 25th regarding the Machine Guns of the 1st Guards Brigade Machine Gun Company, 15 September 1916.

officer who 'was equally dependent upon runners, who would have been useless had a barrage been urgently required'. On 25 September, there were two occasions when the battalion suffered significant casualties from friendly fire. McCalmont described what happened:

> Firstly on reaching the 2nd Line (BROWN) about 1.45 P.M. they were under intermittent shell fire from what appeared to be their Right Rear (from a Southerly direction), and this continued until 2.35 P.M. Secondly on reaching the BLUE LINE at scheduled time, it appeared as if the creeping barrage failed to lift forward for at least 15 minutes, with the result that the Companies found themselves digging-in on the BLUE LINE in the midst of their own barrage, with disastrous results.

McCalmont also identified 'what was a very serious discrepancy'; the blue line on the map that he had been given was in a different location to that of his artillery liaison officer's map.[28]

In his own 'summative' report, Feilding explained that the terrain of the battlefield encountered by the Guards together with the ineffectiveness of the tanks and significant issues with artillery co-operation created many problems in the September attacks. Ginchy stood out as a salient in the Guards' lines; on their right the Germans held the Quadrilateral and a trench running north of it which joined the Flers line. This trench 'was admirably placed as it gave flanking defence to the German line should any attack be attempted from GINCHY. On the left the Germans were in possession of certain trenches between Ginchy and Delville Wood which would also flank any advance that we might attempt to make.' Feilding continued by outlining the fact that the Germans occupied various sunken roads with machine gun posted at various points. Crucially then, the salient made the forming up of the two brigades for the attack 'a very difficult matter. Two brigades had to attack out of a very limited area and out of trenches which were by no means parallel to the first position which was to be assaulted. The 'first objective was 1250 yards distant and between this first objective and GINCHY there would necessarily be a lot of fighting'. Moreover, the men were hampered by the fact that:

> From GINCHY, the top of the tower of the Church of LESBOEUFS was just visible, but from GINCHY the ground fell for about 400 yards in a gentle slope so that once the troops had left GINCHY they had no more (any) landmarks which were really prominent to guide them. The ground then runs in a gentle glaci(e)s to the FLERS line which was heavily wired and a magnificently placed line of defence.

Feilding was very critical of the tanks: 'In this attack great reliance had been placed on the tanks. The barrage was arranged for them. They were expected to clear the enemy out of the trenches between DELVILLE WOOD and GINCHY, out of the Sunken Roads

28 TNA; WO95/1213, 1st Guards Brigade HQ, Report from 1/Irish Guards 4 October, 1916.

in front, and out of the QUADRILATERAL on our right. As a matter of fact none of these things happened' The tanks slow movement was a real handicap.

> The barrage started with the tanks with the result that our infantry as soon as they advanced came under a heavy flank fire from both right and left and also from in front. However, the troops pushed on and by the time they had reached the FLERS line they had suffered not only heavy casualties but they had gone 1250 yards and had taken trenches not marked on any map and fought with the enemy in all sorts of places with the result that they thought they were much further than they really were.

Feilding stressed in his report that:

> The tanks should be used so as to clear the enemy out of such positions as may hamper the immediate formation of trenches for the attack … they should have been used a few days before to assist in taking the QUADRILATERAL and the trenches on our left which would have allowed the 6th Division to come up into line with us for the attack on the 15th.

He continued: The Guards had to 'make an attack with the Division on our right starting 500 yards behind us with the enemy's strong point in line with us and with the enemy on our left having a gap between us and the Division on our left is a hazardous operation. That for a main attack, tanks are of no use'. Continuing with the details of the attack on 15 September, Feilding noted that:

> The Division took the first objective and even pushed as far as 500 yards beyond establishing posts which were most valuable as it was on the line of these posts that trenches were dug from which the attack on the 25th started … The enemy had positions in front of our first objective, positions which were unexpected to our troops and therefore led them to believe that they had taken three lines of trenches when they had really only reached their first objective … in the ground in front of the FLERS line there was one whole battalion whereas in the FLERS line itself there were only two companies. Four machine guns were captured in the Sunken roads alone. This shows how very determined the enemy were that we should only reach the FLERS line after heavy fighting.

Moving on to the attack of 25 September, Feilding outlined that there were significant restraints on the Guards: 'The Division had to take two lines of trenches to get into line with the Division on our right preparatory to the attack on LES BOEUFS.' However, 'a few days before the attack we were ordered to extend our front by 400 yards to our right and extra artillery was given to us for that purpose'. The main problem in this attack was that a 'loop line' in the German trenches was not dealt with properly by the artillery. Ten minutes before the attack was to commence:

> The Captain commanding in this part of the line telephoned and said that the artillery fire was not effective and was very wild. This was too late for remedy; the result was that when the attack was launched there were very heavy casualties and the line of trenches were not captured until the following day. It was eventually captured by the use of a tank.

At another point, 100 yards of wire had not been cut. Feilding concluded that:

> … the Company Officer must be in closer touch with the Artillery Observation Officer and should let them know early whether or not they are satisfied with the shooting of the artillery. Wherever possible, the C.O. or senior officer should go round with a senior Artillery Officer and settle with him what parts of the enemy's line have not been sufficiently treated… the very closest liaison between the Infantry actually in the trenches and the Artillery is absolutely necessary.

In addition, he noted that: 'After the final objective has been gained, the barrage should creep on so as to cross any high ground that there might be in front. On the 25th our troops were stopped from pushing on by our own barrage.'

Concurring with the 2/Grenadiers, Feilding concluded that in an attack: 'Bombing Sections are of no use. These get quickly broken up and even when they can be kept together they are not quick enough. All men should be trained as bombers, and all men should be trained in the use of German bombs of which they will probably find an ample supply'. He also made recommendations with regard to improvements in the use of pigeons, Lewis guns, the allocation of greater numbers of flares to communicate more effectively with aeroplanes, the use of S.O.S rockets and the carrying of lighter shovels. Finally, in light of the machine gun company's suggestions Feilding observed that: 'Machine guns should be given their tasks but told to push forward in their own time, a number always being kept in hand to form a defensive flank.'[29]

Quite simply then, the Guards may have taken their final objectives on the 25 September but there was much to be learnt from their experiences over the two attacks and the loss of life had been dreadful. The casualties suffered by the division during these weeks had been very high indeed. For the period from 10 September to 17 September, over 4,000 casualties were reported.[30] Between 18 September and 30 September there were another 2,340 according to the *Official History* although Headlam puts them slightly lower at 2,280, over 90 percent of which were the result of fighting on 25 September alone.[31] Prior and Wilson estimated that the Guards' casualty figures on this day were 1,900 or 'twice those of any other division of XIV Corps'.[32]

29 TNA: WO95/1213, Guards Division HQ, X1V Corps 'G'. 5 October 1916.
30 Miles, *Military Operations, 1916, Volume 2*, p.350.
31 Headlam, *History of the Guards Division*, p.176.
32 Prior and Wilson, *The Somme*, p.245.

8

The Winter and Spring of 1916–1917

During the coming months, the Guards saw no direct action, and none was anticipated. Nonetheless, Feilding and his staff could afford no complacency. All three of the Guards brigades were moved to the No. 4 Training Area, south-west of Amiens on 1 October.[1] Until the second week in November, there was a routine of drill, route marches and tactical exercises together with musketry, Lewis gun and bombing practice. Clearly such training was a serious undertaking; during October, the 3rd Guards Brigade lost seven men who were accidentally wounded during bombing and trench-mortar practices.[2] Brigadiers were advised that 'It is not unlikely that within the next few months the enemy may carry out a retirement on a large scale with the object of shortening his line, and of thus providing a larger reserve for offensive purposes.' Whilst there would not be time or opportunity 'to exercise units in combined operations', staff officers and senior officers should 'study those portions of F.S.R., Part 1, which deal with moving warfare'.

Interestingly in the light of subsequent events in the following February when German forces began their withdrawal to the Hindenburg Line, it was anticipated 'that it is probable that an enemy retirement would commence after a period of comparative quiet rather than as the result of offensive action on our part'. Planning and thought had to be given in how to deal with rearguard actions and 'frequent counter-attacks'. The document concluded that these situations would necessitate the 'issuing of orders for outposts, advance guards, and attacks, under conditions very different from those to which we have been accustomed during the past two years. The Major General considers that no officer can afford to disponse [sic] with the help that a careful study of F.S.R. will provide in thinking out beforehand how to deal with such situations.'[3]

After several weeks spent in 'elementary training', Feilding instructed his brigadiers on 1 November that he wished them 'to conduct tactical schemes on the ground with Commanding Officers who should subsequently work through similar schemes with

1 TNA: WO95/1192, Guards Division HQ War Diary, 1 October 1916.
2 Headlam, *History of the Guards Division*, p.187.
3 TNA: WO95/1192, Guards Division HQ, App. 1153, 11 October 1916.

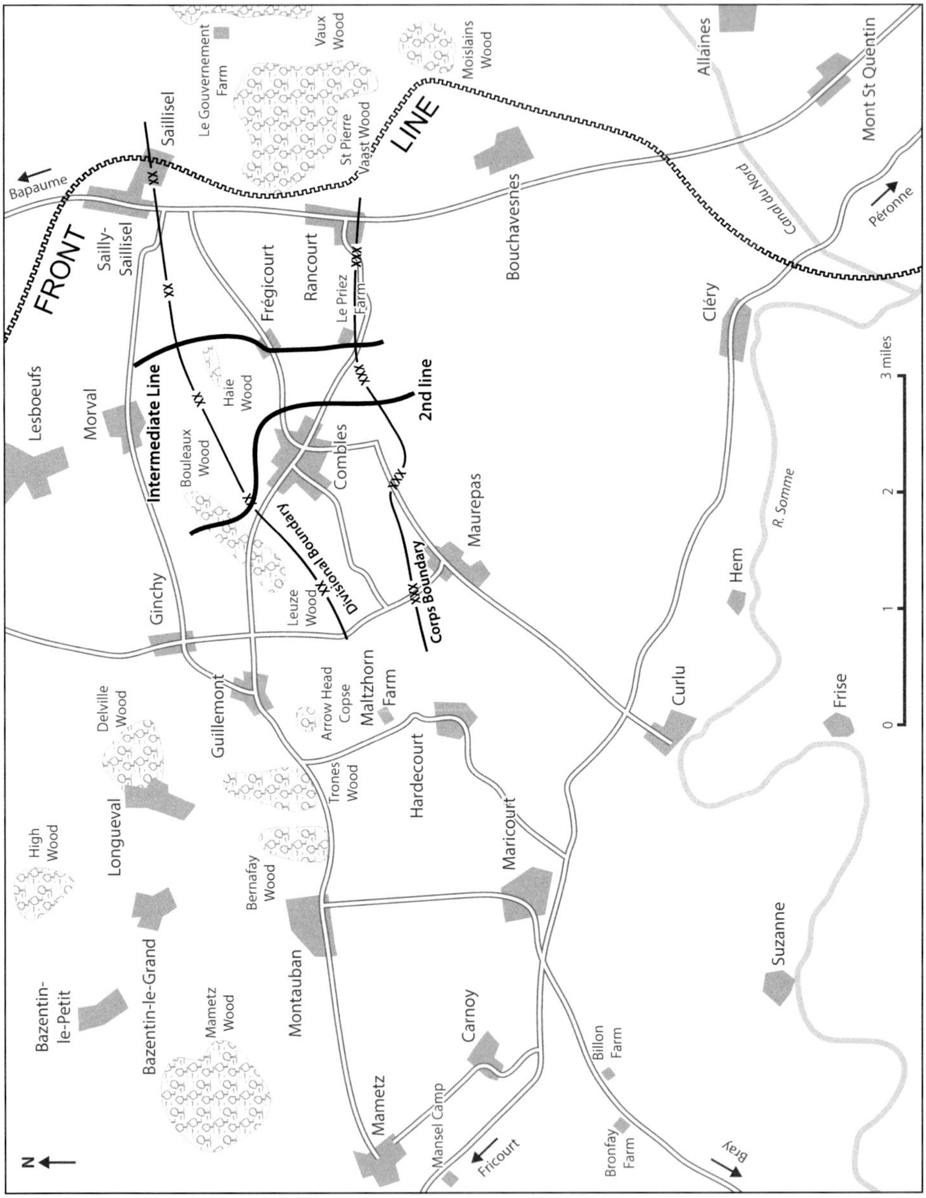

The line at Sailley-Sallisel and St Pierre Vast Wood, winter 1916–1917.

their Company Commanders.' Several scenarios were envisaged such as when 'owing to an enemy retirement, troops in an entrenched line commence a general advance' or 'subsequent to driving in the enemy's protection troops, the development of an attack on an entrenched position which will involve a return to a measure of trench warfare, and the establishment of a line within assaulting distance of the enemy.'[4] However, the reality of moving from the routine training that involved the basic requirements for an effective infantry soldier to more sophisticated tactical exercises proved hopelessly optimistic as the Somme winter embedded itself.

The Guards re-entered the line on 13 November relieving the 17th Division in the left-hand sector of XIV Corps, an area familiar to them between Lesboeufs and Gueudecourt. They were relieved in turn on 21 November by the 5th Australian Division. On 4 December, the Guards relieved elements of the IX French Corps to hold an area that included the high ground at Sailly-Saillisel until 1 January when they were themselves relieved by the 20th Division. The Guards brigades were divided into two groups, each group carrying out their own relief:

> … the idea being that by that system one got shorter hours of duty in the front line, which owing to the awful conditions of the trenches, was essential. On the other hand, under the new system one always seemed to be on the move, never more than three days in one place. Our group consisted of the 1st, 3rd and 4th Battalions Grenadier Guards, the 1st and 2nd Battalions Scots Guards and the Welsh Guards, and was responsible for the left half of the divisional front.[5]

Generally, the winter weather in these months was so severe that the enemy posed little threat except for occasional artillery fire. Nonetheless, the casualties reported by the Guards Division in just the period from 13 to 21 November were eight officers and 257 other ranks.[6]

This extract from Kipling's account of the 2/Irish Guards provides a vivid picture of the appalling conditions that had to be contended with:

> The Battalion was not in position till the 11th of December, when it relieved the 2nd Grenadiers after three or four days' rain which wiped out what communication-trenches had been attempted, and pulped the front line. As for the back-breaking nature of the work – 'Though the first Company (on relief) passed Haie Wood about 4 p.m. it was 11.30 before they had floundered the intervening 3000 yards.' One of the Grenadiers whom they relieved had been stuck in the mud for forty-three hours. Unless the men in the trenches, already worn out with mud-wrestling to get

4 TNA: WO95/1192, Guards Division HQ, App. 1176, 1 November 1916.

5 Fryer, E.R.M. *Grenadier: The Recollections of an Officer of the Grenadier Guards throughout the Great War on the Western Front* (London: Digby, Long & Co., 1923), p.75.

6 Headlam, *History of the Guards Division*, p.191.

> there, kept moving like hens on hot plates, they sank and stuck. ('It is funny, maybe, to talk about now, that mud-larking of ours; but to sink, sink, sink in the dark and you not sure whether they saw ye or could hear you, puts the wind up a man worse than anything under heaven. Fear? Fear is not the word. 'Twas the Somme that broke our hearts. Back, knees, loins, across your chest – you was dragged to pieces dragging your own carcass out of the mud. 'Twas like red-hot wires afterwards – and all to begin it again.')[7]

Meanwhile in some circles, rumours were circulating about Feilding's future and his potential replacement by his well-regarded colleague, Pereira, whose wife wrote to him on 21 December:

> I am full of rumours and excitement. Mother said Archie Strling came to see them,[8] he had been seeing John Ponsonby who rather intimated that you were pretty certain to get the Guards Division almost at once as there was talk of Geoffrey Feilding getting the London District. Putting two and two together from your letter saying Franky Lloyd was looking ill and Geoffrey Feilding saying that you might get the Division, etc… If you did get the Guards Division it would be a big thing, and you would be awfully happy.[9]

There would be no repeat of the 1914 truce and 1915 fraternisation. Kipling remarked that 'The growing quiet on the sector for days past had led people to expect attempts at fraternization on Christmas. Two "short but very severe bombardments" by our Artillery on Christmas morning cauterized that idea.'[10] This was confirmed in Miles Barne's diary: '25th XMAS DAY! Opens with us making a heavy bombardment 8.30 a.m. & others later. Peace and Goodwill! Many severe orders to the contrary are published – at least against our "fraternising" with the Germans, as has been known on former Xmas days in some parts!'[11]

Meanwhile, Pereira replied on the same day to his wife. He did not reject the possibility of his taking over the Guards Division completely: 'I don't think there is much in your rumours, I am not really ambitious but the easier conditions (of a divisional command) would doubtless appeal to me. In some ways I should prefer some other division to the G.D.'[12] Coincidentally, later the same day, he learnt that he would be given command of Second Division. Whether the rumours of his taking command of the Guards had ever been substantial, we simply do not know. Were there any genuine

7 Kipling, *Irish Guards in the Great War, 2nd Battalion*, pp.106–107.
8 Archie Sterling was Brigadier General Archibald Sterling, Scots Guards. He served in Gallipoli and Egypt in First World War.
9 Pereira, *Catholic General*, p.221.
10 Kipling, *Irish Guards in the Great War, 2nd Battalion*, p.109.
11 Nicol, *Barne's Diary*, p.225.
12 Pereira, *Catholic General*, p.223.

concerns about Feilding at the very highest level after such a tough September for the Division? Was Feilding interested in the London Command himself after a tough your as GOC Guards Division? There is no documentary proof of this either way unfortunately. As an interesting footnote, Jonathan Boff has written that in 1918, when the Guards were part of General Sir Aylmer Haldane's VI Corps in General Julian Byng's Third Army:

> Byng engineered the transfer of Major-General G. P.T. Feilding from the Guards Division to command London District, apparently at Haldane's instigation. Haldane thought Feilding 'obstructive'. He is given to call on his imagination freely when he is disinclined to do anything he dislikes. I do not care about him personally, and a division such as the Guards is worthy of a much better commander.[13]

Of course, such machinations over a year afterwards may be completely irrelevant at this juncture.

In January and February 1917, the weather turned much colder as temperatures dropped to record lows. 'The waterlogged craters froze and duck boards laid down over the mud became like polished slides; so that men go slipping and stumbling along communications trenches and fall against snowdrifts all crusted with tiny crystals. The men are 'sticking' the cold as they 'stuck' the wet-as they endure everything in this war, with a stiff upper lip and no moan.'[14] The Guards remained on the Somme and relieved, for example, the 8th Division between Rancourt and Saillisel on 11 January.

Perhaps unsurprisingly, evidence emerged of a 'live and let live' culture on the Guards front line. On 20 January, Esmond Elliot wrote that 'The Huns have shown signs of being friendly. Both sides have been walking about on the top lately with impunity'.[15] Captain Henry Dundas wrote a detailed and rather witty account in his memoir:

> Out of the line once more after an amusing sojourn, which included a visit to the Germans. On the Brigade frontage the line was very close on the right. Up till two days ago a reign of absolute quiet had prevailed. Perfect peace. Every one walked about on both sides. There are no trenches: merely a series of 'islands' and no communication trenches. The other side are in a similar position, except that their islands are on top of a ridge and we can't see anything behind. They of course, can sweep all our islands and the approaches to them, so quiet was essential for any work to be done, or indeed if any existence was to be continued. So peace reigned. People waved bottles at each other across No Man's Land – wha'a bond is Johnny

13 Jonathan Boff, *Winning and Losing on the Western Front: The British Third Army and the Defeat of Germany in 1918* (Cambridge: Cambridge University Press, 2012), p.223.
14 Johnnie Astor and Alexandra Campbell, *Esmond: The Lost Idol 1895–1917* (Solihull: Helion, 2017), p.134 quotes Philip Snowden writing in *The Telegraph*.
15 Astor and Campbell, *Esmond*, p.134.

> Dewar even between enemies – and life was very pleasant. We used to walk round inspecting the islands on the top all the time with the Germans thirty yards away.
>
> But gradually the Divisional Staff decided that this state of affairs must cease. This being so, the Brigadier decided that the Germans must be warned. Accordingly Brodie and I, about seven in the morning, sallied out of our posts across the Bosches' lines. Brodie is an excellent German scholar, so we were well equipped – he with the speech and I with papers inscribed with a message to the effect that 'after dawn on the 19th all Germans exposing themselves would be shot' (printed in English usefully enough). We stayed on their wire shouting for an 'Offizier'. At last, after much excitement, a small man looking like Charlie Chaplin appeared with whom Brodie chatted for about twenty minutes, saying how sorry we were that this state of affairs must cease – telling them that all would be well if there were only head-keeping down by both sides. And so away – not unamusing.[16]

As the dreadful Somme winter of 1916–1917 dragged, the first signs of spring did little to raise spirits. Even the normally upbeat Oliver Lyttelton had been worn down. Given the chance to revisit the trench that he reached on 15 September, his mood had clearly changed. From the euphoria of that day only a few months before:

> This country stinks of corruption … As far as the eye can reach is that brown and torn sea of desolation and every yard there is a grave, some marked with rifles, others with crosses, some with white skulls, some with beckoning hands. But everything is dead: the trees, the fields, the corn, the church, even the prayers of those that went there in their Sunday clothes with their sweaty pennies for the plate: it is all dead and God has forsaken it.[17]

Meanwhile, there had been a significant development for the Guards back home; on 10 February 1917 the Household Officer Cadet Battalion was established. The OCBs were first established by Army Council Instruction No. 357 in February 1916. This has been described as 'a crucial change in the officer development model as men would now only be commissioned after training.' Moreover, this meant that: 'Continuous evaluation and final selection towards the end of the OCB course meant that inefficient men could either be filtered out, or else given the opportunity to pass the course with additional training,'[18] The Household Brigade's OCB, located at The Hall, Bushey in Hertfordshire was the 37th and last OCB to be established. 'Although this battalion was primarily for the training of Special Reserve officers for the Household Cavalry, Household Battalion and Brigade of Guards, there was always a percentage of officer cadets being trained for

16 Henry Dundas, *Scots Guard: A Memoir* (Edinburgh: Blackwood, 1921), pp.150–151.
17 Ball, *The Guardsmen*, p.64.
18 Charles Fair, 'From OTC to OCB; The Professionalisation of the Selection and Training of Junior Temporary Officers in the Great War', in Spencer Jones (ed.), *The Darkest Year: The British Army on the Western Front 1917* (Warwick: Helion, 2022), p.86.

temporary commissions in Infantry regiments of the Line.'[19] It had an original establishment of 200 officer cadets in two companies of 100 men each. This was increased to 250 in October 1917 and eventually to 400 in early 1918. Initially the course lasted four months but this was increased to five and then six months within a year. The majority of the officer cadets were young men aged 18 upwards who were either from or recently from public schools but there were also NCOs sent back home to be trained for temporary commissions together with 'business and professional men of good standing who were recommended for officers' rank. Several representatives of the Foreign Office were trained and commissioned.' Lieutenant Colonel E.L. Pike of the Grenadier Guards, who had taken command of the battalion in May 1917 claimed that:

> It would be impossible to imagine a more mixed and cosmopolitan body than that composing the bulk of the officer cadets of the Household Brigade Officer Cadet Battalion. They varied in age from about 17 and a half to half a century. Alongside the boy straight from school stood the head of a big city firm of bankers; one of the leading lights of the theatrical world listened to a lecture beside an old soldier with seventeen or eighteen years' service.[20]

The course focussed on a high level of fitness initially together with bayonet raining and musketry. Lectures predominated at first before practical instruction took precedence and field exercises were especially important in the third and fourth months. Completion of the course then led to a short period of attachment to a reserve battalion to get some opportunity of commanding men. Charles Fair has argued that 'the OCB system and the broader system of officer development into which it fitted undoubtedly played a part in the improved operational effectiveness of the BEF in 1918'.[21] Although no documentary evidence exists, it is interesting to speculate as to why the Guards Division was so late to develop its own OCB. Perhaps the shocking number of officer losses at Flers-Courcelette and Morval had been a catalyst for change whereas before it had been assumed that the Guards would automatically attract the best who would be seamlessly integrated into the Guards 'way of doing things'.

On 14 March 1917, as the German retreat to the Hindenburg Line began opposite the Guards Division's lines, they moved forward to take possession of the now vacant German front posts and trenches. The German retreat was covered by long-range machine gun fire, artillery and snipers. The instruction had been to stay 'close to the heels' of this retreat without risking any serious commitment to battle. Within a week, German positions in the sector around Nurlu and Manancourt were under the Guards

19 L. Pike, 'Household Brigade Officer Cadet Battalion', *Household Brigade Magazine*, November 1920, pp.35–39.
20 L. Pike, 'Household Brigade Officer Cadet Battalion', *Household Brigade Magazine*, November 1920, pp.35–39.
21 Fair, 'From OTC to OCB', p.109.

control. Consolidation began immediately and a main line of defence was dug and a piquet line wired. Unsurprisingly, the mood of the men lifted:

> The change from the old trench life was most exhilarating. The winter had been severe; the monotony of our life had only been equalled by its discomfort; for four and a half months without relief we had gone backwards and forwards into the same or nearly the same sector; we knew every inch of mud in the place, and we had unpleasant reminiscences of every cross-road. Suddenly all was changed. The first signs of spring began to show; monotony was succeeded by movement; we advanced, new pieces came into view, new interests began to be aroused.[22]

Further evidence of an improvement in the men's spirits can be seen when Feilding visited a Sports Day that involved the 3/Grenadiers during April:

> I want to say how pleased I have been with your bayonet fighting today ... You are out here for one purpose and one purpose only ... to kill Boches. From what I have seen every man here today is good for two or three Boches. That's what I want. You, all of you put any amount of viciousness and beef into your work today, with no fancy work. That's what I want ... Also that you may have an opportunity of showing very soon what you can do against the real thing in the open! To which hundreds of his men cried, 'That's what we want!'. And the General roared with laughter.[23]

From 24 March until 6 May, the Guards Division, both the RE and most of the infantry, were heavily committed to major construction projects: the broad-gauge railway lines from Trones Wood to Rocquigny and from Ham to Peronne together with the restoration of a significant amount of the local road network: Combles through Fregicourt and Sailly-Saillisel to le Transloy, Ginchy through Lesboeufs to le Transloy, and from Manancourt through le Mesnil to Rocquigny.[24] This was seen as vital work in rebuilding the infrastructure that had been so badly damaged in the fighting of 1916.

When the Guards left for Flanders at the end of May to join the Second Army, Rawlinson was fulsome in his praise for the Guards in this message sent to Feilding:

> It is now nine months since the Division joined the Fourth Army, and I cannot allow them to leave without expressing my thanks for the excellent services they have performed, and the high example they have set at all times to the Army in general. Whether in battle, in holding and organising the line, or in work in back areas, they have maintained that standard of discipline and fighting spirit which

22 Dundas, *Scots Guard*, p.156.
23 H. Dearden, *Medicine and Duty: A War Diary* (London: Heinemann,1928), p.50.
24 Headlam, *History of the Guards Division*, pp.210–212.

> has always characterised Guardsmen, and of which all Guardsmen are justly proud. I have been particularly struck at the very excellent work they have done in connection with railway construction, and it is largely due to their labours that the Transportation Services in this area are now in such a satisfactory condition.[25]

Lieutenant Oliver Lyttelton.

Whilst the Guards had played no part in the Battle of Arras during April and May 1917, their move northwards to the Boesinghe sector just north of Ypres was a firm indicator that they would have an important role in what was to become the Third Battle of Ypres, also known as Passchendaele.

25 TNA: WO95/1193, Guards Division HQ App.242, Fourth Army No. G.S. 695.

9

Pilckem Ridge: Preparations

Military Context

Jonathan Boff has explained why the BEF fought at Ypres in the summer and autumn of 1917:

> After the failure of the Anglo-French offensives of spring 1917, two things were clear. Firstly, doing nothing was not an option. Someone needed to attack the Germans to demonstrate commitment to allies such as America, Italy and, especially, a wavering Russia. Secondly, it was unlikely to be the French who did so. They were beset by unrest both in the army and on the home front. That left the British under Sir Douglas Haig, and the only area they could attack was in Flanders. A successful push might have secured Ypres and the supply ports at Calais and Boulogne, threatening the German rail lines behind the front. Cutting these might have forced German submarines from their bases on the Belgian coast, weakening the U-boat campaign against British shipping. And to wear down the German army could do no harm.[1]

When Lloyd George replaced Henry Asquith as Prime Minister on 5 December 1916, he was viewed as a man of decision who would deliver a knock-out blow to Germany. In reality, he was privately doubtful that any breakthrough would be achieved in 1917. Lloyd George did not trust Haig and was persuaded by the French general, Nivelle, that he could mount an attack that would bring about a 'smashing victory' within 24–48 hours. Lloyd George even conspired to place Haig as a sub-ordinate of Nivelle at a joint Allied conference in Calais on 26 February. Nivelle had been successful at Verdun with carefully planned small scale attacks that struck at the weak points in the German defences with overwhelming violence and maximum surprise.

1 Jonathan Boff, *Passchendaele: Why it Failed*, https://www.birmingham.ac.uk/research/perspective/passchendaele.aspx, accessed 13 November 2023.

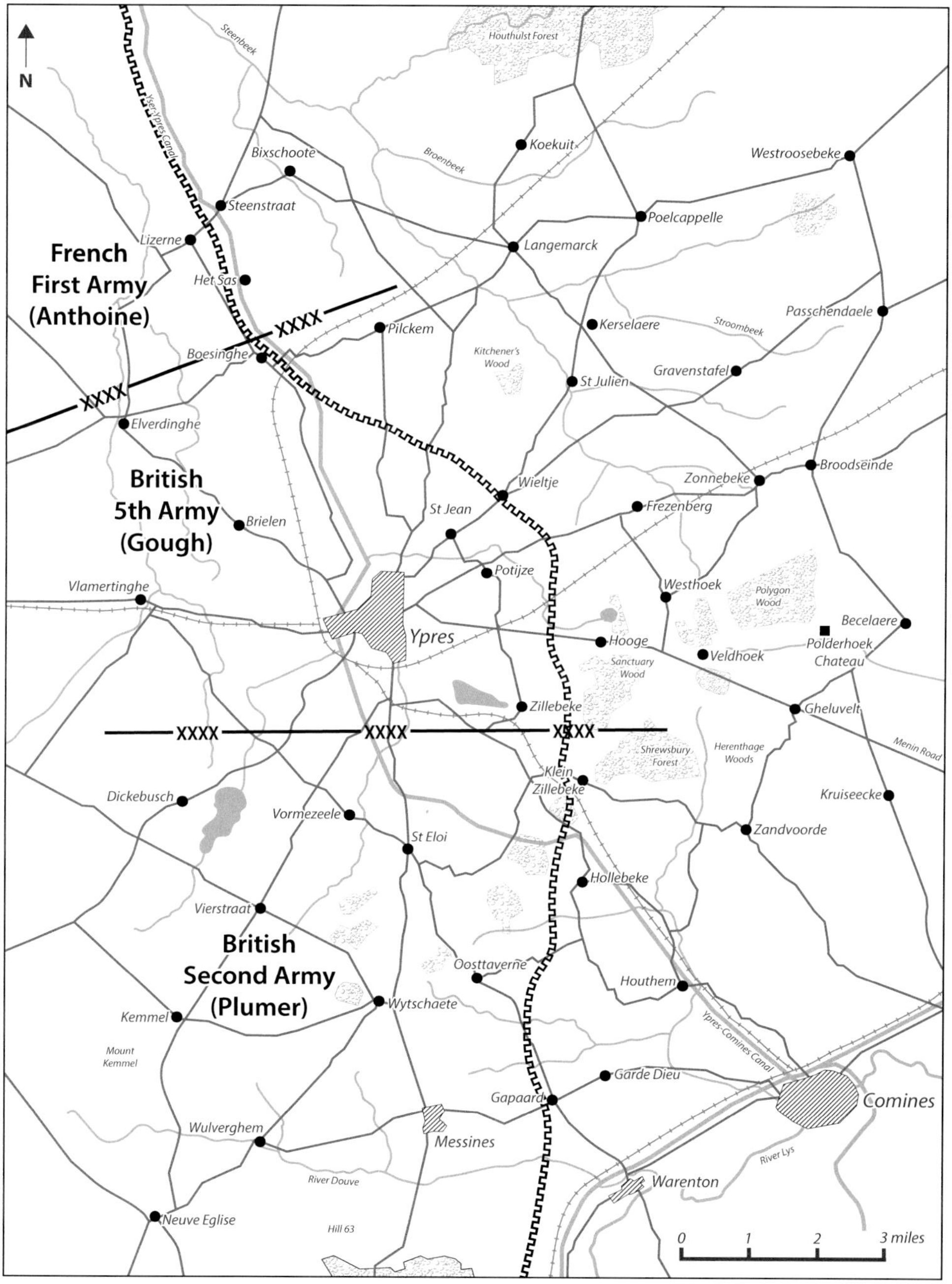

The Ypres Salient, 30 July 1917.

Unfortunately, when the Germans retreated to the Hindenburg Line, they shortened their line of defence and made it a much stronger one in the process. With slack security surrounding French planning, the Germans anticipated the French offensive. It was delayed by poor weather, but by 16 April 1917 it could not be postponed any longer. The British had launched diversionary attacks at Arras on 9 April and would be left in a perilous position if the French did not attack as planned. The resulting offensive on the Chemin des Dames was unfortunately a disaster and resulted in perhaps up to casualties of 187,000 as it dragged on until the middle of May and troops began to mutiny. Nivelle was replaced by Petain.

In fact, the attack at Arras enjoyed significant gains in the opening days. The preliminary bombardment lasted several weeks and was heavier than on the Somme aided by the recent introduction of the 106 fuse which made high explosive shells far more effective. A particular feature of this offensive was the detailed preparation which was to be a clear influence on Feilding's preparations at Pilckem Ridge a few months later. Lieutenant General Edmund Allenby had a large model of Vimy Ridge constructed at First Army HQ which all officers and NCOs were expected to study. The troops were trained on marked out courses, initially walking slowly to familiarise themselves with the objectives before going on to move at the speed set by the creeping barrage. 'Lieutenant General Montagu Harper's message to 51st Division was typical of the post Somme attitude amongst the divisional generals. The men were to fight with their wits and not by a mere display of seeing red and brute courage.'[2] The Canadians soon achieved their objectives on Vimy Ridge and further south there was a successful advance of up to three and a half miles which, was remarkably, further than any attack since the end of 1914. At Bullecourt however, the German defences held before reinforcements arrived to stem the flow. The ensuing attritional struggle led to the offensive being called off on 17 May. The Nivelle Offensive and the associated Battle of Arras had failed to produce the desired breakthrough. The casualty figures at Arras amounted to 158,000.

On 7 May, Haig conferred with his army commanders at Doullens. With the failure of the two spring offensives, planning could now proceed with operations in the north to free the Belgian coast. He envisaged a two-part attack in Flanders. The first part would see the capture of the Messines Ridge early in June in order to secure the southern flank before proceeding with the 'northern operation' which would attack the high ground east of Ypres, destroy the German defensive position in Flanders to facilitate a major advance shortly afterwards.[3] Haig had great faith in the men at his disposal. 'By May 1917 the BEF was approaching its peak … with over 1.8 million men under arms and supported by an impressive array of weaponry and equipment, it was, by some considerable margin, the most powerful army Britain had ever raised.'[4]

2 Andrew Rawson, '*The Learning Process': The BEF's Art of War on the Western Front* 1914–1918 (Warwick: Helion, 2019), p.112.
3 Nick Lloyd, *Passchendaele: A New History* (London: Penguin, Viking, 2017), pp.41–42.
4 Lloyd, *Passchendaele*, p.45.

At the Battle of Messines which took place between 7 and 14 June, General Sir Herbert Plumer led his Second Army to a famous victory. A combined force of New Zealand, Irish, Australian, Canadian and British troops took their objectives within a few hours, captured 7,000 Germans and repulsed their counterattacks. He had been able to concentrate his resources on a very clear and well-defined objective to deliver an attack where 'the infantry and artillery would be coordinated into a set-piece attack that was timed to perfection.'[5] Building on approaches developed at Arras, Plumer had large-scale models together with special training areas built so that his troops could get to grips with their objectives beforehand and ensure that, in the event of officer casualties, the attack would still continue despite their loss. A series of mines were dug, and an 11-day artillery bombardment was the precursor to a simultaneous artillery barrage from all of Second Army's artillery at zero. Despite casualties being taken by troops exposed to German fire on the Messines Ridge, Plumer had control of this elevated position by the evening of 7 June. Nick Lloyd describes this victory as 'perhaps the finest example of a "bite and hold" operation ever conducted, proving that, under the right conditions, the BEF could secure even the most heavily defended locations.'[6]

Haig selected General Sir Hubert Gough to command the next stage of the offensive as early as 30 April, and so on 10 June Gough and the Fifth Army headquarters took over the Ypres salient north of Messines Ridge. Aged just 46, he was the youngest army commander in the BEF. Self-confident and regarded as a 'thruster' by Haig, his appointment has long been regarded by historians as a grave mistake. Despite Plumer's remarkable success at Messines, Haig believed the next stage of the 'northern operation' needed a leader with 'instinctive aggression'. Nick Lloyd points out that even John Terraine, normally sympathetic to Haig regarded: 'The decision to entrust the main role in the Flanders battle to the 5th Army under General Gough must be regarded as Haig's gravest and most fatal error.'[7] For Lloyd, he was, 'A deeply self-confident man who could, in turns, be witty and charming or petty and vindictive, Gough was sadly, a limited soldier. He had suffered the curse of over-promotion and by the summer of 1917 Fifth Army had acquired an unhealthy – if not entirely undeserved – reputation for carelessness with which it prepared attacks.'[8] At least Feilding and his staff could take some satisfaction that they still remained in XIV Corps under Cavan's direction as they moved northwards into the Ypres Salient

5 Lloyd, *Passchendaele*, p.52.
6 Lloyd, *Passchendaele*, pp.56–57.
7 John Terraine, *Douglas Haig: The Educated Soldier* (London: Cassell 2000 [1963]), p.337.
8 Lloyd, *Passchendaele*, p.65.

Preparations

Despite the doubts about Gough's appointment, in keeping with the methodical and carefully planned attacks at the beginning of the Battle of Arras and again at Messines, the next offensive maintained the same approach. Training for the forthcoming attack devolved to each of the individual corps commanders but each of them, Maxse, Watts, Jacob and Cavan worked to a similar programme, devising a training schedule which was then passed down to individual divisional commanders. There were three elements. Firstly, utilising intelligence from aerial photographs, trench raids and observations from front line positions, a replica of the German trench system that was to be taken was made and practiced over. Secondly, a large model of the ground to be traversed was built and thirdly, an extensive training programme for company commanders was introduced.[9]

Before the movement of the Guards Division into the Boesinghe sector just north of Ypres, a series of divisional conferences were held at which Feilding encouraged his brigadiers to study and follow the best practice and doctrine outlined in recent Stationery Services (SS) training manuals as they prepared their men for the next stage of the 'northern operation' in what would be their first major combat commitment since the seizure of Lesboeufs during the previous September. On 2 June 1917, Feilding noted that the division had had only limited training in open warfare, some brigades more than others. To date, there had been a focus on the development of initiative and judgement in junior officers and section commanders. Now Feilding wanted to concentrate subsequent training on 'the initial attack against a well organised and long-established position' in anticipation of such an operation which was 'fairly certain' within the next three months. Feilding outlined the likely scenario in planning for the attack on an assumed brigade frontage of 600 to 800 yards. There would be four objectives which were set out as:

1. The enemy front line.
2. The enemy reserve line, 700 yards from the front line.
3. The enemy 2nd line, 1,300 yards from front line.
4. A ridge not entrenched by the enemy 2,000 yards from the front line.

Two brigades would be allocated to the front line with one brigade in reserve. The leading brigades would be responsible for capturing and holding the fourth objective.

Feilding stressed that SS 135 *(Instructions for Training of a Division for Offensive Action)* plus SS 143 (*Training of Platoons for Offensive Action*) and SS 144 (*Normal formation for Attack*) should be closely studied and adhered to just as the FSR regarding open warfare. Published in December 1916, SS 135 had been designed to consolidate BEF practice in the light of what had been learnt in the Somme campaign. The roles and responsibilities of army, corps and divisions in planning attacks were standardised with

9 Robin Prior and Trevor Wilson, *Passchendaele: The Untold Story* (New Haven: Yale University Press, 1996), pp.79–80.

a clear flow of responsibilities from the army at the top, tasked to draw up the plan for the attack including artillery provision, and then devolve to corps the tasks to be allocated to divisions who, working with their brigades, would then decide upon objectives and appropriate plans for the infantry. In each corps, the General Officer Commanding, Royal Artillery (GOCRA) planned the bombardment plan in conjunction with neighbouring corps artillery commanders as well as co-ordinating counter-battery fire, and howitzer bombardment at zero. Divisions were allowed their own input using any localised knowledge. Another important outcome of SS 135 was that the platoon was now built around sections of firepower.

If facilities for training were 'few', Feilding continued, time would be spent in working through plans of attack in detail on trench maps, 'with the object of making Company and Platoon Commanders familiar with the principles laid down in the manuals'. As a result, 'Officers will be better prepared to train their units when ground is available to carry out practice attacks'. Feilding was of the view that SS 135 was 'excellently written and every officer should be made to read it and visualise its contents'. Whether the men were in a rifle brigade section or a Lewis gun section, it must be impressed upon them 'that the rifle and bayonet is the first and most important arm of the Infantry soldier'.

The Battle of Arras had clearly demonstrated 'the necessity of stimulating fire-control, covering fire and fire tactics'. At Arras, Feilding argued:

> Greater success would have been won if only men had more confidence in their rifles, and more inclination to use them freely. The bomb and the rifle grenade are supplementary weapons, useful in certain circumstances. At the present we are doing all we can to increase proficiency in Musketry … the more that you can do to impress on all ranks that the rifle is their first weapon the better we shall do. Teach your officers and NCO fire control and fire orders.

With reference to the central role of the platoon, Feilding stressed the need to 'Impress on everybody that the platoon is the fighting unit. It is complete in every detail and allows the Platoon Commander to use his brain and teach him to use the various weapons with which he is provided'. Finally, 'In arranging the training, you should do two days open fighting to one day's trench to trench attack. Open fighting trains officers, it teaches them to use their wits and develops their initiative.'[10]

Events now began to move quickly. Within a few days, on 10 June, Feilding called a second divisional conference at which he confirmed that the Guards would be on the left of XIV Corps. It would be the most northern corps of the Fifth Army tasked with the capture of the enemy's positions east and north-east of Boesinghe. At this conference, it was agreed that the initial attack would be carried out by the 2nd and 3rd Guards Brigades with the 1st Guards Brigade exploiting their anticipated breakthrough.

10 TNA: WO95/1193, Guards Division HQ, Appendix 249, 2 June 1917 plus further notes sent out on 5 June 1917.

Ominously, although it was not discussed, a way for the Guards to cross the Yser canal would have to be found.

At a further divisional conference on 18 June, Feilding's focus was firmly focussed on attention to detail and effective training. Discussion centred initially around training for a scenario where either a company commander had to decide to push on against a disorganised enemy or wait if the enemy is set in an organised position until fresh plans could be made, and a new bombardment be organised. He stressed the necessity of all officers knowing thoroughly all landmarks in the attack area with which they were concerned. 'Up to the ridge TELEGRAPH HOUSE-GENERAL FARM WOOD 15 these landmarks can be studied from our trenches. Beyond this ridge oblique aeroplane photographs will be of great assistance. These photographs will, it is hoped, be distributed down to Battalions.' It was anticipated that when the Germans realised that an attack was imminent, it would attempt raids on British lines to gain intelligence about troop dispositions etc. Therefore, 'Good observation and the power of bringing fire to bear on the actual canal, as well as the opposing front line is necessary to repel raids.' At Messines, faults in consolidation had been made. Fire steps to enable men to shoot had often been forgotten and trenches had not been traversed and so 'attention is to be paid to these points when training.'

Once again, the guidelines in SS 135 were to be followed 'as regards preparations for, and carrying out of the attack'. Additionally, SS 161 (*Instructions for Battle*) and SS 158 (*Notes on Recent Operations*) were deemed 'worthy of close study by all officers'. SS 161 had been published in May 1917. It outlined the best methods of procedure to be employed in a large-scale battle such as, for example, a close study of the disposition of the enemy's troops up to the last moment, their likely reinforcements and their approach to the battlefield, the defensibility of the objectives once gained and facilities for artillery support. Further approaches included making a close study of the ground between the enemy's lines of defence to establish likely strong points and machine gun positions beforehand so that artillery fire might be concentrated on them was recommended.

The Guards would prepare for the forthcoming attack in the Herzeele area. Feilding was anxious that, because of delays in obtaining a training ground, 'no time should be lost in commencing training' so a timetable was set out for each brigade. The 3rd Guards would train from 20–30 June inclusive, the 2nd Guards from 2–12 July inclusive and 1st Guards from 15 July to the day of the attack.[11]

It was agreed that, until definite information was received regarding the barrage lifts and pauses on the various objectives, no detailed plan of assembly or advance could be made. However, in broad terms, the provisional plans indicated that the 2nd Guards Brigade would be on the right of the divisional front with the 38th Division on its right. The 3rd Guards Brigade would be on the left with a division of the First French Army on its left. Each brigade was likely to attack on a front of two battalions and would assault

11 TNA: WO95/1193, Guards Division HQ, Conference held at Divisional HQ 18 June 1917, App. 274.

three objectives or lines in turn: 'blue', 'black' and 'green'. Immediately that the blue line was taken, the supporting companies of the battalions that had made the initial attack were to advance and seize the black line. When this second objective had been seized, the remaining two battalions of each brigade were to push forward to the third objective or green line. The task assigned to 1st Guards Brigade (which was finally decided in early July) was to exploit the successes gained by the other two Guards brigades.[12]

This area to be attacked provided a number of challenges. The low-lying ground stretching along the Yser Canal formed a significant barrier between the two hostile trench systems. The Germans had excellent observation of the ground down to the canal as they occupied the high ground of the Pilckem Ridge and also from 'a small detached hill' lying a little to the north-west of Pilckem. Therefore, the enemy could see all the preparations for the attack. The canal itself was especially daunting: 'the canal bed which had a surface of about 70 feet of soft and tenacious mud into which a man sank like a stone, and a narrow, shallow stream of water flowing down the middle, was a formidable obstacle – so formidable, indeed, that neither side had made any serious attempt to cross it during the war'.[13] As Headlam pointed out, it seemed that any advance on the Boesinghe front would depend on 'the rapidity and precision with which this exceedingly difficult movement could be carried out'. After considerable debate, a solution suggested by Belgian advisers was adopted. Ingenious in its simplicity, a number of mats which were 'a yard in width and longer than the canal at its broadest point were constructed from strong canvas reinforced with a backing of wire netting and small wooden slats at close intervals'. A demonstration over the Poperinghe Canal with 500 men was successful and gave confidence that this method would work but some arrangements would have to be made in case heavy rain led to the Yser Canal's water level rising.[14]

Meanwhile, the 76th Field Company RE renovated and realigned four communication trenches in addition to transforming a farmhouse just north of Elverdinghe into a divisional battle HQ. The tunnelling company worked intensively to find pockets of blue clay that were suitable to sink a shaft where a series of chambers for the combined HQs of the two brigades leading the attack would be located. Parts of the canal bank were blown up to facilitate easier access for the pontoons and railway construction continued. This vital work was carried out under frequent artillery fire but remarkably, the bridging operations over the canal were complete by 23 July. Additionally, chambers were built under the bank to store a petrol tin bridge and five wooden footbridges for the attacking infantry. Positioned behind each tunnel leading to the chambers were nine mats and repairing materials. A heavier petrol tin bridge lay at hand to be brought forward through the tunnels if required. This was a remarkable feat of human endeavour. Whilst daylight

12 TNA: WO95/1193, Guards Division HQ, Conference held at Divisional HQ 18 June 1917, App. 274.
13 Headlam, *History of the Guards Division*, p.225.
14 Headlam, *History of the Guards Division*, p.228.

hours were suitable for moving lighter loads, the heaviest loads could only be moved in darkness. As the 76th Field Company's war diary stated: 'During the last fortnight the company has marched an average of 160 miles per man in addition to daily work. A good portion of this has been with heavy loads and all in shelled areas.'[15]

In anticipation of the Guards' attack a short length of a stream which ran through the wooded area in the divisional area had been selected and converted by the RE into an exact model of the Yser Canal to enable troops to practice crossing this important objective. Also, a large sand model was erected of the whole area over which XIV Corps was to operate. The model was laid out to scale and showed the enemy's positions together with the natural and artificial features of the landscape. The idea was to provide a good indication of the ground to be crossed which could then inform the most effective tactics.[16] It included the canal and the British assembly trenches and extended as far as the second objective.[17]

Kipling, never one to hold back if he believed his beloved Irish Guards were being short-changed, described the immense preparations that were made for the Guards Division for the 10 days of special training:

> The whole model was on the same scale as the actual German front-line system. Although the existing features of the ground were puzzling at first, the model proved to be extremely useful as teaching all ranks the lie of the land. The only features not included were the hidden concrete 'pill boxes' supporting each other behind his line, on which the enemy was basing his new and unpleasant system of elastic defence. But, allowing for inevitable unrealities, there is no doubt that training 'on the model' supples and brings a Battalion to hand better than any other device. The men grow keen as they realise by eye what is to be expected; talk it over afterwards (there are certain analogies between trench-to-trench attack and 'soccer'); the N.C.O.'s discuss with the officers, and the Battalion Commander can check some preventable errors before the real thing is loosed.

Kipling went on to describe the sheer intensity of preparation undertaken by the 2/Irish as they repeated the attack in every detail until 'as far as the Battalion was concerned the drill of the attack was reduced almost to perfection'.[18]

On 4 July news had arrived that the King would visit the Guards Division to witness for himself their preparations. For Miles Barne, this was a mixed blessing. On 5 July he:

> Spent a long day out. In morning, we practised the real show, 'popping the Canal' etc, on the trenches we had dug – then dinners, and afterwards we practiced the

15 76th Field Company War Diary quoted in Headlam, *History of The Guards Division*, p.229.
16 Headlam, *History of The Guards Division*, p.228
17 TNA: WO95/1222, 3rd Guards Brigade HQ. Narrative of Operations of the 3rd Guards Brigade in the attack from Boesinghe on 31st July.
18 Kipling *Irish Guards in the Great War, 2nd Battalion*, pp.128–129.

> 'put up show'. July 6 was 'A lovely day – paraded at 9.15 am. and did our 'put up show' for the King and swarms of big wigs – Generals & Staffs of every degree. The King was put in a meadow and shown it all & no doubt was told it was exactly what we were going to do on 'the' day, though it differed in many respects, for the sake of making a good show for him. Very few of the troops even saw the King – and most of those who saw him, saw him only in the distance, as I did and from our point of view it was a total failure, & might have been otherwise – I hope he enjoyed what he saw! No doubt he was anxious not to interfere with our training, but as a matter of fact what we did has all got to be forgotten (not easy) and a good ceremonial parade would have done discipline good and the men would have liked to see the King, and cheered him.[19]

Barne's diary shows, however that the serious preparation soon resumed. On 7 July: 'Did a battalion attack against the Dummy trenches – Many new orders and instructions'. On 8 July: 'In the afternoon did the Battn attack again. The thing is gradually shaping itself.' Finally on 9 July: 'Battalion attack again in the morning … Attended a Brigade Confce … in the evening, and saw "models" from all 4 Battns & Machine Gunners, Riflemen, Bombers, Rifle Bombers, Lewis Gunners, Runners etc dressed up as for the Attack.'[20]

The experience of the 3rd Guards Brigade provides a good example of the intensive activity of these weeks. On 18 June, it had marched into the Herzeele area where it had set to digging the replica of the German trench system that would be used by the rest of the Guards Division. On a daily basis until the end of June, the troops were practiced over the attack ground, each practice being slightly more advanced with specific attention to overcoming strong points that might hold up an attack together with the response to failures by flanking units as well as communications, medical arrangements, carrying parties, working with contact aeroplanes and effective consolidation of any ground gained.

On 1 and 2 July, the brigade moved on to the Divisional Reserve area and then into the line. Then up until 24 July, the brigade provided 23,000 men for working parties in preparation for the attack. The main work was cable burying, carrying ammunition for trench mortars, track making and general support for the RE. Additionally, the left sector of the Divisional front was held from 12–24 July, whilst the garrison worked on the construction of assembly trenches including extra parados, on maintenance of the canal bank, and general improvement of the communication trenches. The attack was originally scheduled for 28 July, but it was postponed to 31 July because bad weather had delayed the French artillery preparation. Consequently, the brigade was pulled out for three days complete rest. 'This rest was very badly needed as many of the men had been without sleep on an average, of two nights out of three … the casualties to carrying parties and to troops holding the line had been severe – about 600 in three

19 Nicol, *Barne's Diary*, p.288.
20 Nicol, *Barne's Diary*, p.288.

weeks.' The Germans had made use of continual gas bombardments that necessitated the wearing of gas masks by carrying parties and by troops moving in and out of the line. Unsurprisingly, this contributed to the troops 'discomfort, fatigue and loss.' The 2/Scots Guards, in particular, suffered very severely from gas; five officers and 200 other ranks were forced out of action by just one bombardment.[21]

The German defenders were themselves subjected to intense artillery fire during these weeks. The artillery was tasked with destroying front line German positions and, when needed, they would be expected to provide protective support in the assault and consolidation phases. Fifth Army had a sufficient amount of artillery to deliver the impact required: 'one 18–pdr per 15 yards and one medium or heavy howitzer (excluding counter-battery guns) per 50 yards of front'. Haig had stressed the vital importance of counter-battery fire before the attack was launched, and Major General Sir Herbert Uniacke (GOCRA) had demanded that fire should '[R]ender useless for further occupation the immediate ground round the gun positions by means of a fierce concentration bombardment by every medium and heavy howitzer than can be brought to bear.' In the artillery planning stages, it was decided that, for example, a 'barrage in depth' approach would be employed in the attack, that divisional artilleries would provide each of their attacking brigades HQs with a battery commander and each attacking battalion's HQ would receive an additional artillery officer. British artillery preparations began formally on 16 July but, 'with the removal of ammunition restrictions on 4 July the tempo of artillery operations increased rapidly' for 24 hours a day. Developments in the methodology used by Royal Engineer Field Survey companies together with the support of Royal Flying Corps observation squadrons and kite ballon sections meant that counter-battery fire could now be more effective.[22] Jack Sheldon notes that '1,000 medium or heavy guns and howitzers and more than 2,000 field guns fired four and a quarter million shells over a two week period into a waterlogged countryside and its precarious drainage system.'[23]

Unsurprisingly, conditions became increasingly difficult for the German defenders in both the forward and rear areas. The reconnaissance flights and air attacks mounted by the RFC went beyond the front lines with relative impunity and the seemingly relentless artillery bombardment of gas-filled mortar bombs and shells poisoned the air for several kilometres into the German lines. All movement of any kind, whether it be in rations or munitions, was stifled and conditions in the limited number of dugouts and pill boxes became increasingly intolerable. *Reserve Leutnant* Rau of the 6th company, *Grenadier Regiment 89*, described the conditions experienced by so many of those along the German front. Suffering in a large, cramped concrete pillbox he commented that:

21 TNA: WO95/1222, 3rd Guards Brigade HQ. Narrative of Operations of the 3rd Guards Brigade in the attack from Boesinghe on 31st July.

22 Simon Shepherd. '"Artillery Conquers, Infantry Occupies". A Study in the Performance of the British Artillery at the Third Battle of Ypres', in Spencer Jones (ed.) *The Darkest Year: The British Army on the Western Front 1917* (Warwick: Helion, 2022), pp.388–392.

23 Jack Sheldon, *The German Army at Passchendaele* (Barnsley: Pen and Sword, 2007), p.45.

'The British soon increased the tempo of their shelling. It was easy to see that large masses of guns, of every calibre from small to super heavy, were being pressed into service to bombard our position.' With increased aerial activity as well, Rau realised that 'an offensive of huge proportions' was imminent. After three or four weeks, his position was now just a crater field and, with the pillboxes standing out so clearly as easy targets, it became necessary to try and take cover in these craters even though they were under what seemed relentless fire. The high water table meant the craters soon flooded and men could easily drown. Wires were cut by the artillery fire and orders could only be communicated by using runners. British intelligence would have been delighted to know that 'Gradually the company losses started to make themselves felt. The average strength dropped to between twenty and forty men. As a result of lack of sleep, insufficient food and over-exertion they became so completely apathetic, that the officers were extremely concerned about their ability to counter attacks launched by fresh British assault troops.'[24]

With the assault becoming imminent, it became imperative to know what the impact of the sustained artillery bombardment and RFC activity had been on the German defences faced by the Guards. Consequently, several remarkably successful raids were made for this purpose. For example, on the night of 19/20 July, the entire front-line defences opposite the Guards Division were raided by the 2/Irish Guards and the 4/Grenadier Guards without any artillery support. The raid confirmed that the Yser Canal's water levels had risen. The muddy conditions were far from ideal but the German trenches were largely deserted. On the night of 22/23 July patrols of the 4/Grenadiers met no opposition and reported that the canal near the railway line was easy to cross but further north the water levels were much higher.

A raid on the night of 24/25 July by the 4/Grenadiers is well documented in the diary of Lieutenant Esmond Elliot. On 17 July, he wrote that:

> The Battalion is probably going to do a raid when we go into the line on the 21st. The CO has warned me and Victor Harbord to be the officers. We go in two parties; each party has two mats and consists of about 25 men. The object of the raid is to get identification: to find out what the Ypres Lys is like, how strongly the line is held, and to kill as many Huns as possible. The whole of my Platoon volunteered for it, which pleases me. I am awfully glad I have been chosen, and only hope all will go well.[25]

On 21 July, Lieutenant Colonel Orr Ewing told Elliot that he would lead the raid alone because a fellow officer had been incapacitated in a mustard gas attack which the Germans were now using for the first time with dramatic effect. On 23 July, Elliot described the dramatic consequences of a seven-hour gas bombardment and later, 'I met

24 Sheldon, *The German Army at Passchendaele*, pp.41–42.
25 Astor and Campbell, *The Lost Idol*, p.177.

two Platoons coming out of the line, some of them totally blind … Our casualties from gas and wounds are now 140-150 men'.[26]

The raid's objectives were straightforward: to ascertain the condition of the German trenches, the location of their strong points and what kind of problems were likely to be faced whilst crossing the canal. As ever with any trench raid, killing the enemy and taking prisoners was an expectation. The plan was an elaborate one. There would be an initial but short-lived bombardment by both trench mortars, machine and Lewis guns which was designed to hold down the Germans and stifle any noise as the mats were placed down. There would be four entry points into the German lines on a front of 300 yards with four raiding parties suitably separated with each party consisting of 16 men with clearly defined roles. Two companies of the pioneer battalion, 4/Coldstream, laid the mats and bridges before the covering party crossed led by an officer would cross to what was known as Baboon Trench. The mat men would cross next followed by bayonet men, sentries over dug-outs and moppers up. Zero hour was fixed for 12:05 a.m. and the raid was expected to last no more than 20 minutes. There was a French raid to the left which Elliot had to be mindful of. These meticulous plans, perhaps unsurprisingly, did not go completely to plan. Elliott described how:

> At 10.30 pm, I went round with the Coldstream officer to see if the mats were ready to be put down. As we went along the line the Hun put over several Gas shells so close that they nearly choked me. I put on my respirator, but had to take it off again for coughing and sneezing. Each man had a Rifle and Bayonet and two Bombs. The Covering Party had three Mills Grenades, and the 'Moppers' had three Phosphorous Bombs for Dug-outs…
>
> I got to the Middle of the Canal, up to my waist in mud and water, when it was passed back to me that the mats were too short and sank considerably and that we could not get across. It would have been useless to have tried to struggle on with no mat. So I decided to take the whole lot back and to cross on the Left Flank mat, 20 yards further down.
>
> Owing to the darkness we missed the mat, but afterwards found it. It was getting late, so I sent the whole party back to our own trench and crossed myself with Sergeant Smart and two men. I found Left Flank, who had met no Germans, and had been as far as the arranged rendez-vous with the French who never turned up. Covered by the Covering Party, I then went on with two to reconnoitre the Yper Lys [Yser Canal], about 200 yards beyond. It could be crossed anywhere.
>
> Baboon Trench was blown to smithereens by our shelling, and clearly untenable. Poor devils, they must have had a bad time as there was practically no trench left! The concrete Dug-outs and Machine Gun emplacements [were] very much damaged. I am sure the Huns hold this trench at night by patrols, and it is just a matter of luck whether one runs into them or not.

26 Astor and Campbell, *The Lost Idol*, p.182.

> We were there for over 20 minutes. We, alas met no Huns! The greatest disappointment to us all – we had so hoped to collar a prisoner or two.[27]

Elliott could be very proud of what he and his men had achieved. Indeed, he remarked that 'The CO has been most awfully nice about the Raid, saying we found out all the information asked for'.[28]

This particular raid certainly provided some more encouraging evidence, but it was not quite 'the game changing moment for Feilding as some have argued.[29] Collectively, reports from the raids offered a mixed picture; the water levels were a continuing concern but on the other hand the artillery bombardment had certainly had the desired effect. The Germans had, without a doubt, been forced to withdraw and were not holding their front-line trenches in any strength. Haig commented later: 'Whether the withdrawal … was due to the desire of the German infantry to escape our bombardment or to their fear that our attack would be inaugurated by the explosion of a new series of mines, is uncertain.'[30] With Feilding still considering the recent intelligence gained, a chance event in the early hours of 27 July appears to have acted as the final catalyst for action. Two wounded British soldiers who had been left behind during a night raid were seen on the far side of the canal, and Lieutenant C.J. Hambro and Private Smith, of the 3/Coldstream Guards, volunteered to go across to bring them in. Having safely recovering the wounded men, Hambro reported back that no Germans had been seen and they had been subject to no hostile fire. In fact, units of the *49th Reserve Division*, especially *Reserve Infantry Regiment 226*, had withdrawn from their positions because of the heavy bombardment.[31]

Feilding decided to seize the moment and, according to the *Grenadiers History*:

> … conceived the audacious plan of seizing the Canal in broad daylight without the aid of an artillery barrage. If the information which he had gained was correct, the enterprise would certainly succeed, but if on the other hand the absence of the Germans was only momentary, as had so often happened, it might prove a costly failure. He decided not to wait but to strike at once, and accordingly sent for Lieut.-Colonel Crawford commanding the 3rd Battalion Coldstream Guards, and told him to send out strong patrols properly supported at 5 p.m. as far as Baboon Support Trench, Artillery Wood, and Cactus Junction. As the matter was urgent, these orders were given verbally, and were later confirmed in writing, but it was not found possible to start before 5.20. The whole scheme, although planned at a moment's notice, was well thought out. The patrols pushed forward closely

27 Astor and Campbell, *The Lost Idol*, p.184–185.
28 Astor and Campbell, *The Lost Idol*, p.185.
29 Astor and Campbell, *The Lost Idol*, p.185.
30 Douglas Haig's 4th Dispatch, <http://www.longlongtrail.co.uk/battles/british-field-commanders-despatches/sir-douglas-haigs-fourth-despatch-bullecourt-messines-third-ypres/>, accessed 16 January 2024.
31 Sheldon, *Passchendaele*, p.42.

> followed by supporting platoons and moppers-up, and succeeded without difficulty in reaching their objectives, where they surprised the Germans who had been left in charge of the trenches. Many prisoners were made, but so quickly and unobtrusively was the raid carried out that the Germans in rear were totally ignorant of what was happening.[32]

The 3/Coldstream Guards remained in these advanced positions for the best part of two days. Any German patrols were allowed to enter the trench before being captured until one particular NCO was able to evade capture and report back on the situation. Unsurprisingly, this brought a swift response from German aircraft and a heavy artillery bombardment began. Fortunately for the Guards, the German attack was launched in great haste with inadequate command and control so that orders were not passed properly down the chain of command. The units of *49th Reserve Division* were already exhausted and unable to mount a credible counter-attack in the face of hostile artillery fire. *Vizefeldwebel* Wellhausen of the 3rd Company, *Fusilier Regiment 73*, *111th Division*, was one of those called on to resist the Guards. His platoon was deployed in shell holes close to the aptly named Artillery Wood. He described how 'the larks were singing and rejoicing up in the sky as shells fell … The earth heaved and rocked. It was like hell on earth' whilst 'British airman circled endlessly above us, machine gunning continuously.' His platoon moved forward at 9:30 p.m. to the front line but 'we were spotted by a British captive balloon crew' and soon 'a hail of shellfire, far worse than anything we had experienced on the Somme came down upon us.' With German units working in isolation from each other, Wellhausen's platoon came across a strong Guards force. 'It seemed as though, instead of a few isolated soldiers, we had come up against something more like a battalion … with shouts of *Hurra*, we launched ourselves forward, but we were too weak.' During the day, a decision was taken by *Leutnant* Ehlert to hold the platoon's position but this was soon discovered by a British aircraft which was nick-named the 'trench inspector'. Wellhausen noted that 'it was here to direct the artillery fire by means of signals and, having dived to roof top height, soon spotted us. I could clearly see the crewman photographing us and taking notes, before flying over to the British trench to throw out a report.' The aircraft then circled and waited for the Guards to move forward. Wellhausen lit a green flare but his request for harassing fire failed to get a response. A desperate retreat then ensued from shell hole to shell hole. 'The British were standing up and shooting at anything that moved' as the Germans continued to suffer heavy losses.[33]

With the Yser Canal now under the Guards' control and the German defences in total disarray, a vital advantage had been secured. The main assault could now start on the far bank which would make ultimate success far more likely with fewer casualties. This was an ideal scenario and a significant achievement for the Guards Division. Feilding's decisive leadership had paid off.

32 Ponsonby, *Grenadiers History*, vol.2, pp.201–203.
33 Sheldon, *Passchendaele*, pp.43–45.

10

Pilckem Ridge: The Attack on 31 July 1917

In the early hours of 31 July, the Guards Division, as planned, attacked on a front of approximately 1,600 yards with the 38th Welsh on the right and the 1st French on the left. Opposing the Guards' front were units of the *111th Infantry Division* which had been formed in Flanders during 1915 and recruited mainly from Lower Saxony. The division was 'composed of young men, part of whom had experience in very active sections'.[1] It comprised the *221st Brigade* and incorporated the *73rd Fusiliers, 76th and 164th Regiments*. Writing after the war *General der Infantarie* Hermann Von Kuhl, chief of staff of *Armee Gruppe Kronprinz* Rupprecht described what happened in the early hours of that day along the front:

> …a hurricane of fire, completely beyond anyone's experience broke out. The entire earth of Flanders rocked and seemed to be on fire. This was not just drum fire; it was as though Hell itself had slipped its bonds. What were the terrors of Verdun and the Somme compared to this grotesquely huge outpouring of raw power? The violent thunder of battle could be heard in the furthest corner of Belgium. It was as though the enemy was announcing to the world: *Here we come and we are going to prevail.*[2]

The Guards' attack was to be made in four bounds with the 2nd Guards Brigade on the right and 3rd Guards on the left. Each had a front of about 800 yards. The first objective (blue line) was the German reserve line about 1,000 yards east of the canal, and about 500 yards on the right and 800 yards on the left from the Guards' front line. This included Artillery Wood on the right and Wood 15 on the left, which both had strong German defences. The second objective (black line) was not defined by any line of enemy trenches. It was about 700 yards from the blue line on the right brigade's front, and about 400 yards on the front of the left brigade. The third objective (green

1 Anon, *Histories of 251 Divisions*, pp.600–602.
2 Sheldon, *Passchendaele*, p.52.

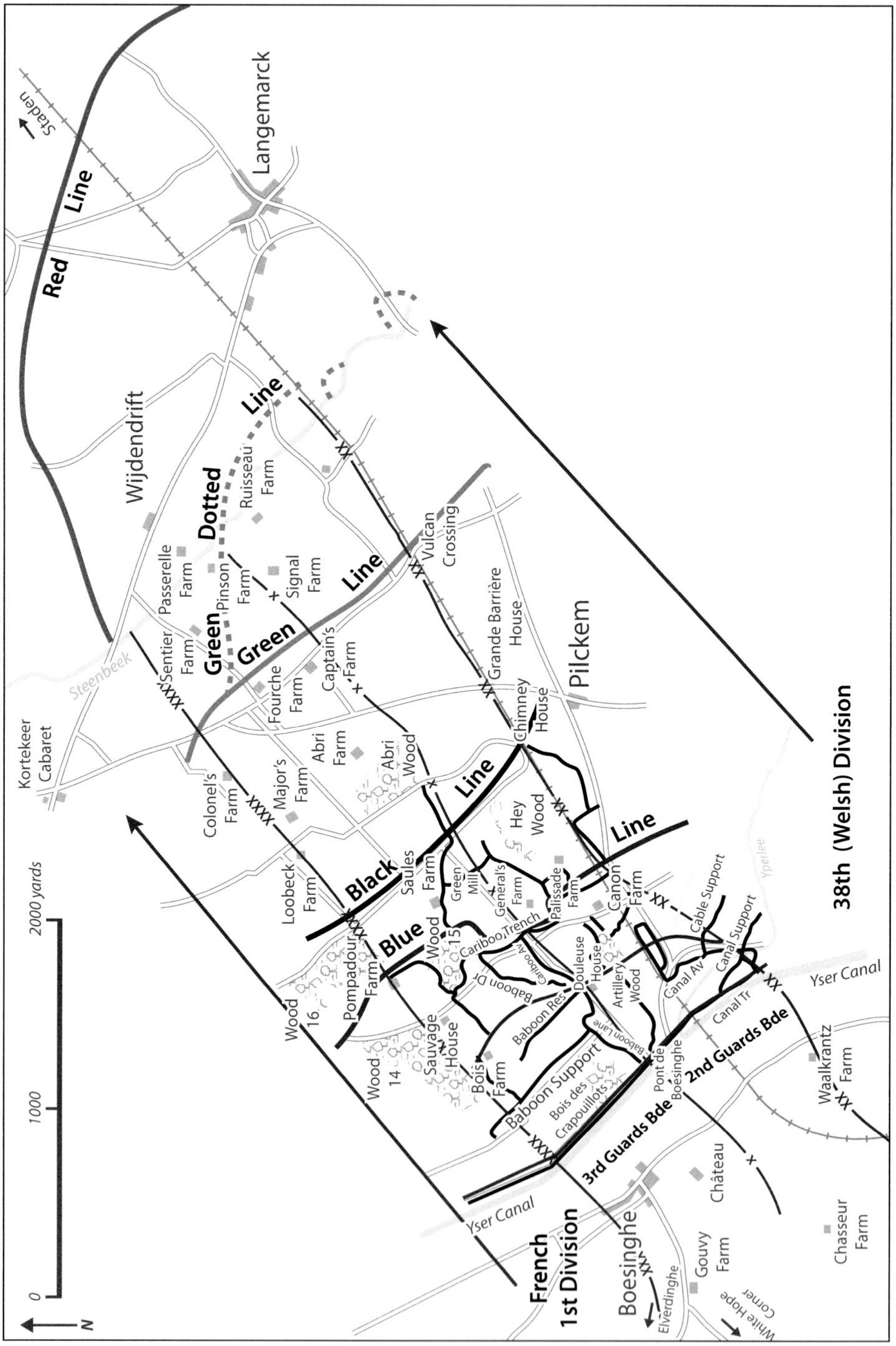

The Third Battle of Ypres, the Battle of Pilckem Ridge, 31 July 1917.

line) was about 1,300 yards from the black line. This formed the last objective of the two leading brigades. The attack from there to the fourth objective was to be made by two battalions of the 1st Guards Brigade. The fourth objective (green-dotted line) included the capture of the eastern bank of the river Steenbeek on the right, a distance of about 900 yards, with a flank brought back on the left to join up with the French on the green line. From there orders would be given to the 1st Guards Brigade to push out patrols and gain any ground abandoned by the enemy up to and including the fifth and final objective (red line) which was the organised enemy trench system running from Langemarck to Wijdedrift.

Because the 1st Guards Brigade had established themselves on the east bank of the canal as far as the enemy support trenches, the attacking brigades were able to assemble for the attack along the new line helped by the fact that several petrol tin and mat bridges had already been made and placed in position. During 30 July, one battalion of each brigade moved up in small lots to their assembly positions. The remainder of the Guards Division started to assemble at 9:15 p.m. The assembly was carried out successfully with few casualties by 1:00 a.m. on 31 July. This was very largely because a gas shell bombardment on the German gun lines was kept up overnight from 10:00 p.m. until 3:45 a.m. At 3:50 a.m. on 31 July the attack was launched but, because the Guards Division held a line in advance of the flanking divisions, the troops did not leave their trenches until zero plus 34 to allow the barrage to come up into the line. The artillery support was extensive; a creeping barrage which advanced at a rate of 100 yards in four minutes plus a machine gun barrage consisting of the guns of two sections of 2nd and 3rd Brigade's machine gun companies, 4th Company and 88th Company, arranged in echelons. The artillery barrage was formed by the divisional artillery consisting of six brigades of field artillery. There was also a barrage formed by the corps heavy artillery which searched the ground between the objectives and lifted back as the field artillery barrage approached. Further, smoke barrages were also made by the barrage guns to hide the assembly of the troops between each objective.

The after-battle narrative in the Guards Division war diary outlines a remarkably efficient and effective attack. Each Guards brigade (2nd and 3rd) attacked with two battalions in front and two in reserve. The two leading battalions, in four waves, attacked the blue and black lines, and the two reserve battalions came through on the black line and attacked the green line. The leading battalions of the 2nd Guards Brigade were the 1/Scots on the right and 2/Irish on the left with the 3/Grenadiers behind the Scots and the 1/Coldstream behind the Irish. The leading battalions of the 3rd Guards Brigade were the 1/Grenadiers on the right and the 1/Welsh on the left with the 4/Grenadiers behind the Grenadiers and the 2/Scots behind the Welsh. The morning was described as 'exceptionally dark and cloudy but not rainy'. At 3:50 a.m. it was almost dark but by 4:24 a.m., when the infantry left their trenches, it was just beginning to get light. At 4:00 a.m. there was a German barrage on the 38th Divisions' trenches but not on the Guards. At 5:00 a.m. an enemy barrage came down on the canal.

Both Guards brigades gained their first objective on schedule but not without loss, on the left from shell fire and on the right from machine gun fire from Artillery Wood, which was able to bring enfilade fire on the third and fourth waves of the 2nd Guards Brigade. Fortunately, this was soon overcome, and the blue line was found to be unoccupied. The 3rd Guards Brigade encountered considerable machine gun fire from the blockhouses in Wood 15 and suffered some casualties.

At zero plus 1:19, the 2nd Guards Brigade advanced to the attack on the black line and at zero plus 2:20, the 3rd Guards Brigade also advanced. German opposition came from machine-gun fire in organised shell holes but fortunately the line was captured without many casualties. At zero plus 3:24, the two reserve battalions of the leading brigades came through and advanced to the attack on the green line. The 3/Grenadiers on the right encountered heavy machine-gun fire from the concrete blockhouses just north of the railway and it was necessary to reinforce the leading waves by one of the companies in the rear with the result that all opposition was overcome. The battalion reached its objective, taking three officers and 50 men prisoner.

Meanwhile, on the left, the 4/Grenadiers came under heavy machine gun fire moving through Abri Wood and the 2/Scots were forced to throw back a defensive flank around Colonels Farm which the French 201st Regiment failed to capture initially but were successful in doing so later. The 3rd Guards trench mortar battery 'rendered great assistance' in clearing up a strong point held by the enemy in Green Mill. Eight machine guns each of the 2nd and 3rd Machine Gun Companies were attached to battalions, two to each, and they were used successfully for the defence of various objectives and exposed flanks.

By zero plus 4:10, the green line had been captured and consolidation had begun. Both flanking divisions (the French and the 38th) had gained their objectives up to this point and 'touch' had been obtained on the blue line and black lines but because the enemy still possessed Colonels Farm on the left flank of the green line, 'touch' was only obtained with the French some 200 yards short of this point. At 8:50 a.m. the two battalions of the 1st Guards Brigade, the 2/Grenadiers and the 2/Coldstream, were close up to the green line and were ready to exploit the progress made by the two leading brigades beyond it. The right-hand company of the 2/Grenadiers came up to the 3/Grenadiers as arranged but the left-hand company, on their arrival on the 'green line', found a gap between the 3/Grenadiers and the 4/Grenadiers on the left as a result of the 1/Coldstream having closed up to the right. The gap was filled and the line consolidated. The 2/Coldstream had no difficulty in finding the troops of the 3/Guards Brigade on the green line.

The advance to the green-dotted line then began. The 2/Coldstream on the left successfully accomplished the difficult manoeuvre of changing front half left to take up the line of the fourth objective, and the left company of the 2/Grenadiers advanced to and crossed the Steenbeek on to its objective taking many prisoners including a battalion commander. The right company was at first unable to advance owing to machine gun fire from the railway and because the troops of 38th Division had not come up on the right. This opposition was, however, overcome with Lewis gun fire and sniping, and the troops began to advance. This enabled the company of the Grenadier Guards to advance within 80 yards of the Steenbeek, 200 yards short of their objective. They were unable to advance beyond this line because of heavy machine gun fire from Langemarck. The line was now consolidated.

The ground on the eastern side of the Steenbeek was found to be strongly held by the enemy; especially along the Langemarck to Wijdendrift road and, as the barrage had become thin, it was not possible to push out patrols in front until dusk, when the 2/Coldstream established posts at Pinson and Sentier Farms. Two sections of the 1st Guards Brigade machine gun company followed closely behind each battalion of the 1st Guards Brigade and these guns were established on and behind the green-dotted line. During the day, two battalions of each of the 2nd and 3rd Guards Brigades were withdrawn into reserve around the Roussel Farm area. Finally, the narrative notes that: 'Signal communications on the whole had worked well; especially pigeon, visual and wireless together with relay runners.'[3]

Therefore, before 10:00 a.m. on 31 July, the Guards had been successful in taking all of their objectives, bar the frontage of one company on the far right of the line, in a well-planned and effectively implemented operation. Their attack had undoubtedly been assisted by the performance of the French First Army which had been required to advance 2,500 yards and establish a defensive flank for the Guards attack and Fifth Army as a whole. Prior and Wilson have argued that the role of the French was very significant:

> Supported by a greater weight of artillery relative to the front attack than any French assault yet mounted, the troops swept forward, meeting little resistance up to their final objective. Even beyond that the Germans had insufficient machine-guns to resist a further advance, so that at the end of the day the French were occupying positions beyond those set down. Losses were fewer than 1,000 in each of the divisions involved.[4]

The French were in no doubt that their success was down to the effectiveness of their artillery preparation and implementation that disabled so many German concrete shelters and blockhouses.[5]

On the face of it, this was very impressive indeed. However, the post-battle narrative of operations by de Crespigny commanding the 2/Grenadiers in the 1st Guards Brigade gives a very good idea of the attack from a battalion and company perspective as they moved to the front line and beyond to the final objective which was some two and a half miles distant. Reading this account, it is possible to see that this was a far from straightforward operation. On the night of 30 July, at about 10:30 p.m., the battalion moved from bivouacs in the forest area about two and half miles west of Elverdinghe to a field near Roussel Farm. The weather was fine and there was no shelling of the battalion

3 TNA: WO95/1193, Guards Division HQ, Narrative of Operations 31 July 1917.
4 Prior and Wilson, *Passchendaele*, p.89.
5 Prior and Wilson, *Passchendaele*, p.89.

during the night. Breakfast was at 3:00 a.m. At 4:00 a.m., the men moved off in platoon 'blobs'. 'Officers for the first time were dressed like men'. The platoons moved forward in two parts and by the scheduled time of 5:20 a.m. the four platoons had met at a point about 1,000 yards west of the Yser Canal. During the early stages of the advance the shelling was very light; it was not until the canal was reached that heavy shelling on both sides of it meant that the battalion began to suffer casualties. Apart from this, the advance to the green line was 'without particular incident' and 'the battalion advanced with perfect steadiness, intervals and distance being kept as though on a field day'. The canal was crossed at about 6:00 a.m. using the temporary bridges. The battalion were now able to make good time 'so that all platoons were able to halt occasionally in shell-holes at the discretion of Company Officers in order to avoid any zones which appeared to receive particular attention from enemy shelling'. However, care had to be taken as 'the enemy were continually shortening the range, and there is no doubt that by moving away from the shelling as necessity demanded, many casualties were avoided'.

At about 2,000 yards from the old front line, the leading companies, No.1 (left) and No.2 (right) came under machine gun and rifle fire and deployed. The other two companies did likewise upon reaching the same point. The advance was continued in two lines to a point about 500 yards southwest of the green line, around 3,000 yards from the old front line. Here the battalion halted as planned until 8:20 a.m. During this period, the 2nd Guards Brigade was timed to advance to and capture the green line, and 25 minutes later at 8:45 a.m., the battalion advanced according to orders through the 2nd Guards Brigade and up to the barrage, which was supposed to stay 200 yards east of the green line for some minutes and then advance to cover the attack of the 1st Guards Brigade.

The green line was not a line of trenches, but only a line of a road which provided a convenient landmark. When the leading companies reached this line, the right company (No.2) found the 3/Battalion Grenadiers digging in as anticipated. Unfortunately, Captain J.N. Buchanan, commanding No.1 Company on the left, could see no trace of the 1/Coldstream who should have been consolidating on the left of the 3/Grenadiers. As his company was slightly in advance of their time, Buchanan commenced to dig in at his position which was on the crest of the hill and exposed to considerable machine gun fire. At that moment, Captain A.T.A. Ritchie MC, commanding the right front company, sent a message to say that his company was held up by machine gun fire and that there was no sign of the battalion on his right. 'The whole line was … under considerable machine gun and rifle fire from farms and strong points at this juncture.' Two officers from No.2 Company were hit by machine gun bullets: Captain Ritchie and Lieutenant R.G.C. Napier. Command then passed to Lieutenant A.S.L. St. J. Mildmay. Captain Buchanan (No.1 Company) decided he ought not to stop whilst it was possible to move on. He continued his advance sending a request to No.3 Company to ask them to garrison the green line for the present. However, Buchanan could not move off straight away because of the delay caused on the left by the absence of the 1/Coldstream who had gone too far to the right and had become mixed up with 3/Grenadier Guards and to the right by the failure of the 17/Royal Welsh Fusiliers. The advance was not continued until after the barrage was timed to move away.

The artillery barrage was, however, extremely uncertain. Sometimes, it dropped across the Steenbeek 800 yards away but sometimes it was so close that the company had to halt. Consequently 'the delay was not the disaster it might have been'. Buchanan's company succeeded in reaching Signal and Ruisseau Farms where 'twenty or thirty' German prisoners, including several officers were captured. Finally, along with a platoon from No.3 Company led by Lieutenant K.O.G. Harvard, Buchanan crossed the Steenbeek and dug in 60 yards beyond the east bank. As de Crespigny remarked: 'The manner in which this Company pushed on under the leadership of Captain J.N. Buchanan and Second Lieutenants R.G. Briscoe and P.A.A. Harbord was quite admirable.'

Meanwhile the position on the right of the battalion was more difficult. When it was found out that the 17/Royal Welsh Fusiliers had failed to advance up to the green line, a platoon of No.4 Company under Lieutenant R.E.H. Oliver at once formed a defensive flank to the right. By this time No.2 Company, by throwing out flank parties with snipers and by Lewis gun fire, had succeeded in silencing some of the opposing machine guns and was again able to advance. Unfortunately, owing to the failure on his right, Lieutenant Mildmay was forced to use half of his company to defend his flank and was thus unable to maintain touch with No.2 Company which had pushed forward on his left. No.4's commander, Lieutenant J.H. Jacob, sent one platoon to assist the advance of No.2 Company and, after consultation with Buchanan, dispatched a third platoon under Second Lieutenant F.H.J. Drummond to extend the right of No.3 Company who had by now advanced in support of No.1 Company. Drummond was then wounded by a shell, which killed a man either side of him, but in spite of this and a later wound in the neck from a bullet. 'He remained at duty until the Battalion was relieved and displayed most conspicuous ability in grasping and dealing with every situation which arose.'

By this time a handful of the Royal Welsh Fusiliers had appeared on the right rear and Mildmay, aware of the importance of pushing on, continued his advance up to within 80 yards of the Steenbeek where they met very heavy German machine gun fire from Langemarck. Mildmay now ordered his men to dig in. During the whole period from the green line, the battalion was under steady German shell fire which caused many casualties. Under the cover of darkness, the line was strengthened and touch established between all units. Overnight drizzle continued with few interruptions until the battalion was relieved by the 1/Irish Guards two days later on the night of 2 August. Enemy snipers were always a threat: 'owing to the exposed position of our line and the impossibility, owing to the wet, of digging deep trenches, the enemy was able to inflict several casualties'. Lieutenant K.O.G. Harvard was a victim, dying of his wounds when he reached the Regimental Aid Post.

De Crespigny observed that, 'We suffered greatly though the proximity of the 38th Division who, day and night, persisted without any counter-attack in sending up S.O.S. Signals, which brought down our barrage, some of which was on our own line and also retaliation from the enemy.' Conditions for the men were very poor throughout with trenches and shell holes waterlogged, and 'little better than those occupied during the past winter'. The casualties: two officers dead, four wounded (two lightly remaining at duty). Other ranks: 44 killed, 191 wounded, 15 missing, 11 slightly wounded remaining at duty. This gave a total of 261 other ranks either killed, missing, or wounded.[6]

The diary of Lieutenant W.B. St Leger, who commanded a company in the 2/Irish Guards, also confirms that, despite the overall success of this day for the Guards Division, losses were still very heavy for some units. His battalion was a follow-up formation to the main attack but nonetheless his orderly was killed by a bullet through the neck and his sergeant (Harris) was hit by a shell that blew away half of his face. Two of his fellow officers (Turner and Leggett) were also killed and three friends ('Lucien', Porrit and Kirk) were seriously wounded in the stomach, neck and chest respectively together with three other friends who received less severe wounds ('Grubby', Day and Publicover). St Leger himself was wounded in the knee and stretchered off the battlefield.[7]

Two VCs were won by the Guards on 31 July 1917: Private Thomas Whitham of the 1/Coldstream Guards and Robert Bye of the Welsh Guards. Whitham was beyond the green line as his battalion fought to consolidate their position:

> …when, during an attack, an enemy machine-gun was seen to be enfilading the battalion on the right. Private Witham [sic] on his own initiative, immediately worked his way from shell hole to shell hole through our own barrage, rushed the machine gun and although under very heavy fire, captured it, together with an officer and two other ranks. The bold action of Private Witham [sic] was of great assistance to the battalion on the right, and undoubtedly saved many lives and enabled the whole line to advance.[8]

Sadly, Whitham struggle to cope with life after the war despite being feted in his town as a war hero. He decided not to return to working on the trams in Burnley but failed to find regular employment as a bricklayer and had to pawn his VC. In 1924 he suffered a serious head injury in a bicycle accident, recovered but died of peritonitis soon after. The Welsh Guards had met no opposition when their attack began as they followed the creeping barrage until they reached Wood 15 where, as the *History of the Welsh Guards* explains that:

> …the right of the line was held by machine guns in a concrete blockhouse on which the barrage had no effect. The barrage passed, and the flanks began to creep round, but were losing distance from the barrage. It was then that Sergt. Bye having crawled within a reasonable distance, rushed forward and succeeded in getting behind the inmates. The first objective was then taken, and the second and third waves went through the Blue Line and advanced on the second objective. On the flank was Wood

6 TNA: WO95/1193, Guards Division HQ, Narrative of Operations by Lt. Col. C.R.C. de Crespigny, commanding 2/Grenadiers, 6 August 1917.

7 Prior and Wilson, *Passchendaele*, p.90. 'The First World War Diaries of Lt. W.B. St Leger'. MC IWM 62.1

8 Doughty, *The Guards Came Through*, p.118 for his VC citation.

> 16, and again machine guns were missed by the barrage; indeed they fired through the barrage and held up the advance. Sergt. Bye, who was truly inspired that day, went forward at a steady amble, stumbling over the uneven ground, so that with each fall he was thought to be dead, and again got behind the blockhouse and bombed the machine gunners. Once more the line swept forward and took its final objective. Sergt. Bye either killed, wounded or captured over seventy men in these blockhouses.[9]

The *Official History* records that between 31 July and 3 August, casualties in the Guards Division amounted to 1,964 of whom 355 were killed and 177 were wounded. The total number of casualties as a whole in Fifth Army were 27,001 for this period.[10]

Prior and Wilson argue that, on the whole, the attack on 31 July achieved some notable successes. The French and XIV Corps together with XVIII and XIX Corps in the centre had broken through two German lines with an advance of 3,000 yards. In capturing Pilckem Ridge, the Germans had lost a dominating position with good observation over the Ypres Salient. To the right, the assault on the Gheluvelt Plateau had achieved a more limited advance in taking the German front line and approximately 1,000 yards beyond with valuable German observation points at Bellewaarde Ridge and Stirling Castle. 'Fifth Army, therefore, could point to some solid achievements' due to effective pre-battle training and the ability of the artillery to neutralise numerous German strongpoints. However, the failure to take the Gheluvelt Plateau left the areas captured on the left and centre exposed to enfilade fire. 'But the nature of the failure lay much deeper than that. The most that 'could follow from what had been achieved was a succession of similar operations, carried out spasmodically.'[11] This, of course did not escape the attention of the ordinary Guardsman: 'From the individual soldier's point of view ... the capture of one ridge always exposed another on which the enemy was firmly entrenched.'[12] Then the rain came. Starting at noon on 31 July, it rained incessantly for seven days except for a few hours on 5 August. Only three days in August were rain free and the total rainfall for the month was twice the average. As the earlier artillery bombardment had destroyed the water table, there was no drainage for the deluge and quickly the battlefield landscape changed as shell holes filled with water and the earth was transformed into mud that stuck to the troops and horses alike. The pattern for the remaining months on the Salient was now set.

In brief, the Guards remained in the line until they were relieved by the 29th Division on 7 August but the conditions were so bad that the men were rotated through the line with reliefs every 48 hours. On 27 August, they returned to the line on a front line from the Ypres-Staden Railway line towards the Broembeek stream. For the next three weeks, they were under heavy German artillery fire on a frequent basis and repulsed several attacks. The Guards were

9 Dudley Ward, *History of the Welsh Guards*, pp.66–67.

10 James Edmonds, *Military Operations, France and Belgium 1917, Volume 2* (Tennessee: Battery Press, 1995 [1948]), p.178.

11 Prior and Wilson, *Passchendaele*, pp. 94–96.

12 Dudley Ward, *History of The Welsh Guards*, p.157.

finally withdrawn on 17 October having taken part in two attacks in this area during the month. In the fighting between 9 and 15 October, the Guards Division lost 24 officers killed and 56 wounded, 399 other ranks killed, 1,621 wounded and 164 missing. The total losses, therefore, were not insignificant, amounting to 2,264.[13]

Lieutenant Esmond Elliot. (Courtesy of Lord Astor)

Sadly, neither Esmond Elliot nor Miles Barne were to survive Third Ypres. Elliot died of his wounds on 6 August. He was commanding G Company of the 2/Scots Guards in the trenches on the western side of the Steenbeek. Crossing a moonlit road, 'a bullet struck him in the left upper arm. It pierced his side, just below the armpit, travelled through his lung, shattering two ribs, and exited his upper back.' Elliot died shortly afterwards at the 1/Grenadiers Casualty Dressing Station. The doctor treating him believed it was unwise to move him. Dosed up with morphine, his last words were: 'I'm very tired, I think I'll go to sleep'. He was just 22 years old.[14]

Miles Barne died on 17 September, aged 43. He had been writing a letter home in his tent whilst the battalion postman, Private Samuel Allen waited close by. Their tragic deaths were described in an official report by Lieutenant Trafford on 19 September. At about 12:30 p.m. Trafford saw a British aeroplane approaching:

> I saw the aeroplane directly over the lines, and a small object which proved to be a bomb, dropping from it. This bomb fell directly on the tent ... As a result of the explosion, this Private [Allen] was killed outright and Major Barne was so severely injured, that he subsequently died. Five other Privates who were standing near were also wounded. After dropping the bomb the aeroplane, still flying very low, proceeded and was seen to alight a short distance away. Subsequently I saw the Pilot in charge of the aeroplane, Lieut. H. Turner No. 9 Squadron R.F.C., who stated that he was unaware that he had dropped a bomb, as he had supposed that he dropped those all over the German lines, and that he attributed the fact of this not having been done to a mechanical defect. He also stated that he was flying low and looking for a place to alight owing to shortage of petrol.[15]

13 Headlam, *History of the Guards Division*, p.286.
14 Astor and Churchill, *Lost Idol*, pp.198–199.
15 Nicol, *Barne's Diary*, p.304.

Conclusion: An Elite Division?

Looking back at the Guards Division's contribution to the three major battles of these two years it is fair to say that they had a mixed record. At Loos, they were kept in reserve for far too long and then fed into the battlefield in a chaotic fashion as shown by the experience of the Irish Guards who had no rest for 48 hours beforehand. Command and control became especially challenging and inadequacies in artillery co-ordination were sharpened in the fog of war. The fact that units of the Welsh Guards reached up to the German defences on Hill 70 was a testament to the drive, bravery and determination of the division as a whole. Cavan did come out of the attack with some credit however and his growing reputation was further enhanced by his leadership during the Guards' stint at the Hohenzollern Redoubt in October where he showed his ability to develop and refine new bombing techniques. Indeed, this is a good early example of the learning process within the BEF and was a worthy attempt to disseminate good practice. During the winter of 1915/1916, Cavan and then Feilding sought to dominate the Germans in their sector by a series of well executed trench raids although Cavan's inept handling of the Christmas fraternisations probably succeeded only in raising emotions and tensions.

The division's experience on the Somme in September and October 1916 was a very challenging one. Much attention had been paid to training and preparation for the Battle of Flers-Courcelette and yet, starting from an awkward jumping off point and fighting on a narrow frontage, they soon lost direction because of intense German fire to their right from the Quadrilateral. Hindered rather than helped by their allocated tanks, and with neither flanking division able to make sufficient headway, they failed to get beyond their first objective. Despite some remarkably brave fighting and the desperate attempts by battalion commanders to find direction and momentum, losses were very heavy indeed. Unquestionably 15 September was the darkest day in the war for the division. Despite Lesboeufs being taken a few days later with a significant intake of inexperienced reinforcements, the division's reputation had been tarnished. Nonetheless, after-battle reports revealed a capacity to reflect and learn from these tumultuous experiences.

However, the Guards Division bounced back at Pilckem Ridge in July 1917. The British Army was progressing and learning quickly; the Battle of Arras in April had seen encouraging early breakthroughs and at Messines in June a significant victory had been won. On both occasions, training and preparation had been detailed, appropriate and effective, and Feilding's own preparation for the attack reflected these new approaches which was part of an emerging methodology within the BEF. The influence of the growing number of Stationery Services manuals was apparent, and replica training areas were built which provided the Guardsmen with more realistic and finely tuned training. The Yser Canal provided a formidable challenge, yet the attack was planned meticulously whilst intelligence on German weaknesses was brilliantly exploited to gain an impressive victory in just a few hours on 31 July. Importantly, Feilding offered decisive leadership in choosing when to move forces across the Yser Canal ahead of the main assault. The Guards had proved that they could learn and adapt to change.

The Guards Division was always ferocious and highly committed in attack and their historic pedigree cannot be doubted. The training of new recruits at Caterham left them in no doubt as to what kind of regiments they were joining and the fact that all Guards battalions, brigades and ultimately the division itself could only be led by a fellow Guardsman placed it in a unique position within the BEF. With its officers drawn from an interconnected social class at the very apex of British society, the division was expected to function as *the* elite unit of that army. Yet a feature of the First World War was that there were typically significant constraints on the battlefield performance of British army divisions; hastily constructed plans that needed to be modified in the heat of battle, stiff enemy resistance, the performance of neighbouring units, ineffective or erratic command and control, indifferent artillery support etc. However well trained and led a division or units within it were, failure or only partial success were an inevitability on occasion. At Loos and on the Somme, there was both disappointment and a measure of success whereas, at Pilckem Ridge, better training and leadership reflected the fact that the division was learning to fight effectively. This aligned with some good fortune to produce an impressive battlefield performance. Between their foundation in the summer of 1915 and the first stage of Third Ypres at the end of July 1917, the Guards Division performed as well as the circumstances allowed. The division believed that it was an elite force, behaved as such and within the constraints imposed upon them, functioned as one.

Appendix

Infantry Composition of the Guards Division with respective GOCs, 1915–1917.

1st Guards Brigade:
G.P.T. Feilding 20/8/15 to 2/1/16
C.E. Pereira 9/1/16 to 26/12/16
G.D. Jeffreys 30/12/16 to 21/9/17
2/Grenadier Guards
2/Coldstream Guards
3/Coldstream Guards
1/Irish Guards

2nd Guards Brigade:
J. Ponsonby 23/7/15 to 19/11/16
Lord H. Seymour 28/11/16 to 20/3/17
J. Ponsonby 21/3/17 to 21/8/17
B.N Sergison-Brooke 22/8/17 to 23/3/18
3/Grenadier Guards
1/Coldstream Guards
1/Scots Guards
2/Irish Guards

3rd Guards Brigade:
F.J. Heyworth 18/8/15 to 9/5/16
C.E. Corkran 15/5/16 to 20/3/17
Lord H.C. Seymour 21/3/17 to 7/4/18
1/Grenadier Guards
4/Grenadier Guards
2/Scots Guards
1/Welsh Guards

Bibliography

Archival Sources

Churchill Archives Centre, University of Cambridge (CAC)
The Papers of Field Marshal Lord Cavan, GBR/0014/CAVN,

The National Archives, Kew (TNA) War Diaries:
First Army HQ: WO 95/158
X1 Corps HQ: WO 95/880
Guards Divisional HQ: WO 95/1190, WO 95/1192, WO 95/1193
1st Guards Brigade HQ: WO 95/1212, WO 95/1213
2nd Guards Brigade HQ: WO 95/1217
3rd Guards Brigade HQ: WO 95/1221
2nd Bn, the Grenadier Guards: WO 95/1215/1
2nd Bn, the Coldstream Guards: WO 95/1215/2
3rd Bn, the Coldstream Guards: WO 95/1215/3
1st Bn, the Irish Guards: WO 95/1216/1
3rd Bn, the Grenadier Guards: WO 95/1219/1
1st Bn, the Coldstream Guards: WO 95/1219/2
1st Bn, the Scots Guards: WO 95/1219/3
2nd Bn, the Irish Guards: WO 95/1220/1
1st Bn, the Grenadier Guards: WO 95/1223/1
4th Bn, the Grenadier Guards: WO 95/1223/2
2nd Bn, the Scots Guards: WO 95/1223/4
1st Bn, the Welsh Guards: WO 95/1224/1

British Newspaper Archive
Whitstable Times and Herne Bay Herald 26 February 1916
Sheffield Daily Telegraph 19 May 1925
Sheffield Independent 20 October 1926

Memoirs and Papers

Asquith, Lady Cynthia, *The Diaries of Lady Cynthia Asquith, 1915–18* (London: Century Hutchinson, 1968)
Astor, Johnnie and Campbell, *Alexandra. Esmond: The Lost Idol 1895–1917* (Solihull: Helion, 2017)
Beach, Jim (ed.), *The Military Papers of Lieutenant–Colonel Sir Cuthbert Headlam* (Stroud: The History Press, 2010)
Blackler, John (ed.), *Have You Forgotten Yet? The First World War Memoirs of C. P. Blacker M.C., G.M.* (Barnsley: Pen & Sword, 2000)
Blake, Robert (ed.), *The Private Papers of Douglas Haig* (London: Eyre & Spottiswoode, 1952)
Cliff, Norman, *To Hell and Back with the Guards* (Braunton: Merlin, 1988)
Dearden, Harold, *Medicine and Duty: A War Diary* (London: Heinemann, 1928)
Dundas, Henry, *Scots Guard: A Memoir* (Edinburgh: Blackwood, 1921)
Ewart, Wilfrid, *Scots Guard on the Western Front, 1915–1918* (Stevenage: Strong Oak Press Reprint, 2001 [1934])
Fildes, G., *Iron Times with the Guards: The Experiences of an Officer of the Coldstream Guards on the Western Front During the First World War* (Uckfield, Naval & Military Press 2016 [1918])
Fryer, E.R.M., *Grenadier: The Recollections of an Officer of the Grenadier Guards throughout the Great War on the Western Front* (London: Digby, Long & Co., 1923)
Graham. Stephen, *A Private in the Guards* (London: Macmillan, 1919)
Graves, Robert, *Goodbye to All That* (London: Penguin, 1960 [1929])
Hamilton, R.G.A., *The War Diary of the Master of Belhaven* (London: John Murray, 1924)
Jolliffe, John (ed.), *Raymond Asquith: Life and Letters* (London: Collins, 1980)
Lyttelton, Oliver, (Lod Chandos) *From Peace to War: A Study in Contrast 1857–1918* (London: The Bodley Head, 1968)
Lyttelton, Oliver, (Lord Chandos) *The Memoirs of Lord Chandos* (London: The Bodley Head, 1962)
MacGill, Patrick, *The Great Push: An Episode of the Great War* (London: H. Jenkins, 1917)
Macmillan, Harold, *Winds of Change: 1914–1939* (London: Macmillan, 1966)
Nicol, Randall, *Miles Barne's Diary: A Suffolk Countryman at War 1915–1917* (Warwick: Helion, 2018)
Pereira, Edward, Jones, Spencer and Locicero, Michael (eds), *Catholic General: The Private Wartime Correspondence of Major-General Sir Cecil Edward Pereira, 1914–19* (Warwick: Helion, 2020)
Sheffield, Gary and Bourne, John (eds), *Douglas Haig: War Diaries and Letters, 1914–1918* (London: Phoenix, 2006)
Street, Cecil J.C., *With the Guns* (London: Eveleigh Nash & Co, 1916)

Official Histories

Edmonds, Brigadier Sir James. *Military Operations, France and Belgium 1914, Volume 2* (Tennessee: Battery Press, 1995 [1925])
Edmonds, Brigadier Sir James, *Military Operations, France and Belgium 1915, Volume 2* (Uckfield: Naval and Military Press Reprint, 2021 [1928])
Edmonds, Brigadier Sir James, *Military Operations, France and Belgium 1916, Volume 1* (Tennessee: Battery Press,1995 [1932])
Edmonds, Brigadier Sir James, *Military Operations, France and Belgium 1917, Volume 2* (Tennessee: Battery Press, 1995 [1948])
Falls, Captain Cyril, *Military Operations, France and Belgium 1917, Volume 1* (Tennessee: Battery Press, 1995 [1940])
Miles, Wilfrid, *Military Operations, France and Belgium, 1916 Volume 2* (I.W.M./Battery Press, 1995 [1938])

Regimental Histories

Headlam, Cuthbert, *History of the Guards Division in the Great War, 1915–1918, Volume 1* (London: Murray, 1924)
Kipling, Rudyard, *The Irish Guards in the Great War: The First Battalion* (Staplehurst: Spellmount, 2007 [1923])
Kipling, Rudyard, *The Irish Guards in the Great War: The Second Battalion* (Staplehurst: Spellmount, 1997 [1923])
Nicol, Randall, *Till the Trumpet Sounds Again: The Scots Guards 1914–1919 in Their Own Words* (Solihull: Helion, 2016)
Petre, Loraine, Ewart, Wilfrid and Lowther, Major-General Sir Cecil, *The Scots Guards in the Great War* (London: Murray, 1925)
Ponsonby, Frederick, *The Grenadier Guards in the Great War* (London: Macmillan, 1920)
Ross-of-Bladensburg, John Foster, *The Coldstream Guards 1914–18* (London: Oxford University Press, 1928)
Ward Dudley, C.H. *History of the Welsh Guards* (London: Murray, 1920)

Other Secondary Printed Sources

Anon., *Histories of Two Hundred and Fifty-One Divisions of the German Army Which Participated in the War (1914–1918)* (Uckfield: Naval and Military Press 1989 [1920])
Attwood, Rodney, *General Lord Rawlinson: From Tragedy to Triumph* (London: Bloomsbury, 2018)
Ball, Simon, *The Guardsmen, Harold Macmillan, Three Friends and the World They Made* (London: Harper Collins, 2004)

Barr, Niall, 'Command in the Transition from Mobile to Static Warfare, August 1914 to March 1915' in Gary Sheffield and Dan Todman, *Command and Control on the Western Front: The British Army's Experience 1914-1918* (Staplehurst: Spellmount, 2004)

Beckett, Ian, *Johnnie Gough VC: A Biography of Brigadier-General Sir John Edmund Gough V.C., K.C.B., C.M.G.* (Staplehurst: Spellmount, 1989)

Bidwell, Shelford and Graham, Dominick, *Fire-Power: The British Army, Weapons and Theories of War 1904–1945* (London: George Allen & Unwin, 1982)

Boff, Jonathan, *Winning and Losing on the Western Front: The British Third Army and the Defeat of Germany in 1918* (Cambridge: Cambridge University Press, 2012)

Bond, Brian, *Survivors of a Kind, Memoirs of the Western Front* (London: Continuum, 2008)

Bond, Brian, *The Unquiet Western Front: Britain's Role in Literature and History* (Cambridge: Cambridge University Press, 2002)

Cherry, Niall, *Most Unfavourable Ground: The Battle of Loos 1915* (Solihull: Helion, 2005)

Churchill, Alexandra, *Blood and Thunder: The Boys of Eton College and The First World War* (Stroud: The History Press, 2014)

Clark, Alan, *The Donkeys* (London: Hutchinson, 1961)

Corrigan, Gordon, *Loos 1915: The Unwanted Battle* (Staplehurst: Spellmount, 2006)

Curragh, Brian, 'A Great Victory All But Gained', in Spencer Jones (ed.), *Courage without Glory: The British Army on the Western Front 1915* (Solihull: Helion, 2015)

Doughty, Simon, *The Guards Came Through* (London: Third Millennium, 2016)

Duffy, Christopher, *Through German Eyes: The British and the Somme 1916* (London: Phoenix, 2007)

Fair, Charles, 'From OTC to OCB; Fair, Charles. The Professionalisation of the Selection and Training of Junior Temporary Officers in the Great War', in Spencer Jones (ed.), *The Darkest Year: The British Army on the Western Front 1917* (Warwick: Helion, 2022)

Gliddon, Gerald, *VCs of the First World War: The Somme 1916* (Stroud: Alan Sutton, 1995)

Green, Andrew, *Writing the Great War: Sir James Edmonds and the Official Histories, 1915–1948* (London: Routledge, 2003)

Griffith, Paddy, *Battle Tactics of the Western Front: The British Army's Art of Attack, 1916–1918* (London: Yale University Press, 1994)

Hodgkinson, Peter, 'Infantry Battalion Command on the Somme 1 July–18 November 1916', in Spencer Jones (ed.), *At All Costs: The British Army on the Western Front 1916* (Warwick: Helion, 2018)

Hodgkinson, Peter, *A Complete Orchestra of War* (Warwick: Helion, 2019)

Jones, Spencer (ed.), *Courage without Glory: The British Army on the Western Front 1915* (Solihull: Helion, 2015)

Jones, Spencer. (ed.), *At All Costs: The British Army on the Western Front 1916* (Warwick: Helion, 2018).

Jones, Spencer (ed.), *The Darkest Year: The British Army on the Western Front 1917* (Warwick: Helion, 2022).
Jones, Spencer, '"To make war as we must, and not as we should like": The British Army and the Problem of the Western Front, 1915', in Spencer Jones (ed.), *Courage without Glory: The British Army on the Western Front 1915* (Solihull: Helion, 2015)
Kearsey, Lieutenant-Colonel A., *1915 campaign in France: the battles of Aubers Ridge, Festubert and Loos considered in relation to the field service regulations* (Uckfield: Naval and Military Press, 2002 [1929])
Lee, John, 'The SHLM Project – Assessing the Battle Performance of British Divisions' in Paddy Griffith (ed.), *British Fighting Methods in the Great War* (London: Routledge, 1998)
Levine, Joshua, *Forgotten Voices of the Somme.* (London: Ebury, 2008)
Liddell Hart, B.H., *The Real War, 1914–1918* (London: Faber and Faber, 1930)
Lloyd, Nick, *Loos 1915* (Stroud: Tempus, 2006)
Lloyd, Nick, *Passchendaele: A New History* (London: Penguin/Viking, 2017)
MacGill, Patrick, *The Great Push: An Episode of the Great War* (London: H. Jenkins, 1917)
Marble, Sanders, *The Infantry Cannot Do with a Gun Less: The Place of the Artillery in the British Expeditionary Force 1914–1918* (New York: Columbia, 2003)
Marden, T.O., *A Short History of the Sixth Division* (London: Hugh Rees, 1920)
Oldfield, Paul, *Victoria Crosses on the Western Front: Somme 1916, 1 July1–3 November* (Barnsley: Pen & Sword, 2016)
Peaple, Simon, *Mud, Blood and Determination, The History of the 46th (North Midland) Division in the Great War* (Solihull: Helion, 2015)
Philpott, William, *Bloody Victory: The Sacrifice on the Somme and the Making of the Twentieth Century* (London: Little, Brown, 2009)
Philpott, William, *Attrition: Fighting the First World War* (London: Little, Brown, 2014)
Pidgeon, Trevor, *The Tanks at Flers: An Account of the First Use of Tanks in War at the Battle of Flers-Courcelette, the Somme, 15th September 1916* (Cobham: Fairmile, 1995)
Pope, Stephen, *The Tanks Corps in the Great War: Volume 1. Conception, Birth and Baptism of Fire, November 1914–November 1916* (Warwick: Helion, 2022)
Prior, Robin and Wilson, Trevor, *Command on the Western Front: The Military Career of Sir Henry Rawlinson 1914–1918* (Oxford: Blackwell, 1992).
Prior, Robin and Wilson, Trevor, *Passchendaele: The Untold Story* (London: Yale University Press, 1996)
Prior, Robin and Wilson, Trevor, *The Somme* (London: Yale University Press, 2005)
Rawson, Andrew, *Loos – Hill 70* (Barnsley: Leo Cooper, 2002)
Rawson, Andrew, *The Learning Process: The BEF's Art of War on the Western Front 1914–1918* (Warwick: Helion, 2019)
Robbins, Simon, *British Generalship on the Western Front, 1914–1918: Defeat into Victory* (London: Routledge 2006).
Saunders Anthony, *Raiding on the Western Front* (Barnsley: Pen & Sword, 2012)
Senior, Michael, *Lt. Gen Sir Richard Haking: A Dutiful Soldier, XI Corps Commander 1915–18: A Study in Corps Command* (Barnsley: Pen & Sword, 2012)

Senior, Michael, *Victory on the Western Front; The Development of the British Army* (Barnsley: Pen & Sword, 2016)

Senior, Michael, *Field Marshal the Earl of Cavan: Soldier and Fox Hunter* (Barnsley: Pen & Sword, 2023)

Sheffield, Gary and Dan Todman, *Command and Control on the Western Front: The British Army's Experience 1914–1918* (Staplehurst: Spellmount, 2004)

Sheffield, Gary, *The Somme* (London: Cassell, 2003)

Sheldon, Jack, *The German Army at Passchendaele* (Barnsley: Pen & Sword, 2007)

Sheldon, Jack, *Fighting the Somme: Challenges, Dilemmas and Solution* (Barnsley: Pen & Sword, 2017)

Shephard, Simon, '"Artillery Conquers, Infantry Occupies". A Study in the Performance of the British Artillery at the Third Battle of Ypres', in Spencer Jones (ed.), *The Darkest Year: The British Army on the Western Front 1917* (Warwick: Helion, 2022)

Simpson, Andy, *Directing Operations: British Corps Command on the Western Front 1914–1918* (Staplehurst: Spellmount, 2005)

Simpson, Andy, *Directing Operations: British Corps Command on the Western Front 1914–1918* (Warwick: Helion 2019), revised edition

Simpson, Andy, 'British Corps Command on the Western Front, 1914–1918', in Gary Sheffield, and Dan Todman (eds), *Command and Control on the Western Front: The British Army's Experience 1914–1918* (Staplehurst: Spellmount, 2004)

Stevenson, David, *1914–1918: The History of the First World War* (London: Allen Lane, 2004)

Terraine, John, *Douglas Haig: The Educated Soldier* (London: Cassell 2000 [1963])

Travers Tim, *The Killing Ground: The British Army, the Western Front & The Emergence of Modern Warfare 1900–1908* (Barnsley: Leo Cooper, 2003)

Warner, Philip, *The Battle of Loos* (London: William Kimber, 1976)

Woods, Michael, 'Gas, Grenades and Grievances: The Attack on the Hohenzollern', in Spencer Jones (ed.), *Courage without Glory: The British Army on the Western Front 1915* (Solihull: Helion, 2015)

Journal Articles

Lloyd, Nick, '"With Faith and without Fear": Sir Douglas Haig's Command of First Army during 1915', *The Journal of Military History*, vol.71, no.4 (October 2007), pp.1051–1076

Pike, L., 'Household Brigade Officer Cadet Battalion', *Household Brigade Magazine*, November 1920

Reeve, John S., Capt., 'Little Sparta in the War', *Household Guards Magazine*, Victory Edition (1920), pp.89–91

Ponsonby, Frederick, Lieutenant Colonel, 'The finest achievements of the Household Brigade in the War, *Household Brigade Magazine*, Victory Number 1920, p.45

Trappes-Lomax, Capt. T.B., 'Artillery Support at Loos', *Household Brigade Magazine*, Spring Number 1930, pp.87–89

Theses

Wood, Roger, *The Evolution of Infantry Brigade Command in the British Army on the Western Front, 1916-1918*, PhD thesis, University of Wolverhampton, (2020)

Internet Sources

Jonathan Boff, *Passchendaele: Why it Failed,* <https://www.birmingham.ac.uk/research/perspective/passchendaele.aspx>, accessed 13 November 2023

Diary of Sir Ian Colquhoun, <http://www.valeofleven.org.uk/contributions/iain-colquhoundiary.html>, accessed 23 November 2023

The Great War Forum, <https://www.greatwarforum.org/topic/245966-are-there-any-factual-german-assessments-of-british-divisions-regiments-etc/#comment-2477003>, accessed 22 December 2023

David Hutchinson, *FSR: An Analysis*, <https://fieldserviceregulations.co.uk/>, accessed 20 December 2023